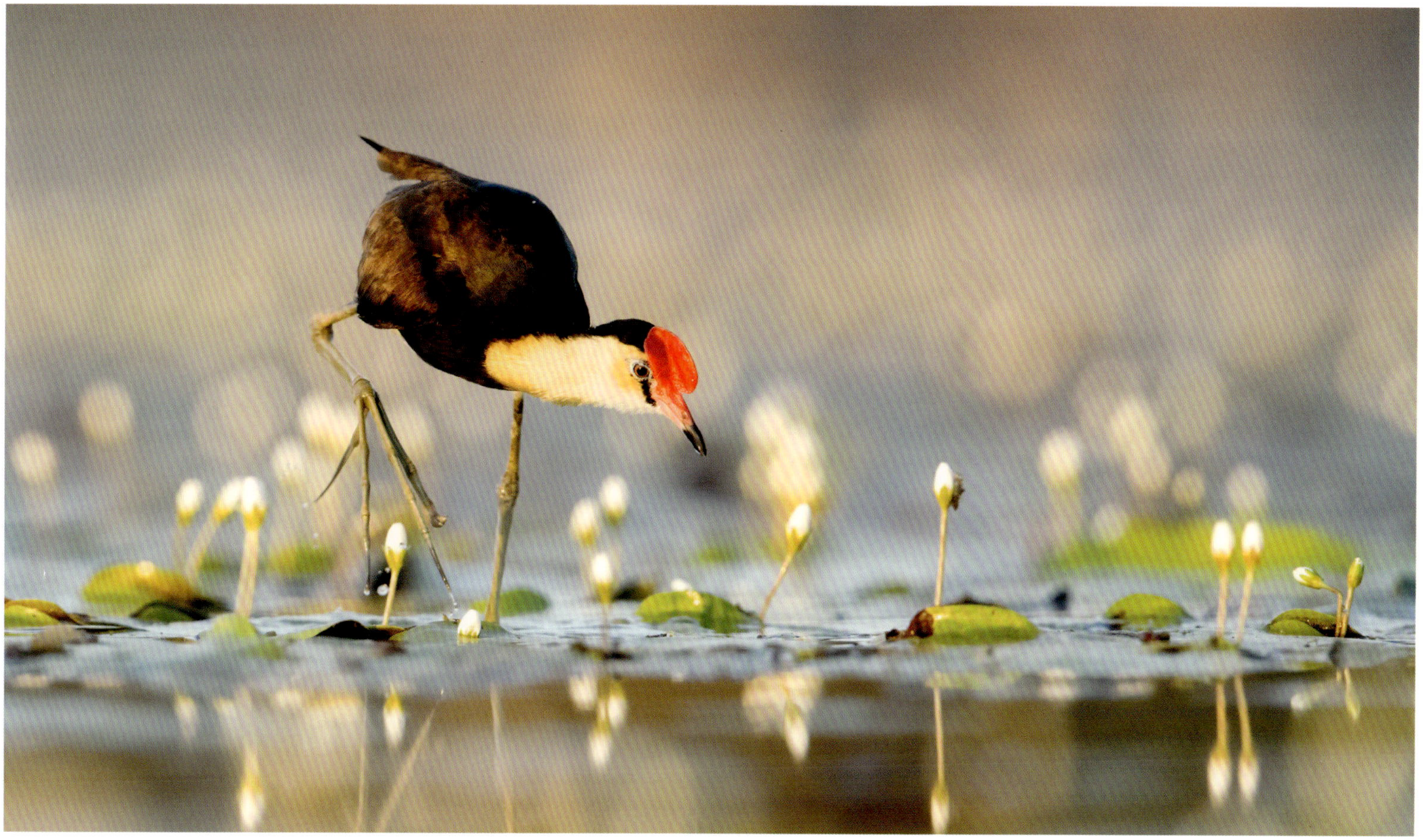

EIGHTEENTH EDITION

Nature Photographer of the Year

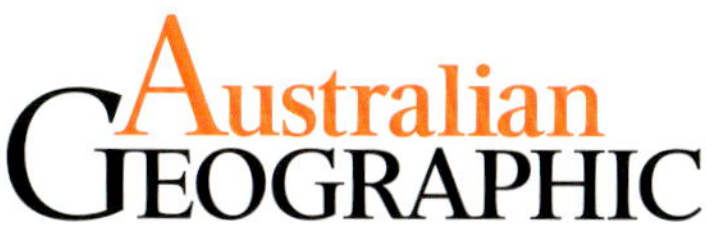

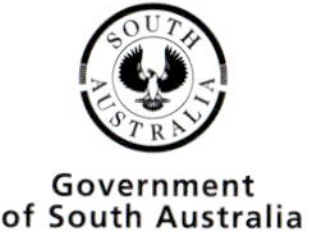

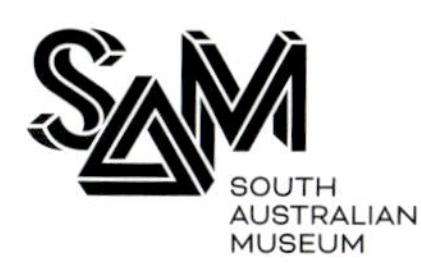

Nature Photographer of the Year:
The year's best wildlife and landscape photos
18th edition

First published in 2021 by
Australian Geographic
52–54 Turner Street, Redfern NSW 2016
Telephone 02 9136 7214
Email editorial@ausgeo.com.au
australiangeographic.com.au

ISBN: 978-1-922388-26-1

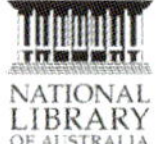

A catalogue record for this book is available from the National Library of Australia

The Australian Geographic Nature Photographer of the Year competition
is run by the South Australian Museum
North Terrace, Adelaide SA 5000
Email NPOTY@samuseum.sa.gov.au
naturephotographeroftheyear.com.au

Managing Director, Australian Geographic: Jo Runciman
Australian Geographic Editor-in-chief: Chrissie Goldrick
Creative Director: Mike Ellott
Editors: Lauren Smith and Katrina O'Brien
Assistant Editor: Peter Tuskan
Commercial and Rights Manager: Simone Aquilina
Image Management: Luke Chenoweth and Tim Gilchrist

Printed in China by C & C Offset Printing Co., Ltd

Front cover
Mudskipper
Mudskipper (Oxudercidae)
Scott Portelli, New South Wales

Back cover
Ghost Mushrooms
Ghost mushroom (*Omphalotus nidiformis*)
Callie Chee, New South Wales

Title page
Comb-Crested Jacana
Comb-crested jacana (*Irediparra gallinacea*)
James White, Victoria

Page 5
Cockatoo
Sulphur-crested cockatoo (*Cacatua galerita*)
Aidan Cimarosti, New South Wales

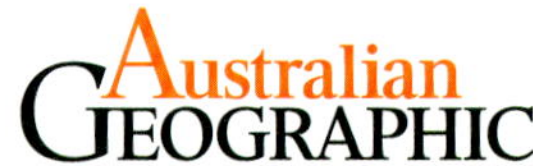

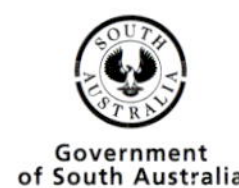

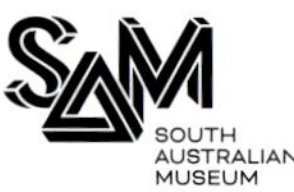

Contents

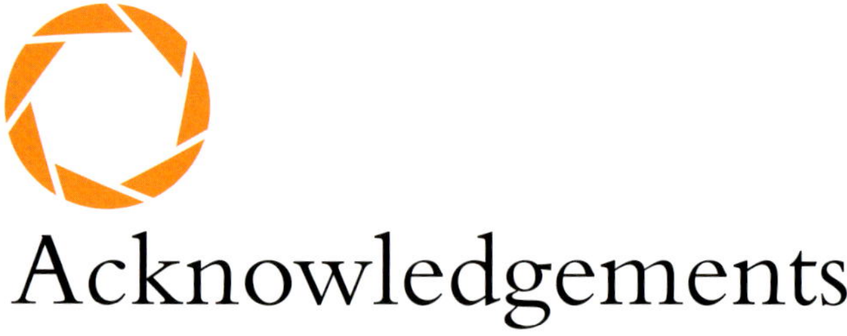

Acknowledgements

The South Australian Museum gratefully acknowledges the support of Dr Stuart Miller AM, founder and patron of the Australian Geographic Nature Photographer of the Year (formerly known as ANZANG), and his sister Mrs Alison Huber in memory of their parents, Dr Robert and Mrs Clarice Miller, both late of Waikerie, South Australia.

The South Australian Museum would like to thank our sponsors, who in 2021 have so generously supported the 18th cycle of this competition and exhibition.

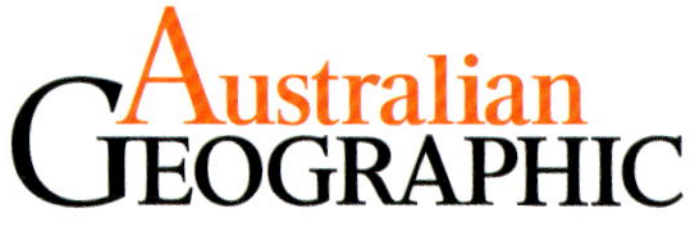

Principal Sponsor

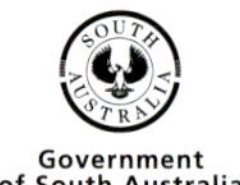

Government of South Australia

SAM
SOUTH AUSTRALIAN MUSEUM

Producer

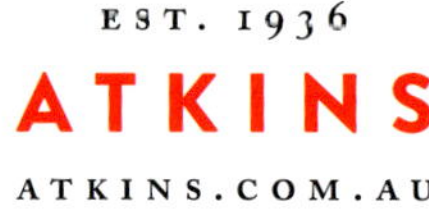

Production Partner

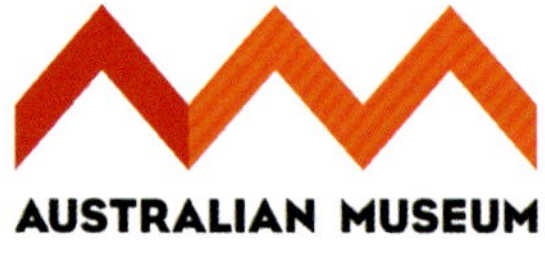

Touring Partner

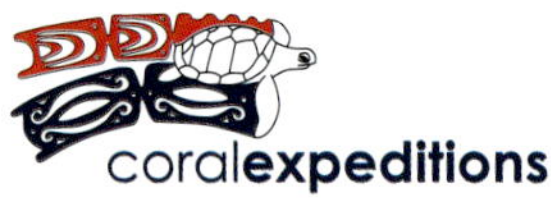

Holiday Prize Sponsor

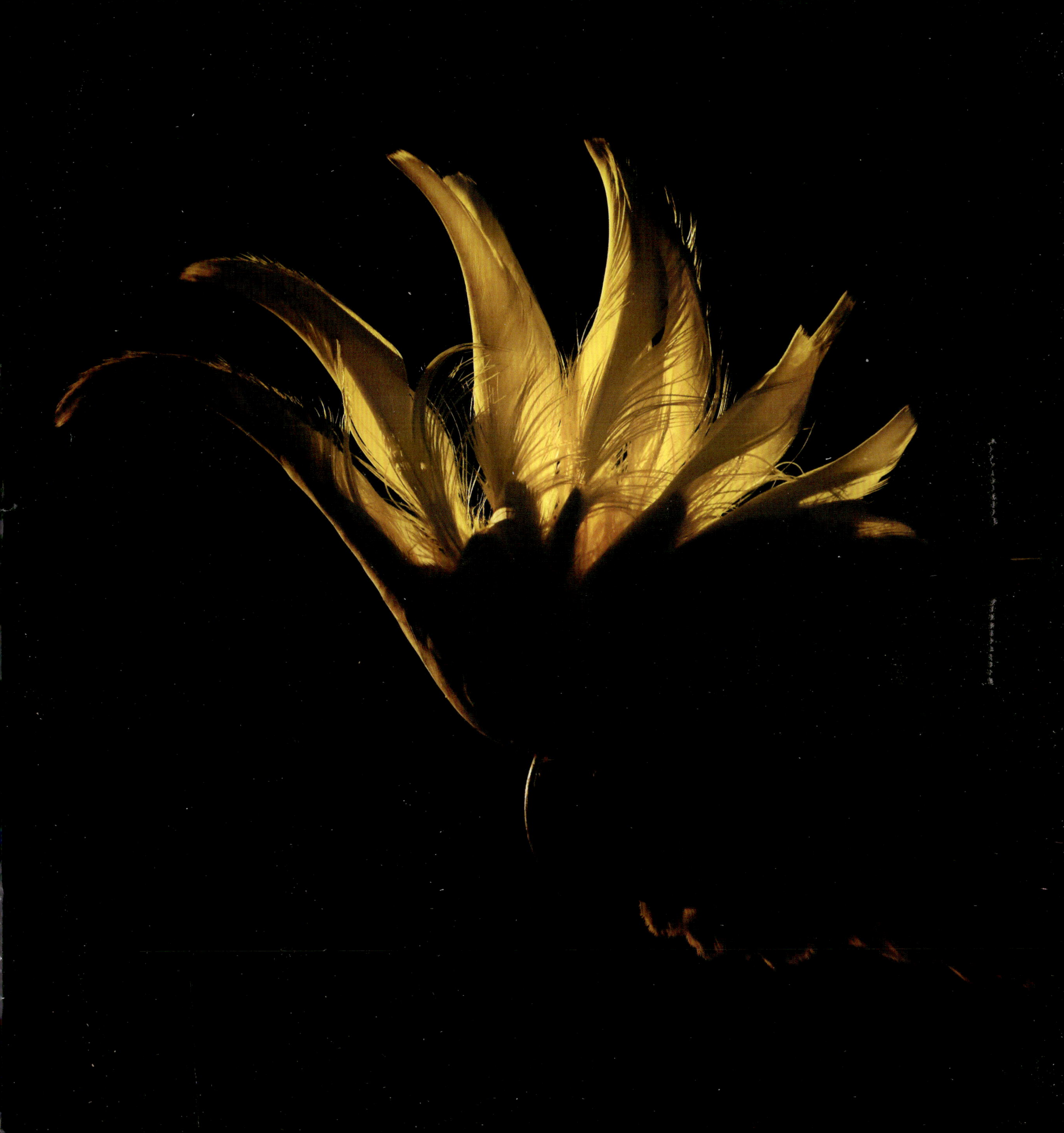

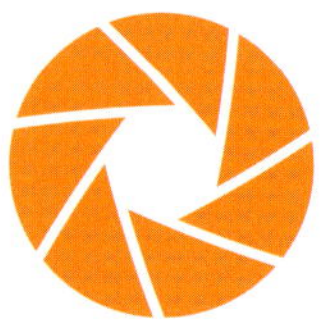

Premier's statement

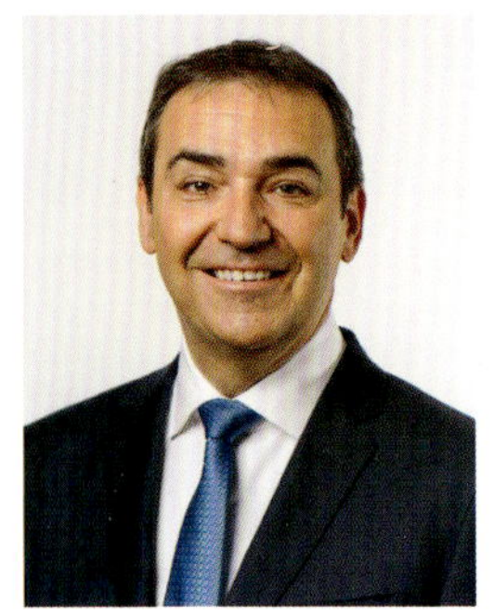

To paraphrase Albert Einstein, if we look deep into nature we will understand everything better. Through the photographs featured in the South Australian Museum's Australian Geographic Nature Photographer of the Year, we take that deep look and have an opportunity to appreciate and understand the splendour of our region.

With lenses focused on the ANZANG region, including Australia, New Zealand, Antarctica and New Guinea, photographers from around the world have used their craft to share the spectacular scenes they have been fortunate to witness firsthand.

Through these photographers we are offered the chance to see wonders of our natural world. We can visit locations that may otherwise be out of reach and witness intimate moments in the lives of plants and animals. We are also afforded the opportunity to pause and contemplate the human impact on the environment. After a period of staying close to home, it's a wonderful tonic to see images taken across our region to remind us how special it is.

I congratulate all of the photographers featured in this book and the accompanying exhibition. Thank you for taking time to share your work.

I also congratulate all of the nature photographers focusing their lenses on the ANZANG region who aren't featured. It's wonderful to know you share our love and excitement for this part of the world, and I hope all of you will have your chance to share work in a future Australian Geographic Nature Photographer of the Year.

Hon. Steven Marshall MP
Premier of South Australia

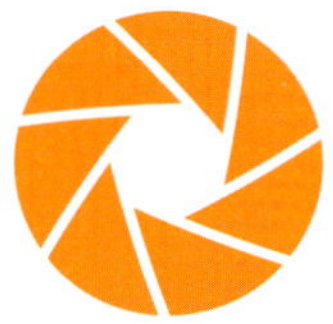

From the Director of the South Australian Museum

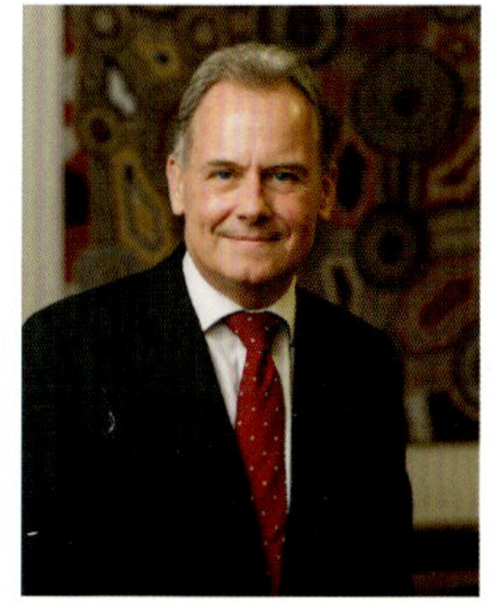

There is nothing like a period of reflection to make one look at life differently. The whole world had time to reflect in 2020 as we all grappled with the impact of Covid-19. There was the necessary requirement to be 'socially distanced' and occasionally to be in 'lockdown'. Some of us have not been able to pursue our usual occupations. The long-distance travel that we had all taken for granted has been curtailed. These enforced changes have given us time to reflect and reacquaint ourselves with our immediate surroundings. For many it rekindled a renewed appreciation and an increased value being placed on what we had rediscovered in our backyard.

This certainly seems to be the case with nature photographers who have seemingly refocused their energies and examined the world about them with renewed vigour. They have delivered extraordinary new visions of Australia, New Zealand, Antarctica and New Guinea. This year's competition has seen an exciting coming together of the photographer's view of the natural world.

It was wonderful to see this year's competition show a strong increase in the number of photographs submitted. In all, 2206 photographs were received from 403 photographers in 17 countries. I would like to thank them all for sharing their personal vision of the natural world.

I would also like to thank this year's judging panel, who have approached their daunting task with their usual discipline, professionalism and candour. Finally, I would like to thank Australian Geographic for their wonderful support over many years – it is a relationship which the South Australian Museum truly values.

Brian Oldman
Director, South Australian Museum

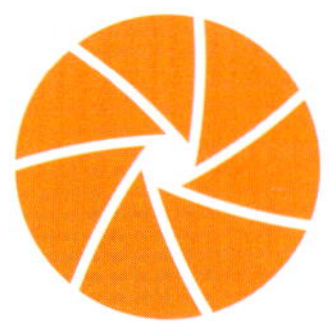

The Judges

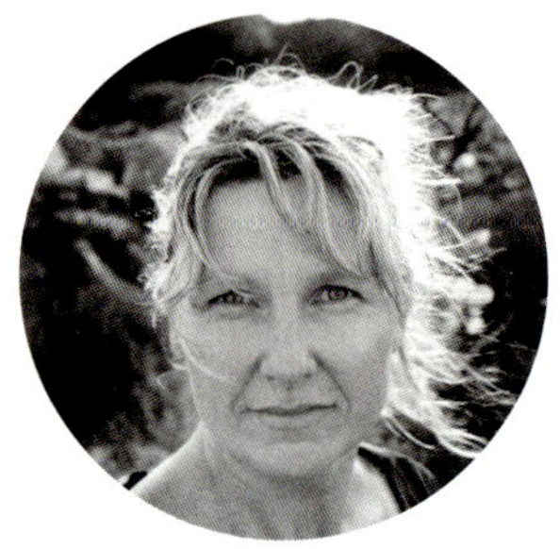

NARELLE AUTIO

Narelle Autio's vibrant and award-winning images of Australian outback and coastal life have won her impressive national and international acclaim. Growing up in Australia she has had a lifetime relationship with the ocean and is fascinated by the need for many of us to return to water. Her sophisticated, cinematic use of colour, light and composition create photographs that evoke the complex beauty of Australia's landscape, which is otherwise eroded by postcards and clichés.

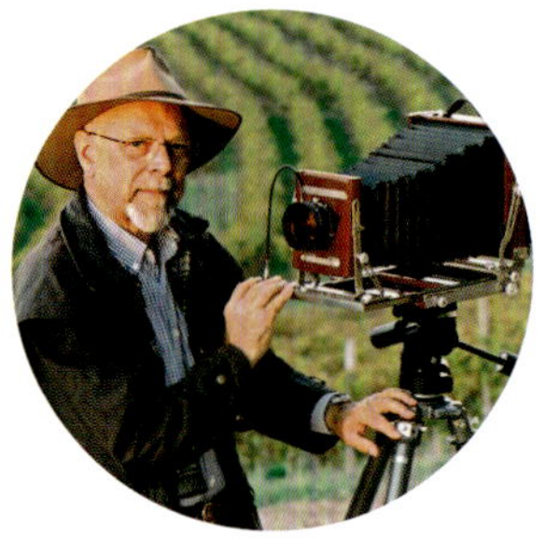

STAVROS PIPPOS

Stavros Pippos is a landscape photographer whose interest began as a 12-year-old boy, taking photos, processing film and contact-printing negatives in a makeshift darkroom. This desire to create ultimately led him to a career in television where he worked his way from sweeping floors to the role of Managing Director at Channel Seven in Adelaide. Following his retirement, Stavros focused on photography, documenting the South Australian landscape and developing a passion for alternative photographic printing methods and the characteristic charm of old wooden cameras.

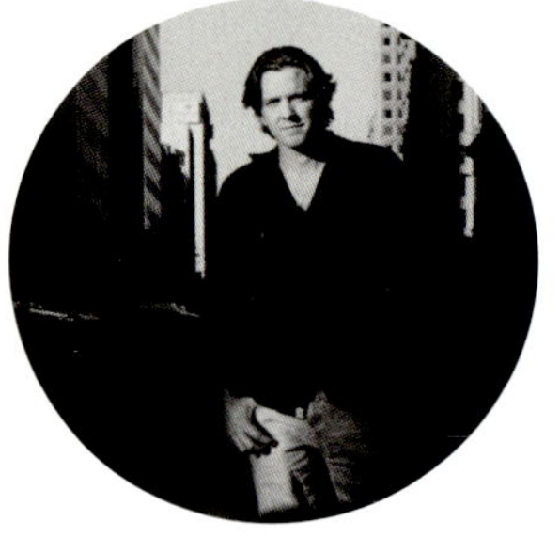

TRENT PARKE

Trent Parke is one of the most innovative photographers of his generation. He is known for his poetic, often darkly humorous photography that offers an emotional and psychological portrait of his home country of Australia – from the southern outback to its busy beaches. Though rooted in documentary, his works sit between fiction and reality, exploring themes of identity, place and family life.

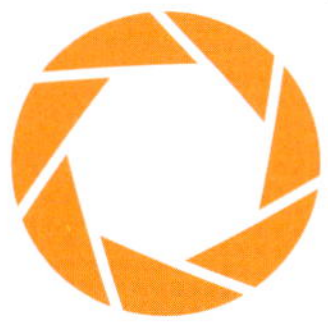

Introduction

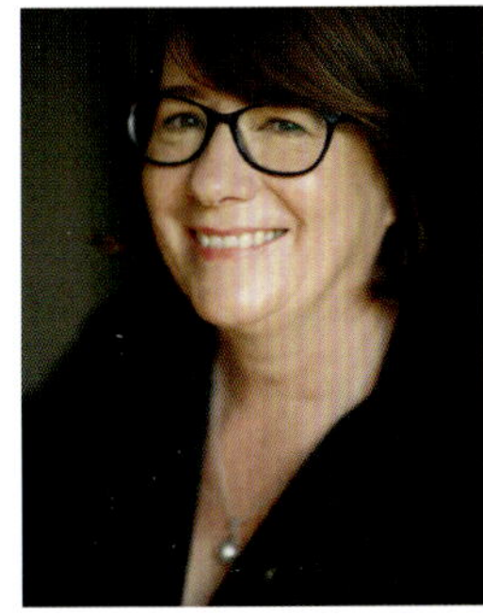

I found myself lingering for a long time over the landscape entries in this year's Australian Geographic Nature Photographer of the Year. Maybe the unprecedented restrictions throughout the pandemic have made me particularly wistful for the vistas and landforms that these talented photographers are such experts at capturing. Their powerful evocations of the unique landscapes of our region provide inspiration to embrace all opportunities to explore locally during this time of limited travel. Populating these scenes, mostly hidden from all but the keenest eye, is an array of birds, animals, invertebrates, fungi and plant life found nowhere else on the planet. The photographers featured here are equally gifted at documenting this world. They go below the ocean's surface to reveal an underwater world. They spotlight tiny insects and arachnids, replacing fear with fascination. They allow us to study animals close up, and poignantly remind us of the fragility of the natural world and of the role we play in accelerating its demise. They provoke us and galvanise us into action.

That's the power of great photography, and the reason that this popular celebration of nature goes from strength to strength with every year. The quality of this year's photography is outstanding, and I would like to thank every photographer who entered. I congratulate all who made the shortlist and are featured in this book and exhibition, with a special shout-out to portfolio prize winner Tim Wrate, the category winners, and the runners-up. Scott Portelli's engaging leafy seadragon portrait is a worthy overall winner. Scott is a great advocate for the protection of our oceans and his win well earned. Well done to the judges, all talented photographers in their own right, for their insight and expertise. Finally, I would like to acknowledge our valued partner, the South Australian Museum, and its director Brian Oldman, for their continued, excellent custodianship of this event. Special thanks from all here at Australian Geographic to Tim Gilchrist for his calm professionalism and support of the photographic community through this competition over so many years.

Chrissie Goldrick
Editor-in-Chief, Australian Geographic

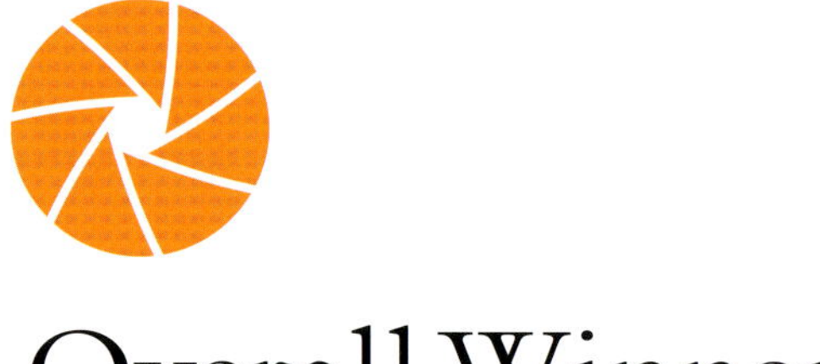

Overall Winner

Leafy Night
Leafy seadragon (*Phycodurus eques*)
Scott Portelli, New South Wales

In the temperate waters of the southern parts of Australia, a unique wonder lies hidden, camouflaged by nature, an evolutionary chameleon of the ocean. Leafy seadragons inhabit shallow reefs and seagrass meadows. They use their environment to camouflage themselves and avoid predators and this is a key component to their survival.
Fleurieu Peninsula, South Australia

Olympus OMD EM1 Mk II, 60mm macro, 1/250, f/22, ISO 100, Olympus strobes, underexposed to highlight details in the appendages

Judges' comments:

A unique and striking image. The backlighting has transformed the seadragon from a tiny sea creature into the illusion of a mythical beast. Beautifully framed, the dragon emerges from the darkness, glowing with a sense of fire within.

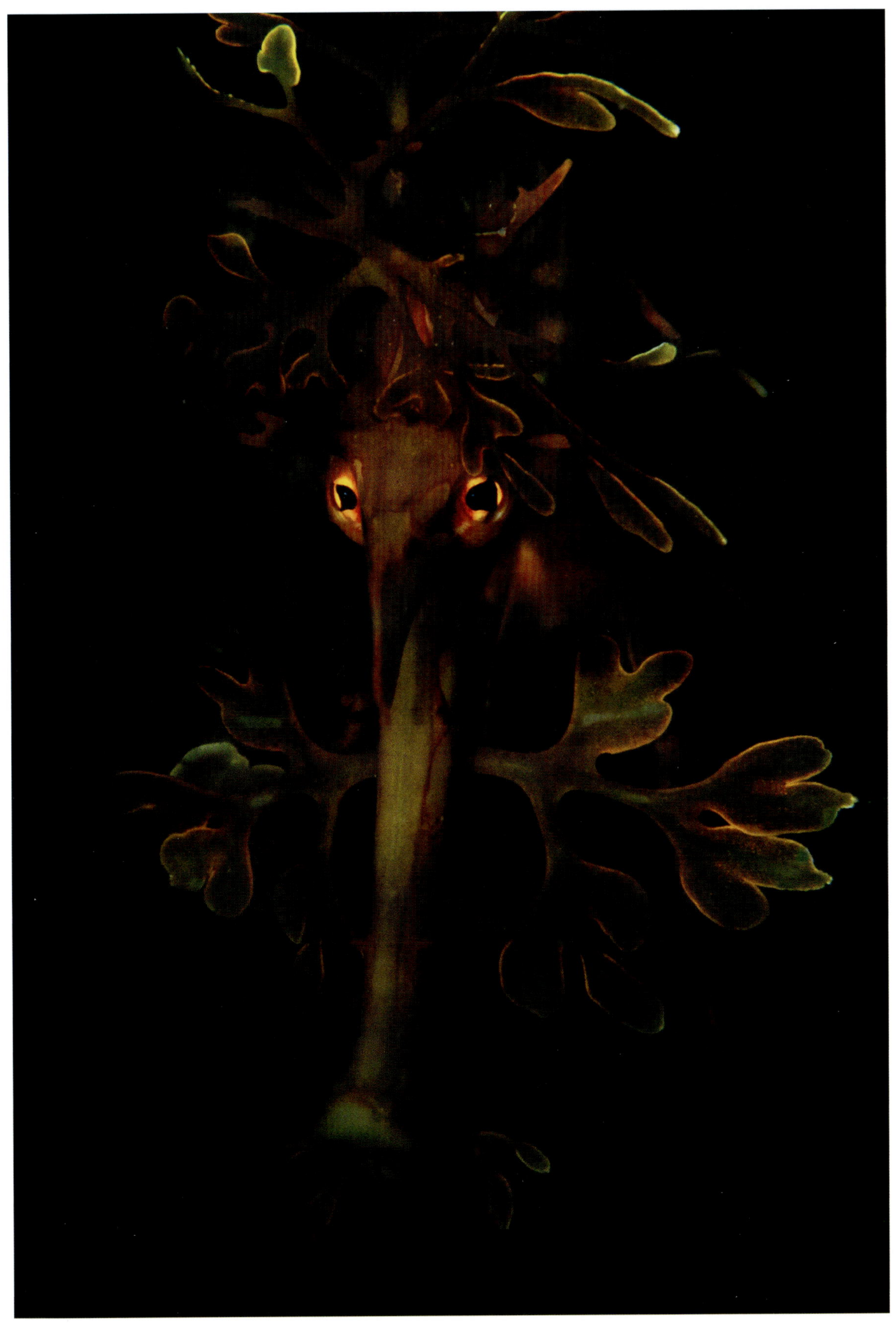

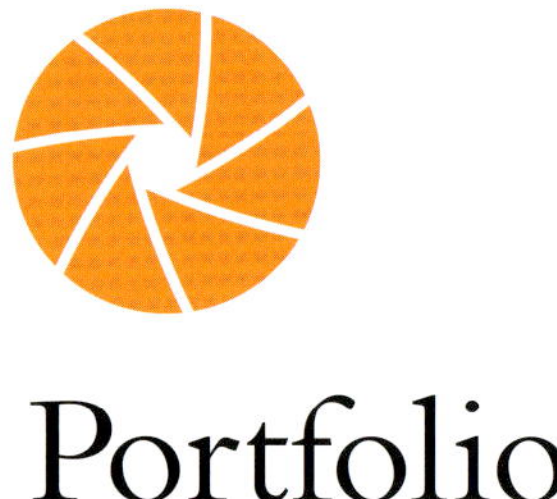

Portfolio

Rise

Tim Wrate, New South Wales

Captured above ephemeral floodplains, the electric colours and intricately textured patterns are where the waters of a standing swamp have seeped out on to the extensive floodplain network. The colours are primarily the result of a mix of high salinity levels, algae, and a long, hot dry season.

Southern Arnhem Land, Northern Territory

Fuji GFX 100, GF 110mm f/2, 1/2500, f/5.0, ISO 400, handheld, captured from a Cessna 210 at 2000 feet

Judges' comments:

The colours of Australia are celebrated in the shapes and forms caused by the incredible forces of nature. Viewed from above, the landscape has been abstracted into a painterly aesthetic. Demonstrating a keen eye for colour, structure and composition, the resulting portfolio creates curiosity and invites us to consider the landscape in a way that might not be possible from ground level.

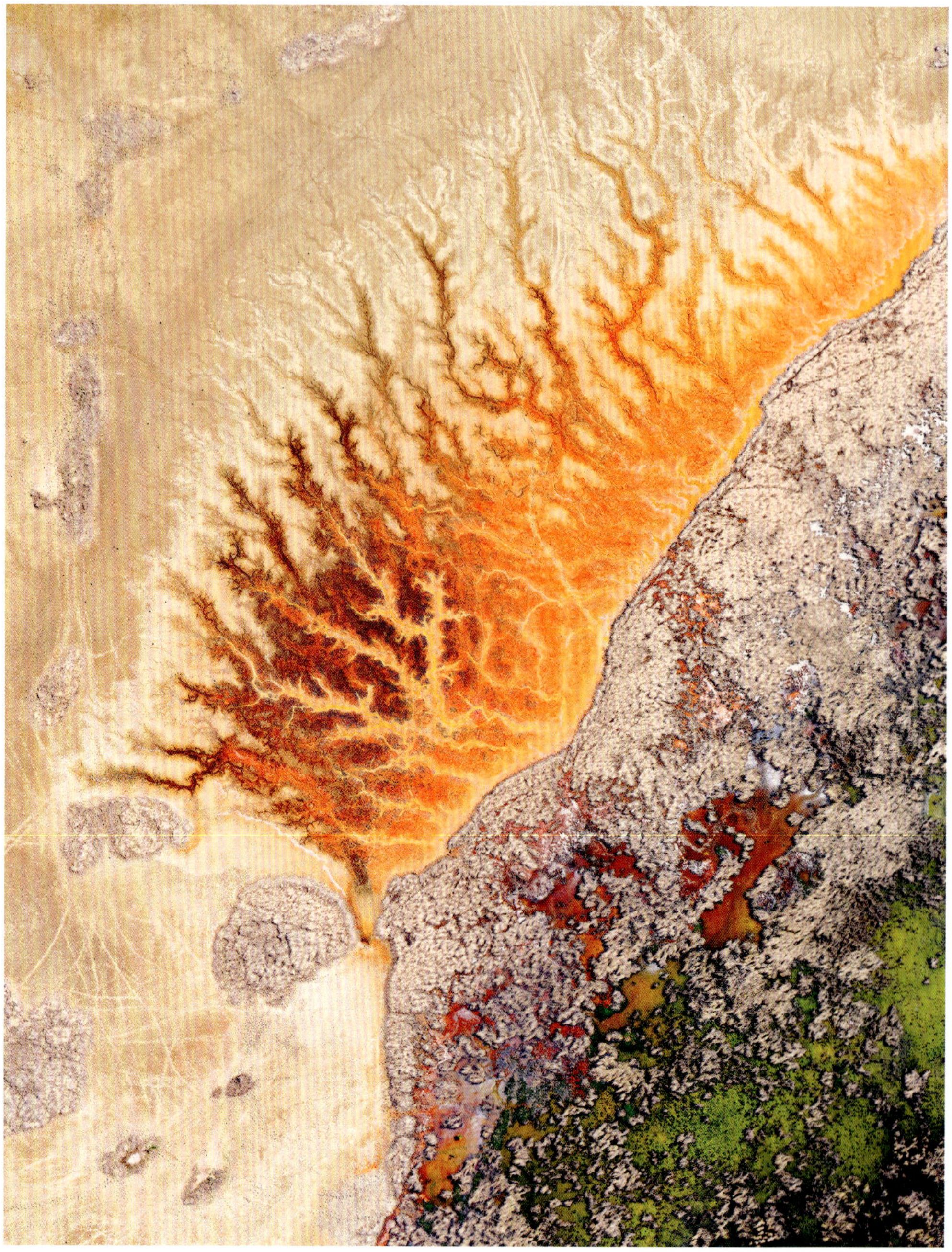

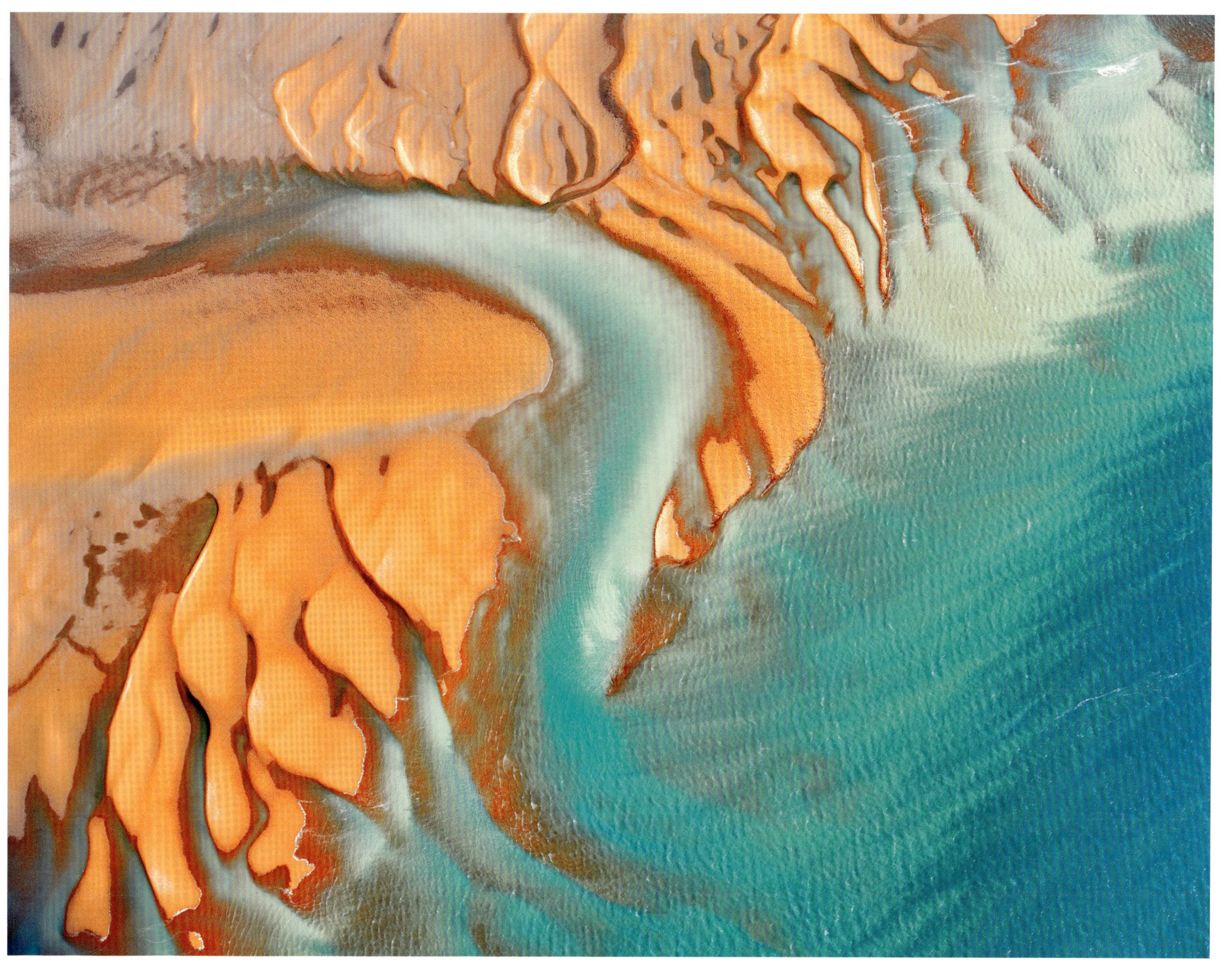

Ebb & Flow

Tim Wrate, New South Wales

Ebb & Flow was captured at 2500 feet above Bynoe Harbour, where the tidal variations of 5.8m expose extensive seabeds and variations in sand banks that contrast wonderfully with the impossibly blue water of the Northern Territory.
Bynoe Harbour, Northern Territory

Fuji GFX 100, GF 110mm f/2, 1/1900, f/5.0, ISO 200, handheld, captured from a Cessna 210 at 2500 feet

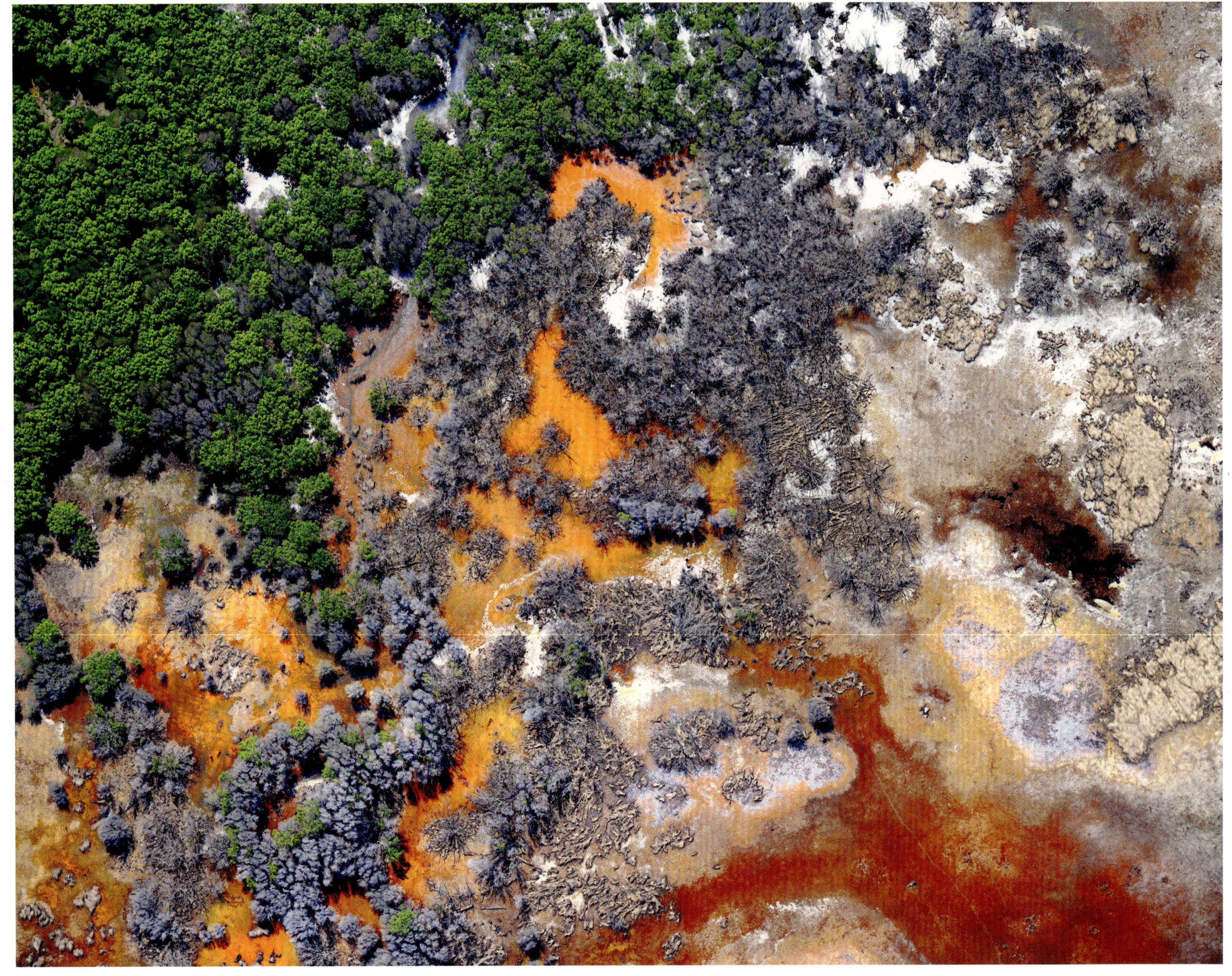

Mangrove Dieback

Northern grey mangrove

(*Avicennia marina eucalyptifolia*)

Tim Wrate, New South Wales

During the summer of 2015–16, one of the worst mangrove dieback events ever recorded devastated around 7400ha of mangrove forests along more than 1000km of Gulf of Carpentaria coastline.

The unfortunate consequence of unseasonably high temperatures and dry wet seasons caused by climate change.

Southern Arnhem Land, Northern Territory

Fuji GFX 100, GF 110mm f/2, 1/750, f/5.0, ISO 200, handheld, captured from a Cessna 210 at 1500 feet

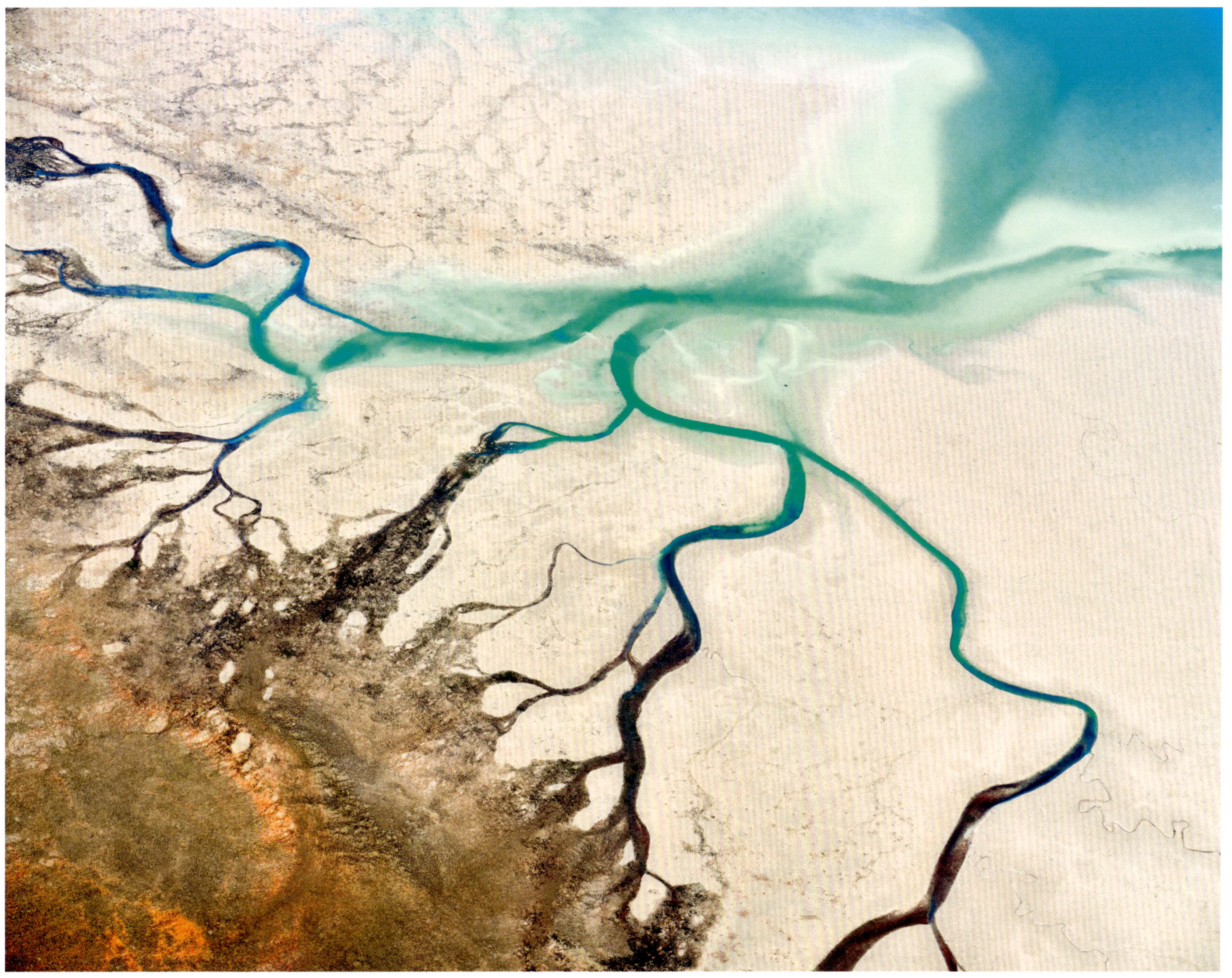

Balance

Tim Wrate, New South Wales

Low tide exposes the seabed and rock shelf of Bynoe Harbour. The patterns created by the receding water are really intriguing and the warmth in the bottom left balances the cool of the top right perfectly, giving the image a sense of rhythm.
Bynoe Harbour, Northern Territory

Fuji GFX 100, GF 110mm f/2, 1/2500, f/5.6, ISO 320, handheld, captured from a Cessna 210 at 2000 feet

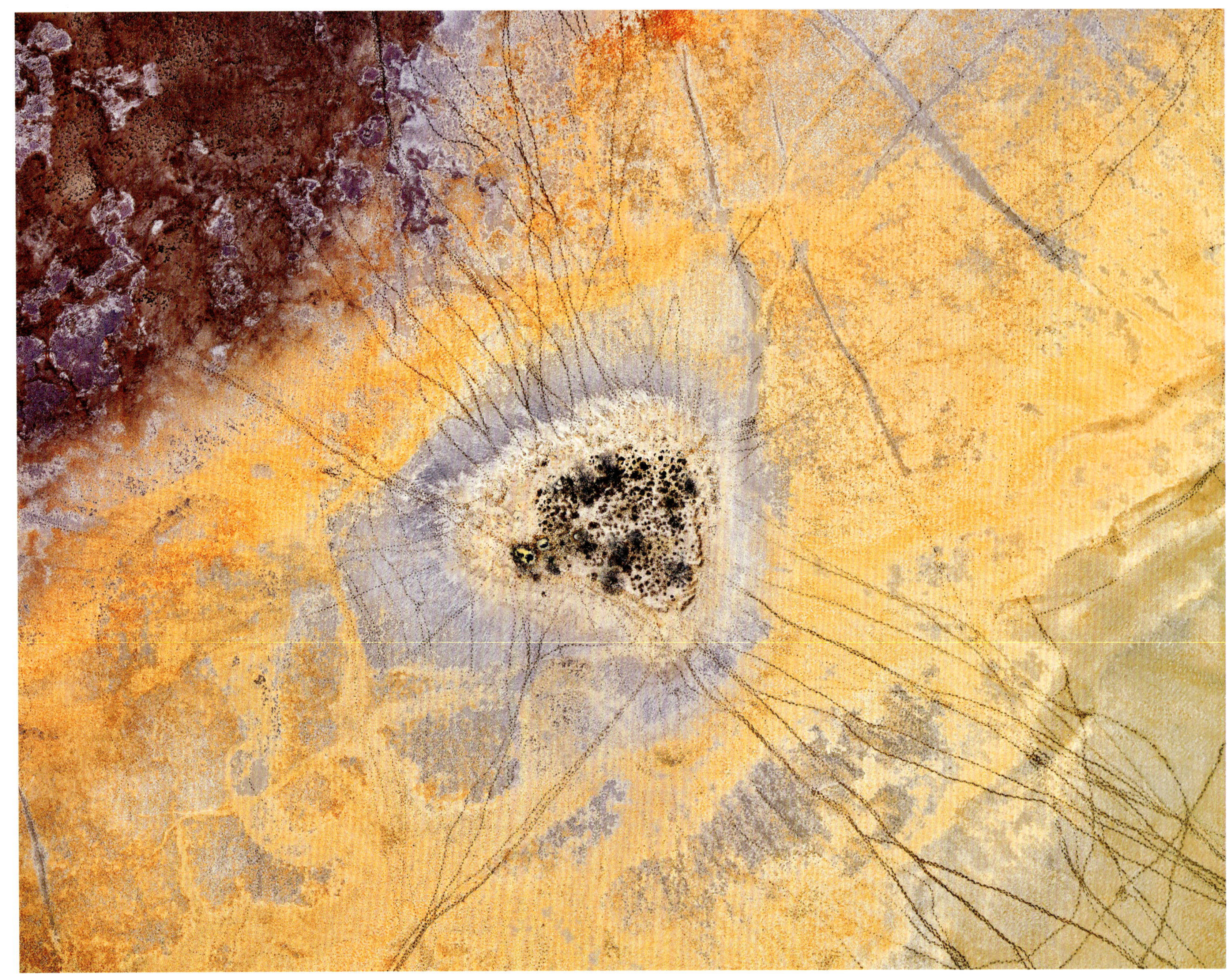

Tracks

Tim Wrate, New South Wales

This picture was captured at 2000 feet above the intertidal floodplains between the Roper and Limmen Bight Rivers on the remote shores of the Gulf of Carpentaria. The floodplain is punctuated by water buffalo tracks meandering to and from the island. Look closer and you may find water buffaloes basking in mud wallows. *Southern Arnhem Land, Northern Territory*

Fuji GFX 100, GF 110mm f/2, 1/2700, f/4.5, ISO 160, handheld, captured from a Cessna 210 at 2000 feet

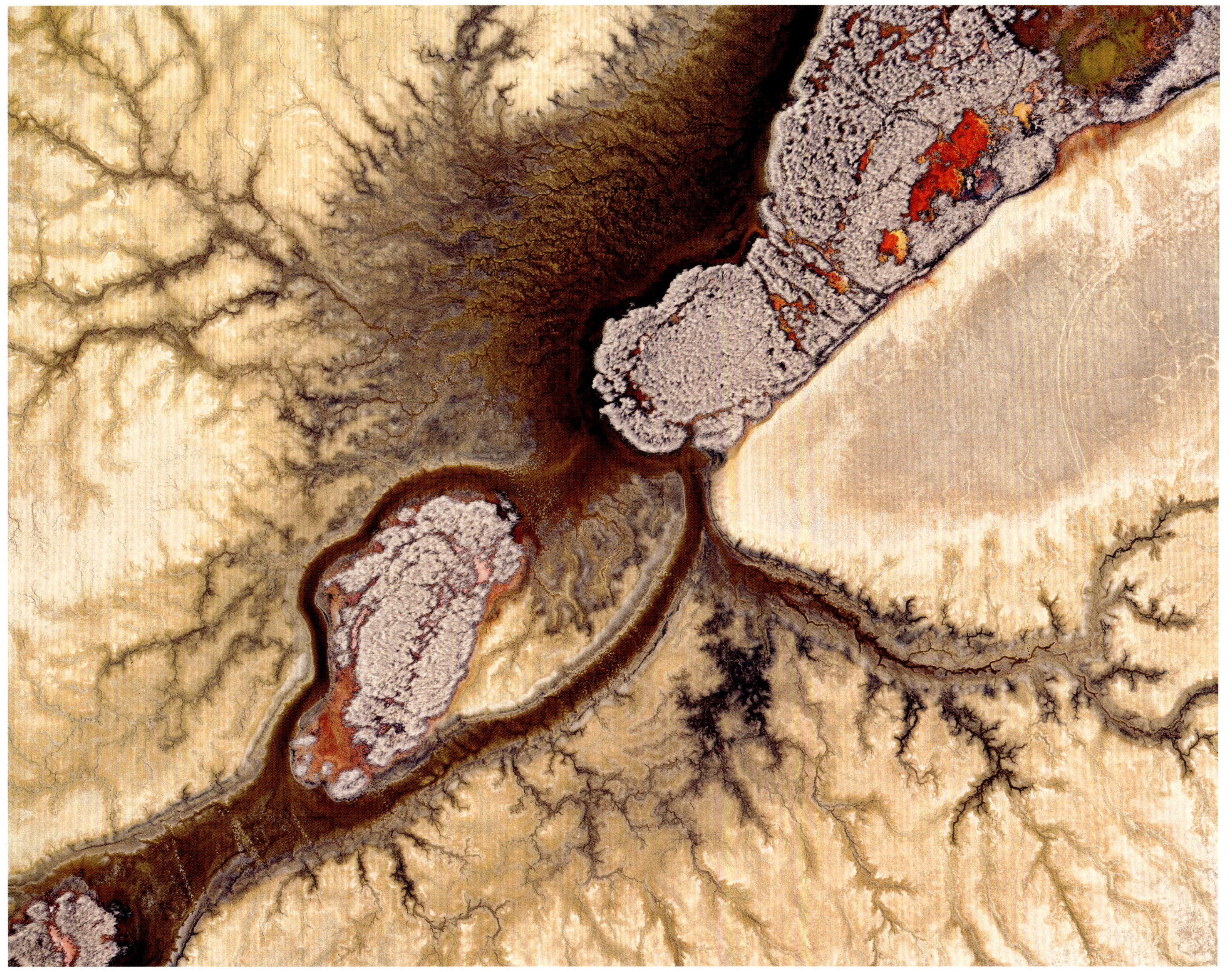

Fabrica
Tim Wrate, New South Wales

Flying over the remote Limmen Bight region of the far western Gulf of Carpentaria was one of the single most incredible experiences of my photographic career. What may be ordinary from the ground can be extraordinary from above – this image is the perfect example of that.
Southern Arnhem Land, Northern Territory

Fuji GFX 100, GF 110mm f/2, 1/1800, f/5.0, ISO 250, handheld, captured from a Cessna 210 at 2000 feet

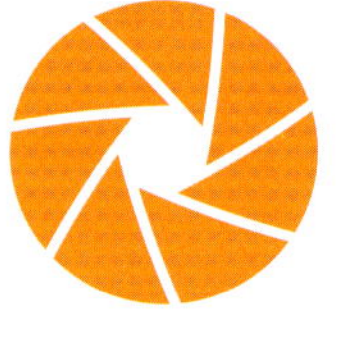

Animal Portrait

Animal Portrait Winner

A white-capped at sunset

White-capped mollymawk (*Thalassarche cauta*)
Doug Gimesy, Victoria

White-capped mollymawks aka white-capped albatrosses, mainly eat squid, fish, krill, salps, and offal from the ocean surface. They rarely dive for food. Their largest threat is now longline and trawl fishing, especially in the seas off southern Africa. Please eat less fish and buy only MSC certified produce.
Foveaux Strait, Stewart Island, New Zealand

Nikon d750, Nikon 80–400mm f/4.5–5.6, 1/640, f/7.1, ISO 800, handheld

Judges' comments:
There is a surreal quality to this albatross, flying sternly across the sky with anthropomorphic determination. The sharpness highlights the bird's facial features, colour and shape. The angles and lines of the bird caught mid-flight have been used to advantage, contrasting against the soft pastel background of clouds.

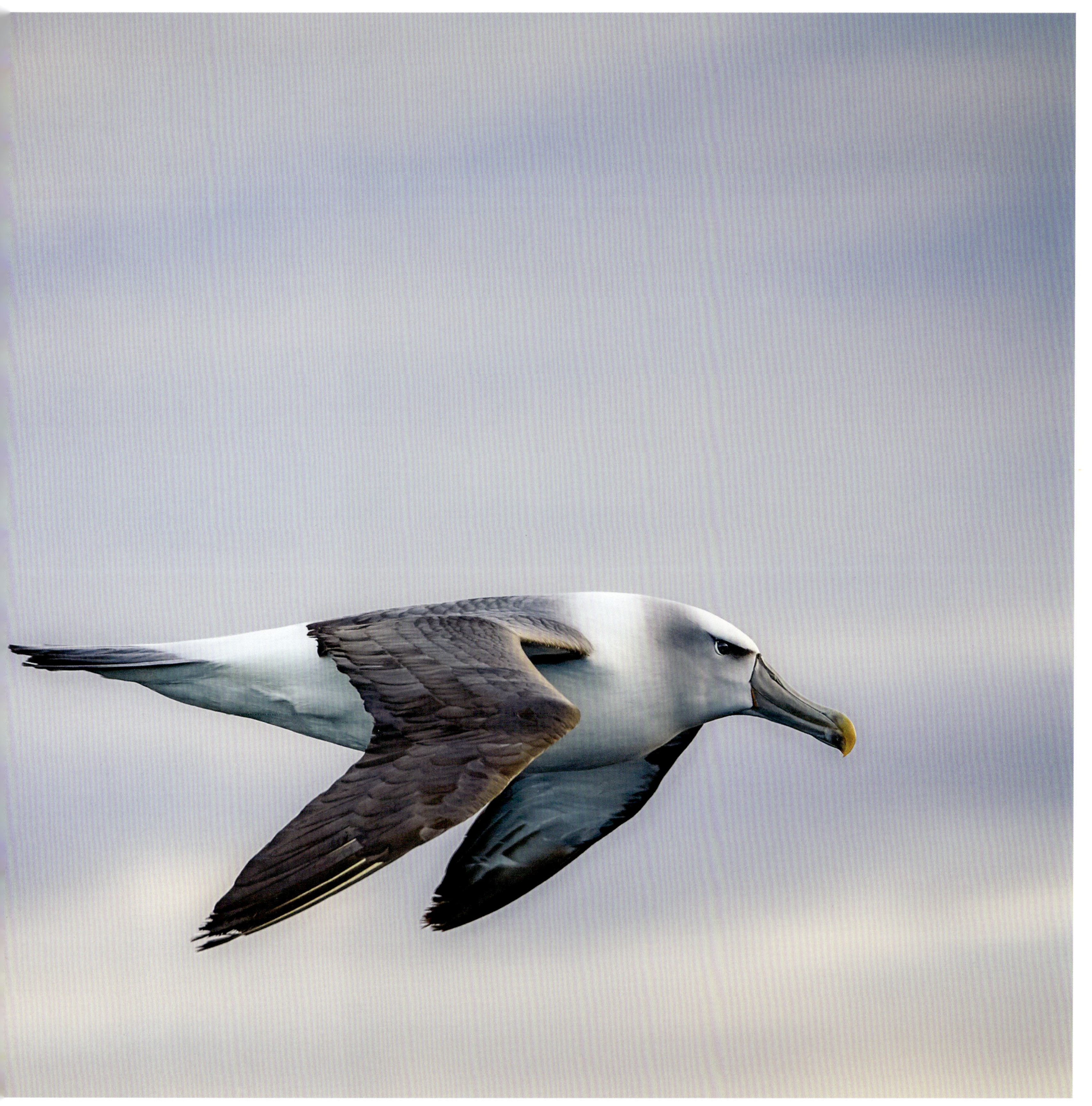

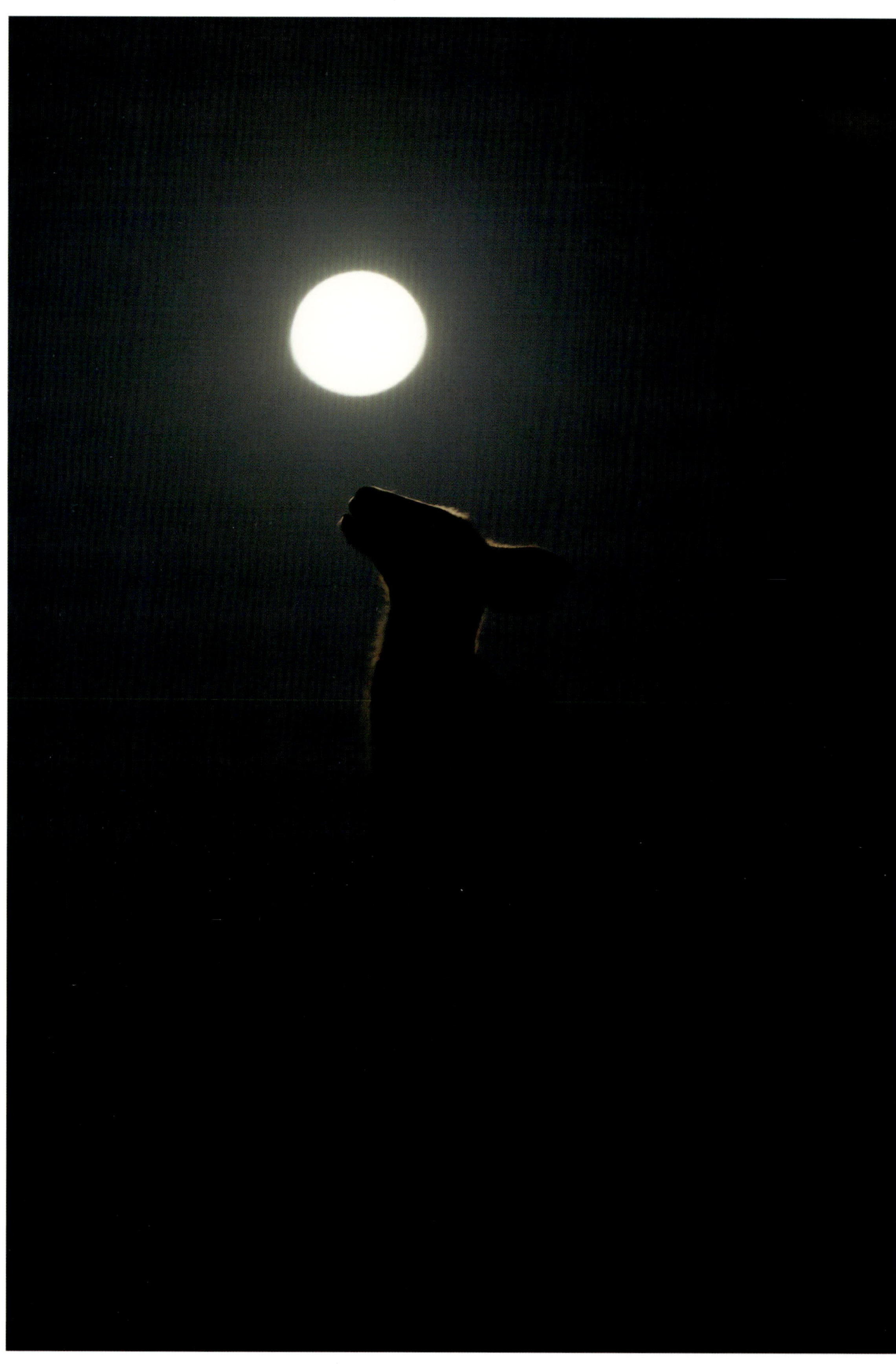

Animal Portrait Runner-Up

Howling at the moon

Eastern grey kangaroo
(*Macropus giganteus*)
Mike George, New South Wales

I spotted some eastern grey kangaroos on the headland. I had to crawl through long grass downhill from them to try and get close enough to backlight one against the rising full moon. As I took a few shots my model tilted its head back and opened its mouth slightly.
Woolgoolga, New South Wales

Canon EOS 5D Mk II, Canon EF 70–200mm f2.8L IS USM, 1/60, f/2.8, ISO 4000, handheld, manual exposure and manual focus

Judges' comments:
Delicately backlit, the likelihood of a kangaroo positioning itself so perfectly beneath a full moon makes this a miraculous capture. This is a powerful image and well executed by the photographer.

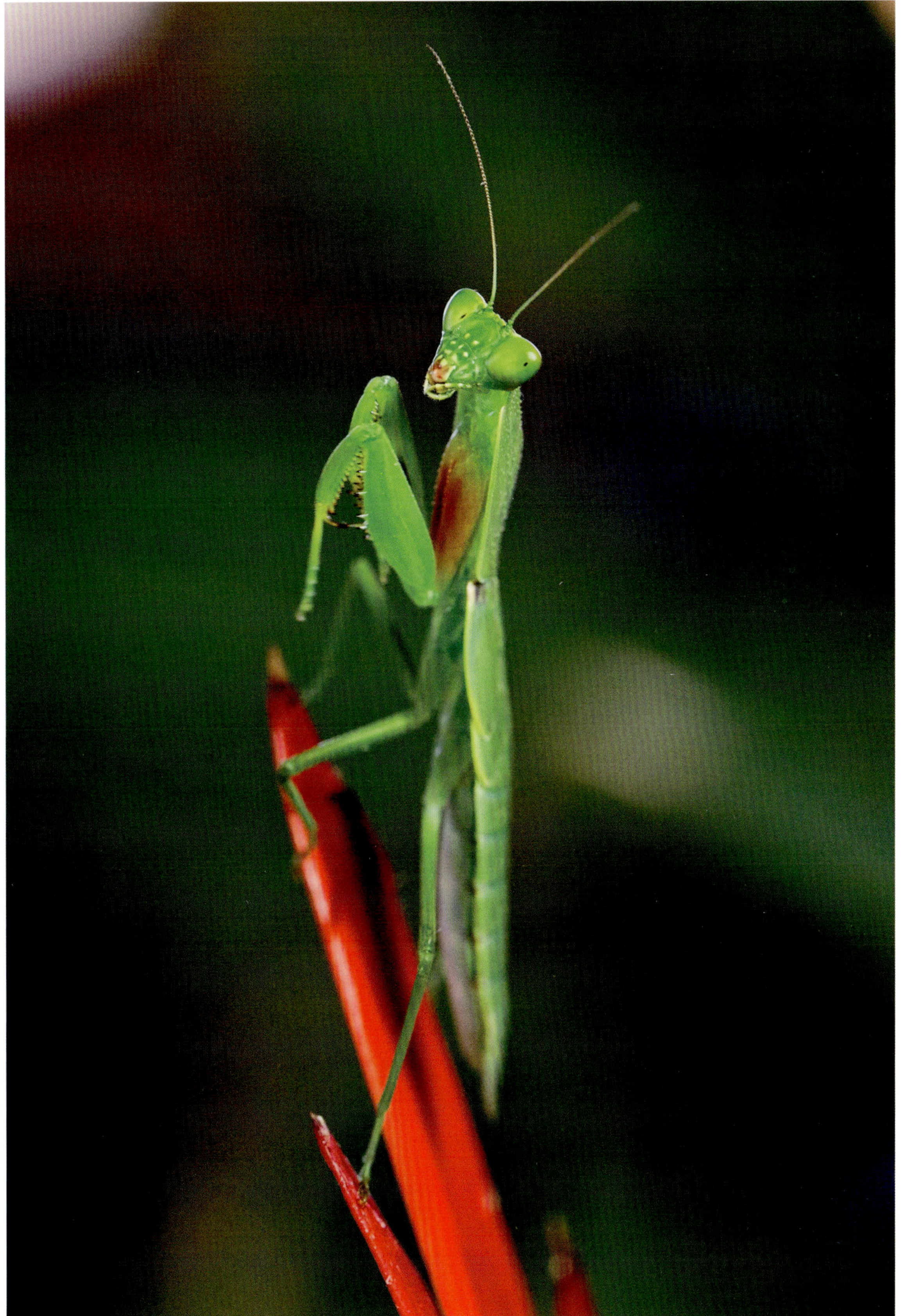

Elegant

Praying mantis (Mantodea)
Sharron Marks, New South Wales

My camera is never far away when I am in the garden. You never know what you might find, as was the case with this praying mantis, suspended elegantly on this red spear. I appreciated its willingness to strike a pose, the green on its body contrasted greatly with the spear's red.
Port Kembla, New South Wales

Canon EOS 5D Mk III, Canon EF 100mm f/2.8L macro IS USM, 1/160, f/8.0, ISO 4000, handheld

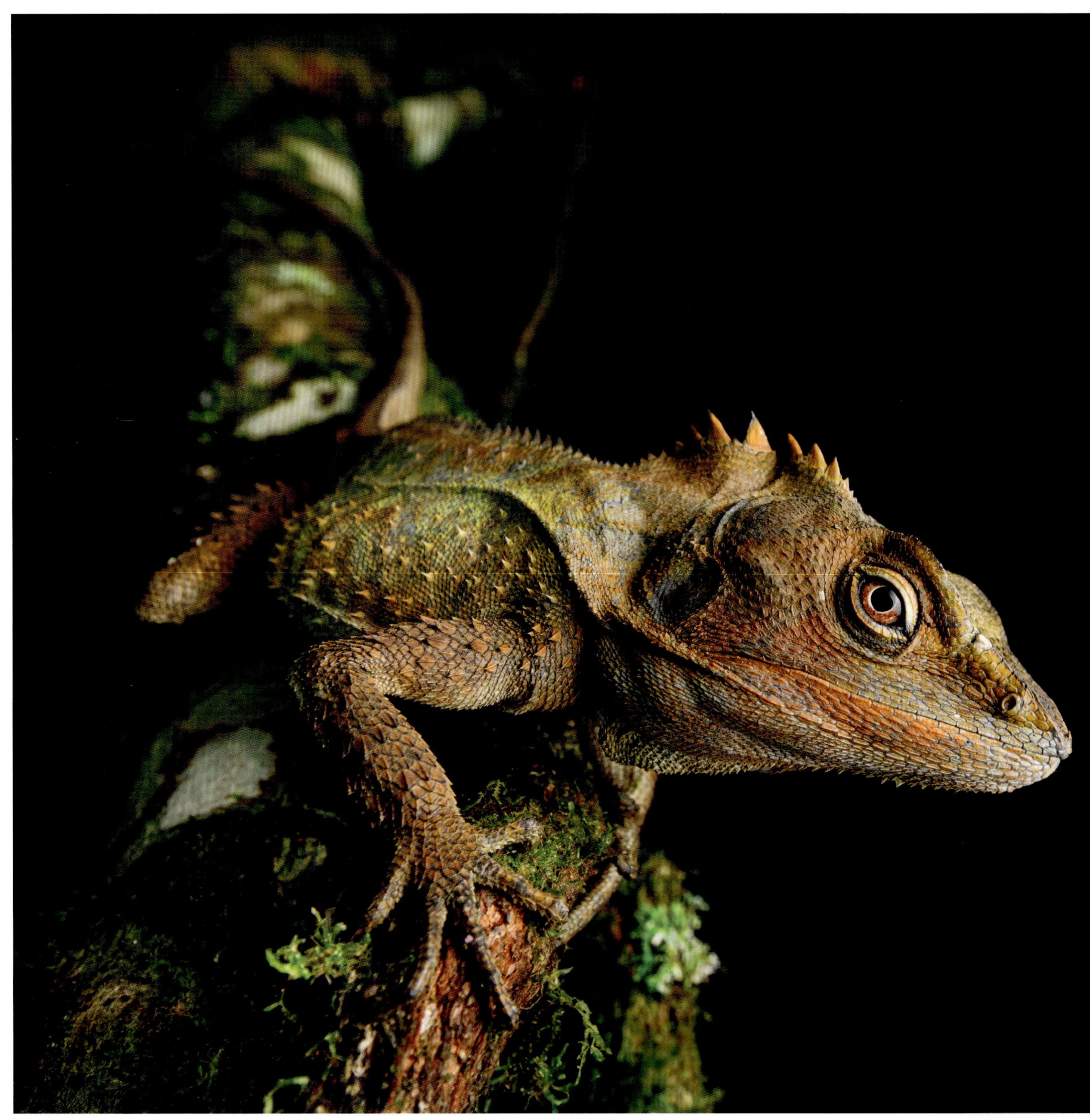

Forest Dragon

Cryptic forest dragon,
(*Lophosaurus spinipes*)
Isaac Wishart, Queensland

The cryptic forest dragon is my favourite reptile to photograph. Although common, this species is rarely seen. The forest dragon is often overlooked due to its effective camouflage and slow-moving nature. These dragons are sexually dimorphic, coming in a range of colours.
Springbrook National Park, Queensland

Nikon D850, Tamron 15–30mm f/2.8, 1/200, f/11, ISO 125, off camera flash, handheld

---

Rufous Fantail

Rufous fantail (*Rhipidura rufifrons*)
Matt Oliver, Victoria

Mt Macedon on a cold, wet, windy, overcast day. I saw a couple of rufous fantails enter a large clump of ferns with a lichen-covered branch at the edge and waited until one came out to look at me briefly.
Mount Macedon, Victoria

Nikon D500, Nikon AF-S Nikkor 500mm f5.6E PF ED VR Nikon TC-14E III 1.4X teleconverter, 1/1000, f/8, ISO 12800, handheld

OVER PAGE

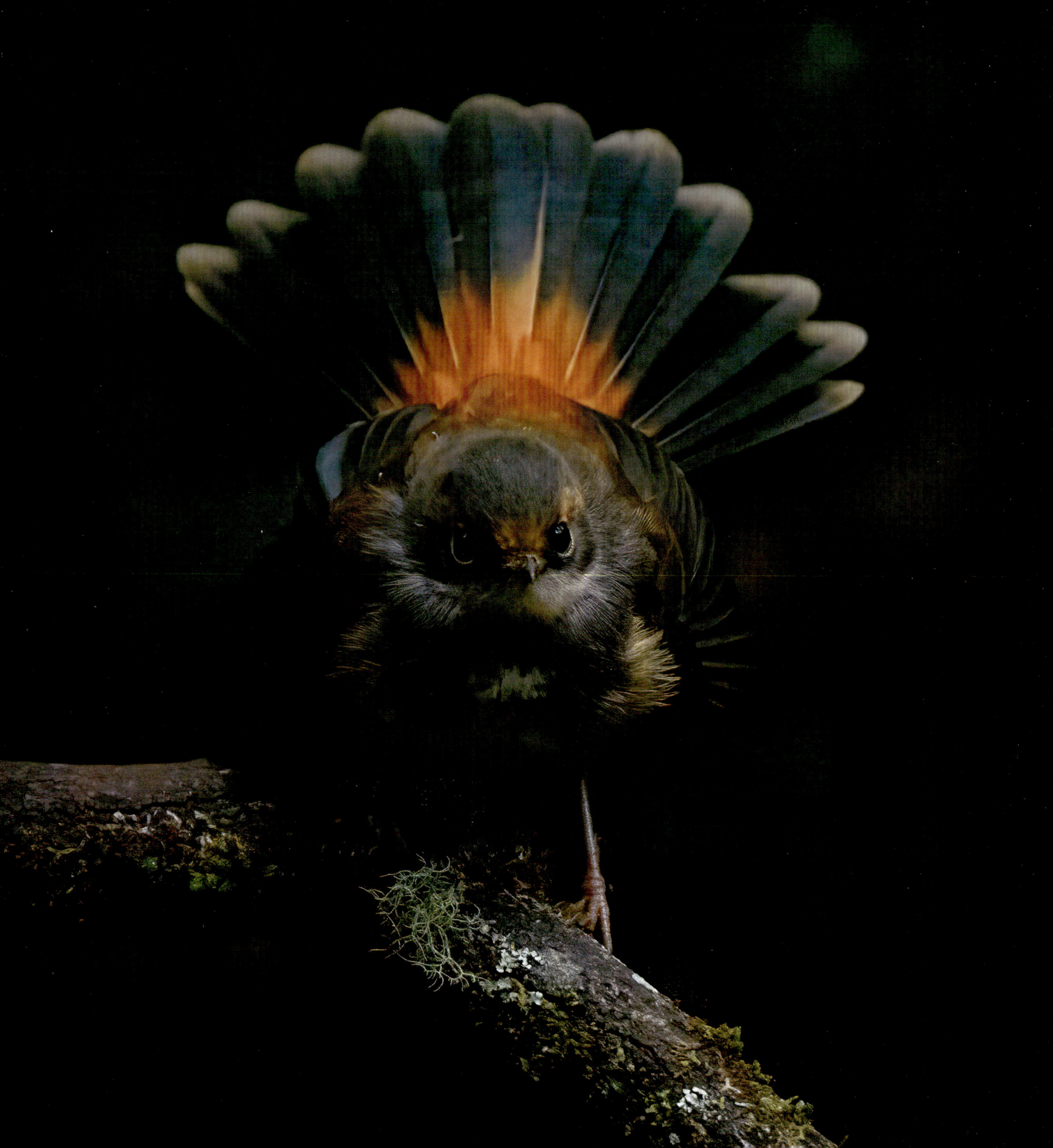

Masked Hero

Eastern fiddler ray
(*Trygonorrhina fasciata*)
Pete McGee, New South Wales

Fiddler rays cover their beautifully marked bodies with sand to help prevent detection. I saw the eyes of this one protruding rather obviously and was amused by its comical appearance. Its misplaced confidence in its own camouflage allowed me to approach closely and photograph the 'masked hero'.
Cabbage Tree Bay, Manly, New South Wales

Sony NEX7, Sony E 10–18mm f/4 OSS (focal length 13mm), 1/100, f/9, ISO 200, twin Inon strobes (external), handheld

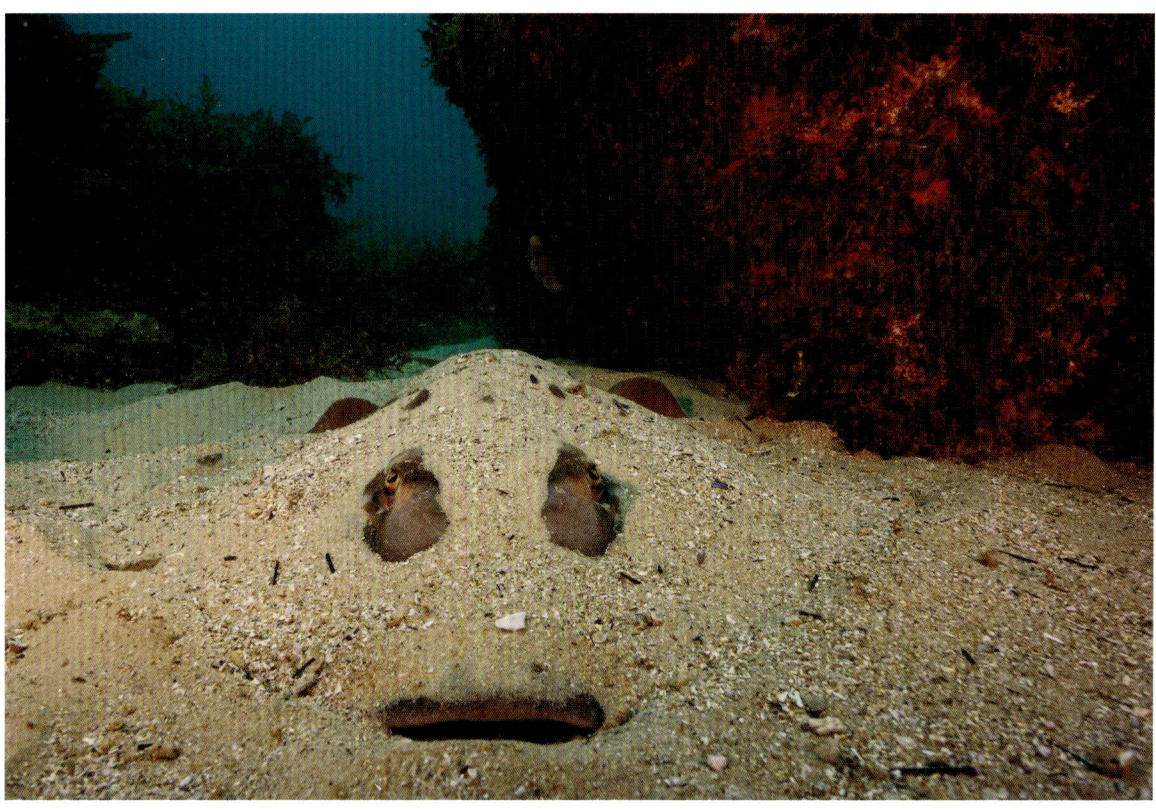

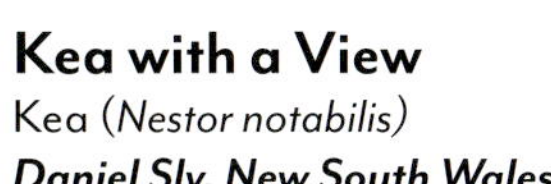

Kea with a View

Kea (*Nestor notabilis*)
Daniel Sly, New South Wales

The kea is the only parrot species in the world that can be found in the alpine environment. I came across this particularly inquisitive individual who was more than happy to pose on a rock for me with the beautiful Lake Wakatipu in the background.
South Island, New Zealand

Nikon D7200, Sigma 17–50mm f/2.8 EX DC OS HSM, 1/640, f/4.0, ISO 100, handheld

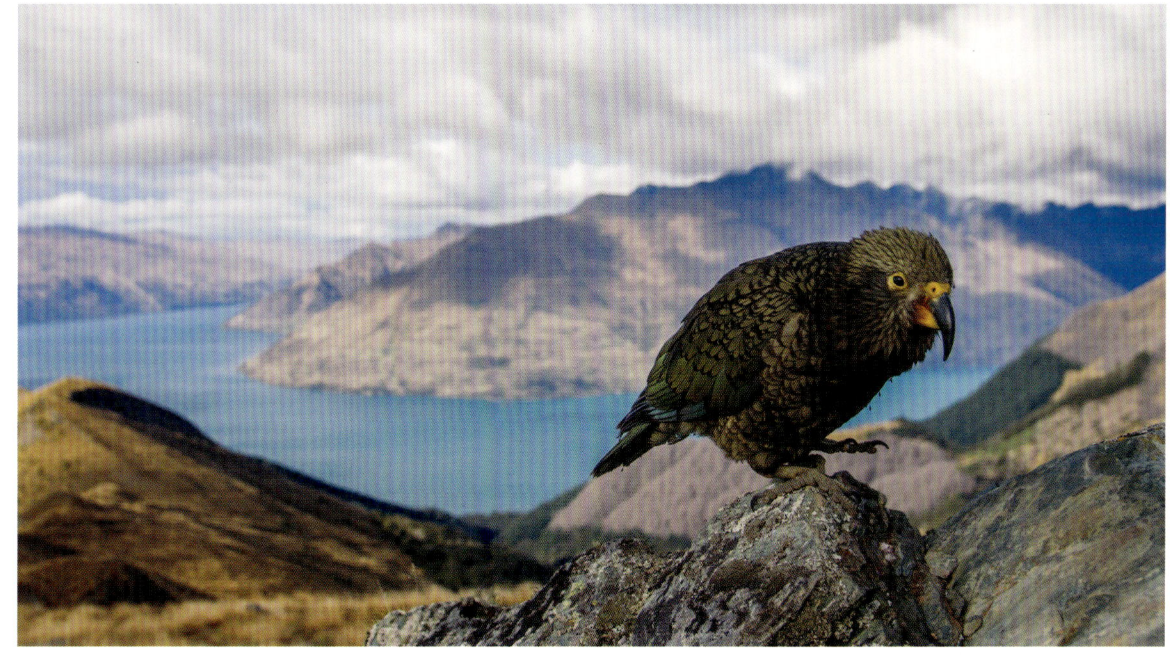

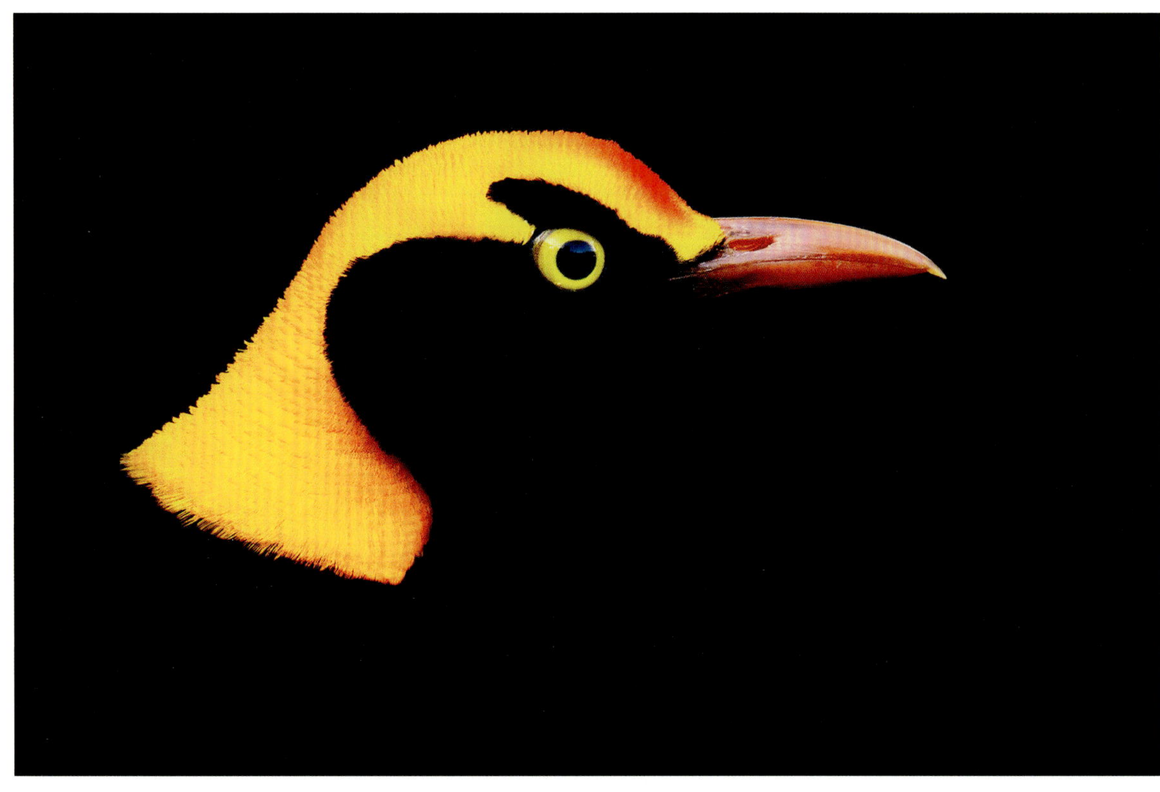

Regent of the rainforest

Regent bowerbird
(*Sericulus chrysocephalus*)
Craig Greer, South Australia

A truly exotic species, the regent bowerbird features high on any bird photographer's bucket list. In late 2020, I made a short trip to the Gold Coast's Lamington National Park, a stronghold for this most striking of birds, and was happy to come away with this image.
Lamington National Park, Queensland

Nikon D500, AF-S Nikkor 500mm f/5.6E PF ED, 1/320, f/5.6, ISO 800, handheld

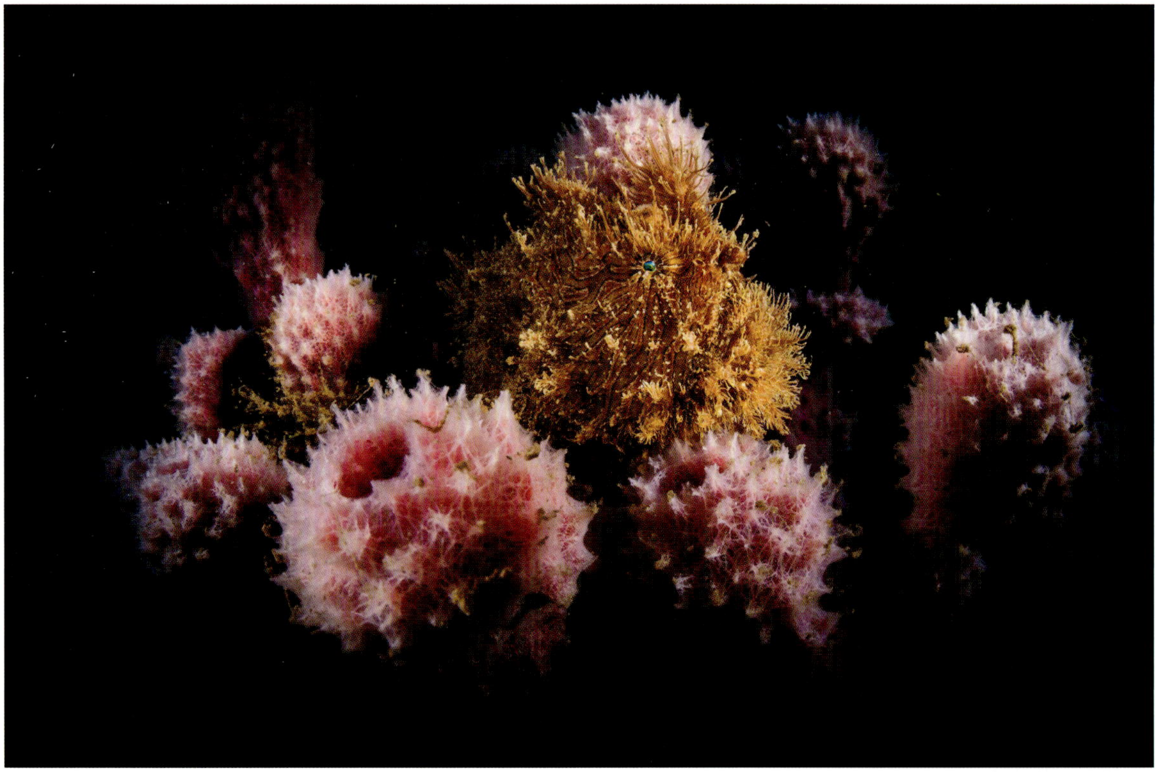

Now You See Me

Striate anglerfish (*Antennarius striatus*)
Matty Smith, New South Wales

The striate anglerfish is a master of disguise. They are very poor swimmers yet highly predatory. They wait motionless for prey. When I found this one, I had the wrong lens to make a captivating portrait of it. I swapped lenses for the next dive, hoping it was still there.
Nelson Bay, New South Wales

Nikon Z7, Nikkor 8–15mm f3.5–4.5 E ED fisheye, 1/200, f/22, ISO 200, 2 x Sea & Sea YS-D3 flashed, Aquatica AD6/7 underwater housing

Nocturnal Nightmares

Common stargazer
(*Kathetostoma laeve*)
Richard Smith, United Kingdom

As night falls, the stargazer, a fish about a foot in length, emerges from beneath the sand to ambush its hapless prey. With the naked eye, it blends in seamlessly, however, I was using special techniques to show off its biofluorescence; the fish glows an eerie neon yellow.
Wakatobi, Indonesia

Nikon D850, Nikon 105 mm VR with yellow blocking filter, 1/160, f/13, ISO 640, dual INON strobes with 'excitation' filters, Nauticam underwater housing, handheld on scuba

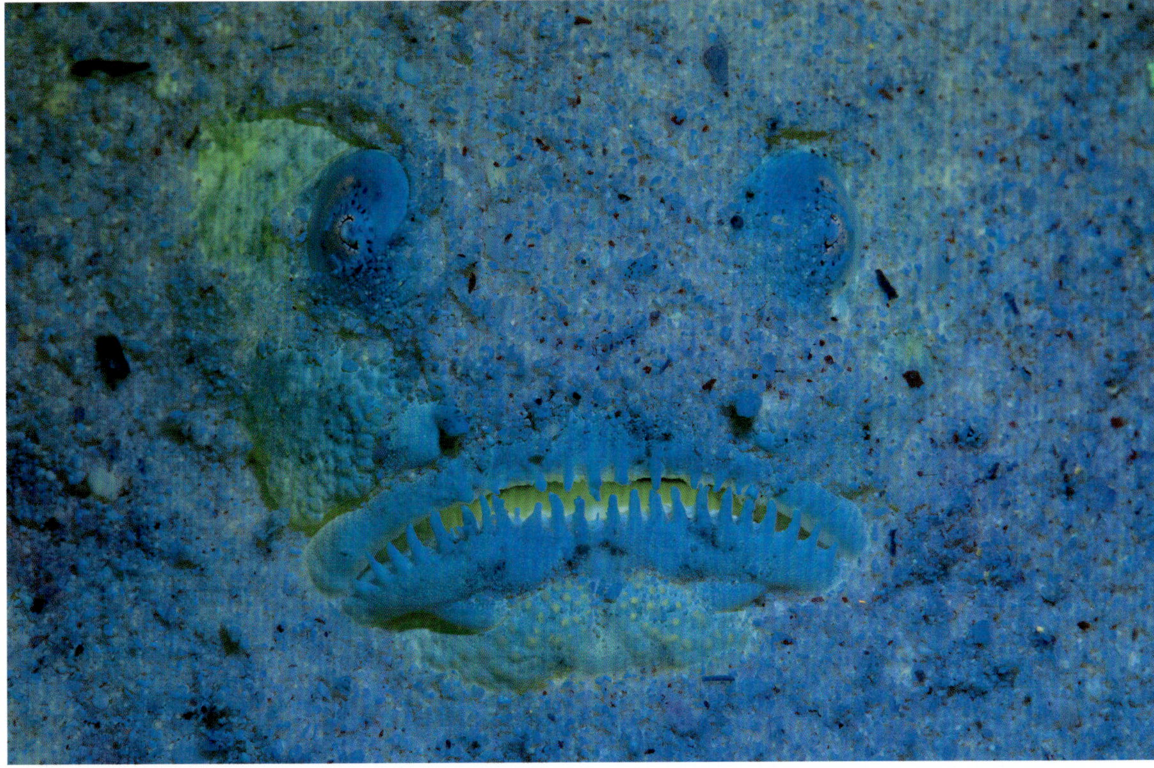

Checking me out

Australian fur-seal
(*Arctocephalus pusillus doriferus*)
Alex Pike, Australian Capital Territory

A playful Australian fur-seal swimming by me for a closer look. These mammals are seriously nimble swimmers, using their powerful flippers to shoot through the water.
Jervis Bay, New South Wales

Canon EOS 5D Mk IV, Canon 35mm f2.0, 1/1250, f/2.0, ISO 100, Ikelite housing, handheld

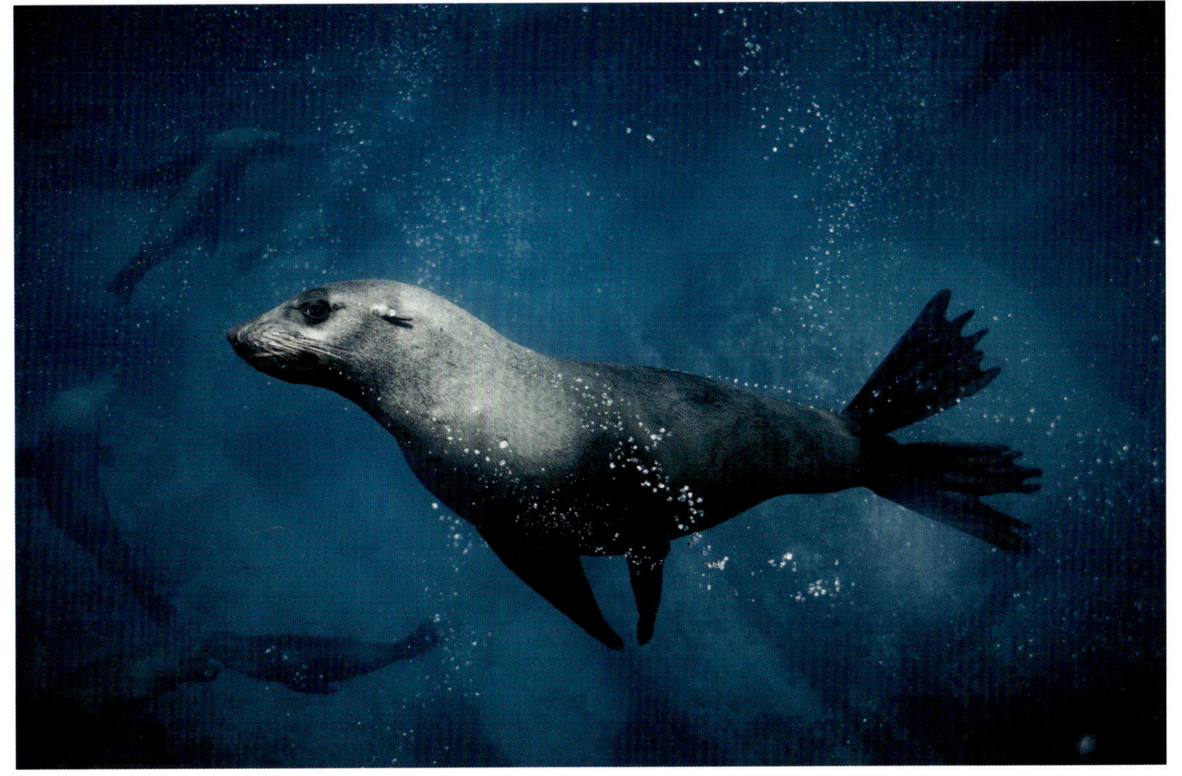

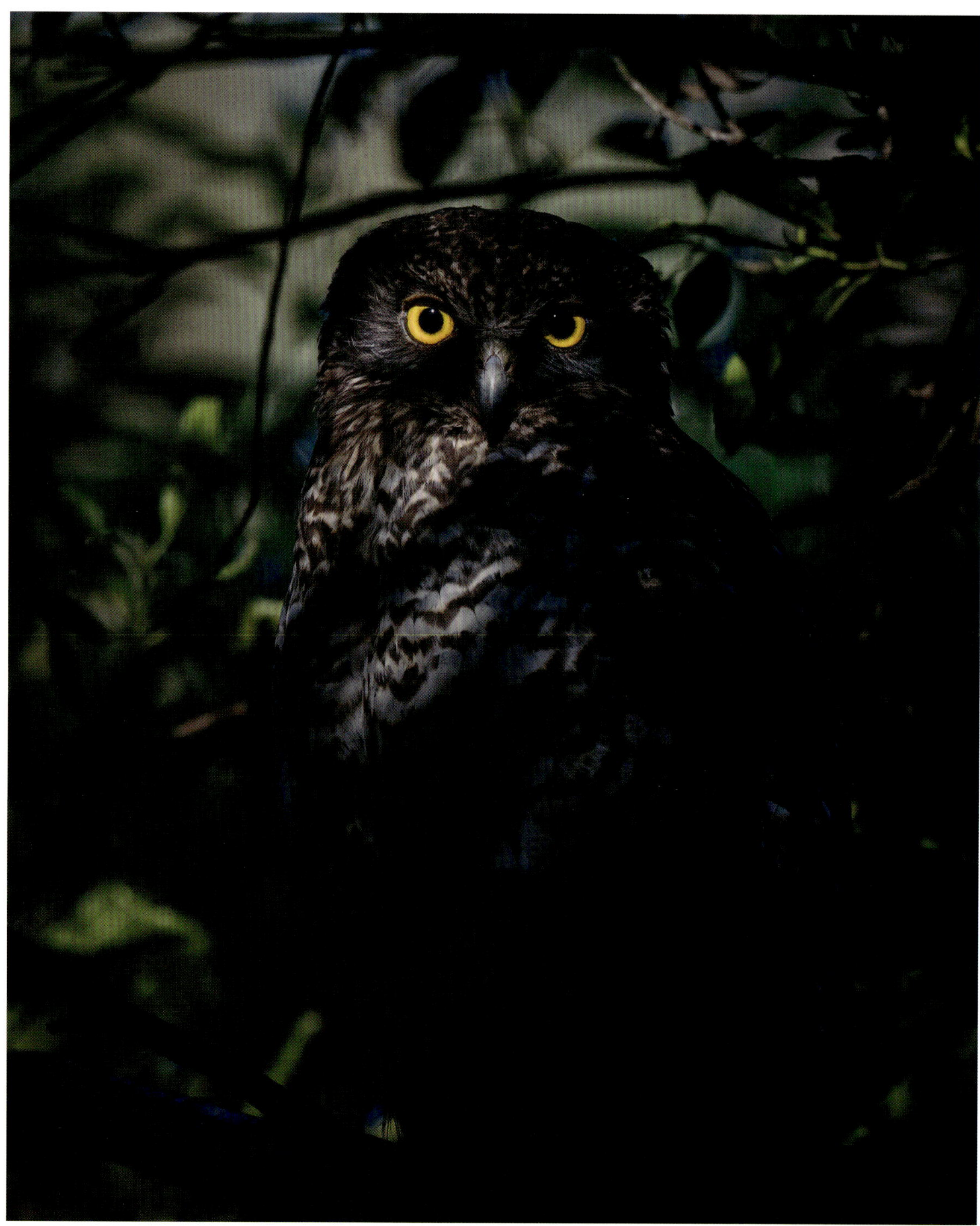

Powerful Stare

Powerful owl (*Ninox strenua*)
David Stowe, New South Wales

The late afternoon sun caught the eyes of this powerful owl while it was roosting along a creek line, giving it an intimidating look!
Sydney, New South Wales

Canon 5D Mk IV, Canon 500mm f4L IS II + 1.4X, 1/125, f/8, ISO 800, Gitzo tripod and Mongoose gimbal head

---

Snake Eel

Snake eel (species unknown), Periclimenes shrimp (*Periclimenes* sp)
Neil Vincent, New South Wales

Snake eels bury themselves in the bottom substrate and move easily through the sand, exposing only their head during the day, then coming out to hunt in the open at night. This eel is being cleaned by *periclimenes* shrimp, removing dead skin and parasites from its body.
Lembeh Strait, Sulawesi, Indonesia

Nikon D700, Nikkor 60mm micro, 1/250, f/20, ISO 500, 2 x Ikelite D160 underwater strobes, handheld in Subal housing

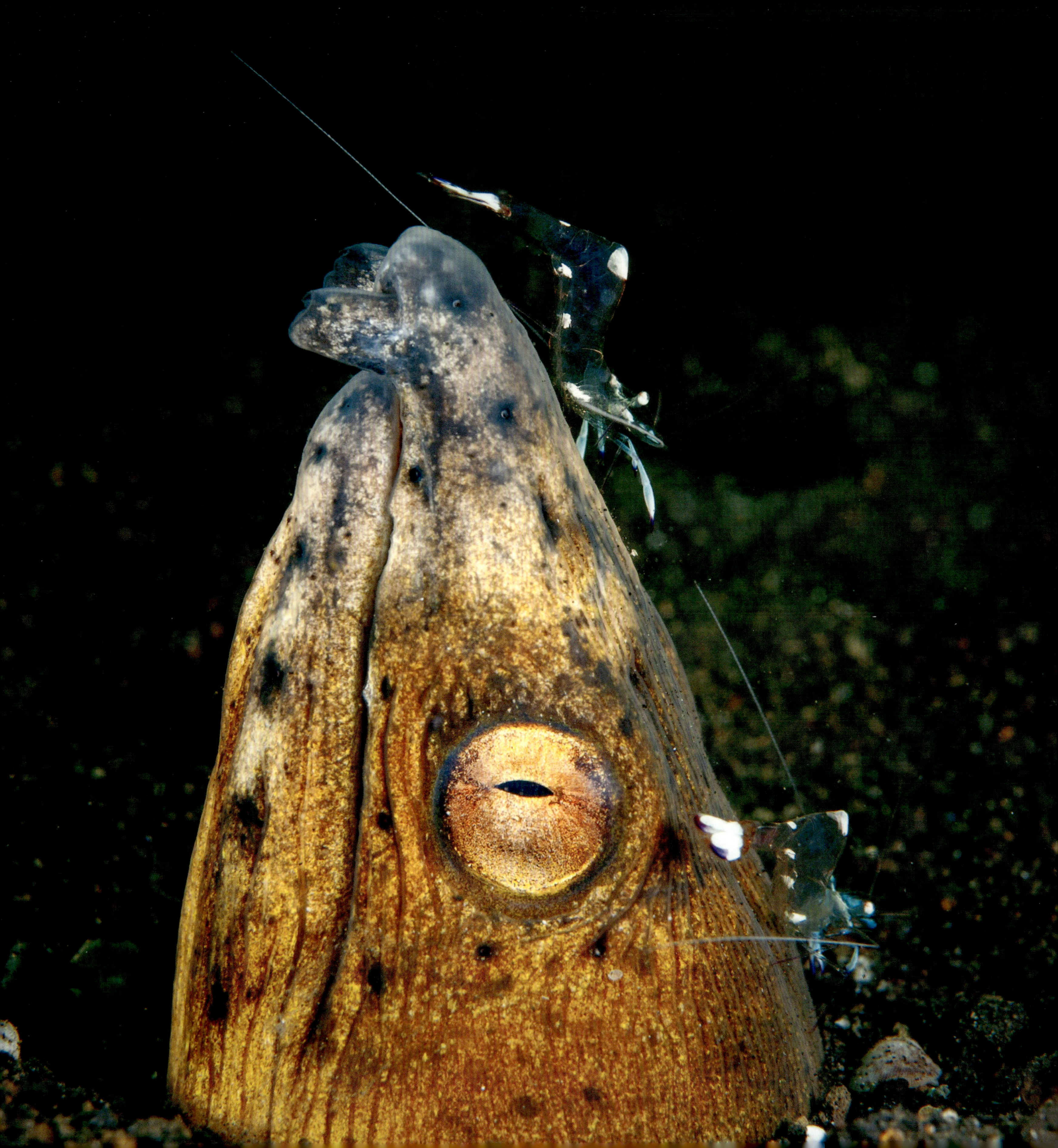

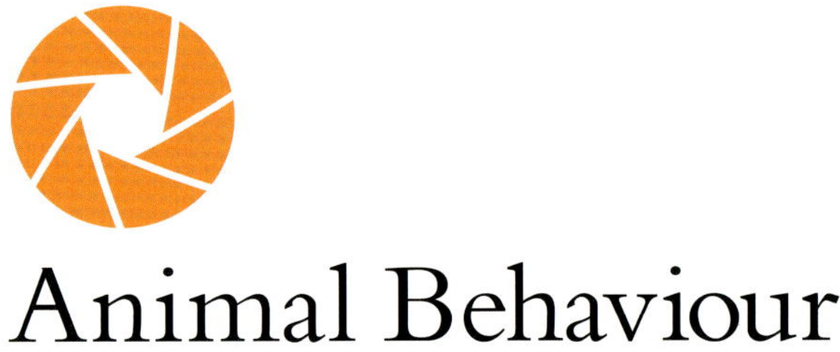

Animal Behaviour

Animal Behaviour Winner

Next generation

West Australian seahorse
(*Hippocampus subelongatus*)
Tammy Gibbs, Western Australia

I've spent many hours underwater at night photographing our West Australian seahorses giving birth. It's the male seahorses that 'get pregnant' and brood the babies in their pouch. Photographing them having their babies takes lots of patience, persistence, good timing and a hint of luck.
Perth, Western Australian

Nikon D850, Nikkor 60mm macro, 1/200 sec, f/13, ISO 320, 2 x Inon Z240 strobes, Nauticam NA-D850 underwater housing with 230mm dome port, handheld

Judges' comments:
Beautifully composed and technically difficult, this is an incredible capture of such an extraordinary moment. Subtle colour helps to achieve a mystical, magical quality, like something out of a dream. Dedication, patience and good timing have all come together to create a stunning image.

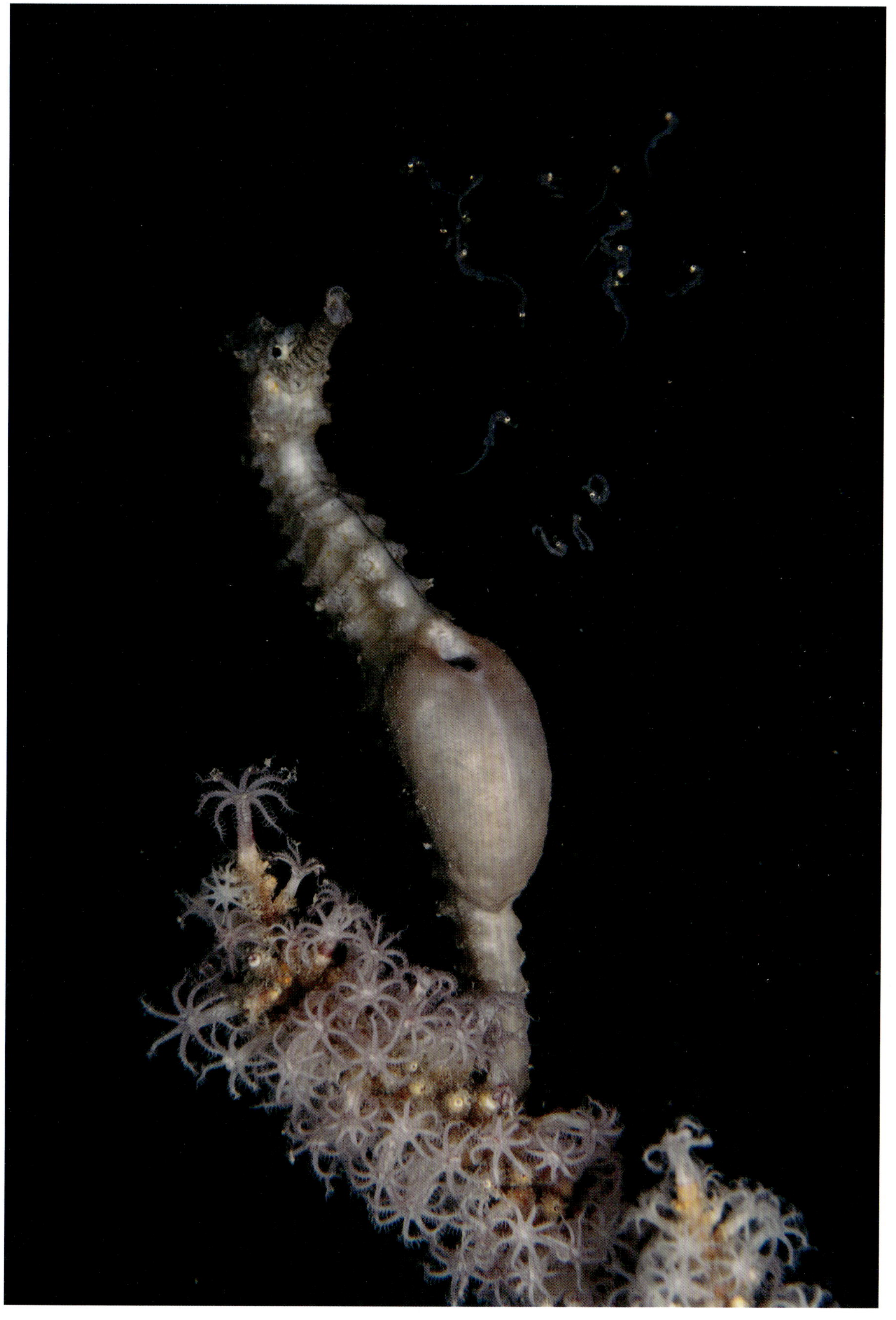

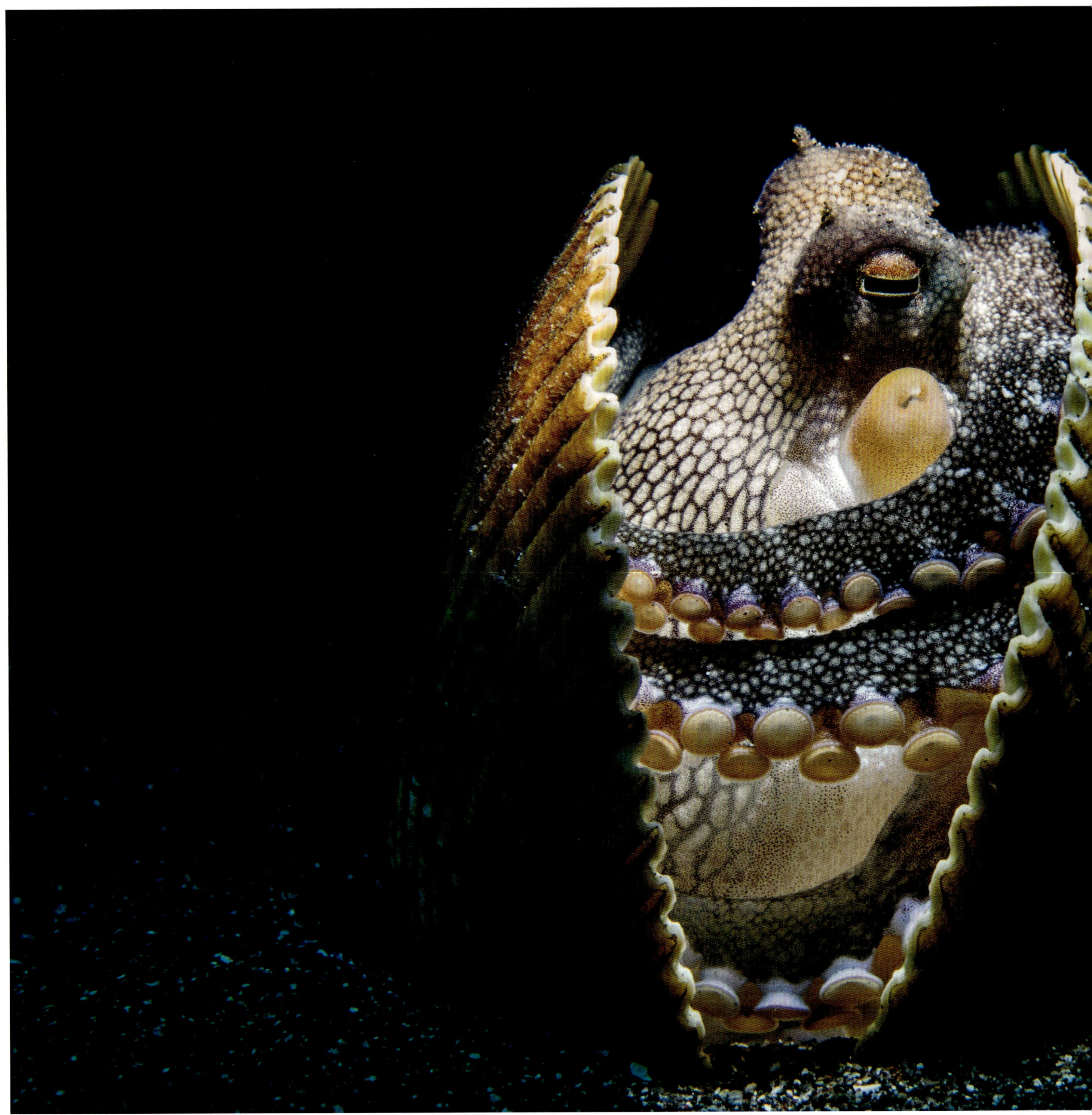

Animal Behaviour Runner-Up

Dreaming

Veined octopus
(*Amphioctopus marginatus*)
Franco Tulli, Italy

The animal inside the seashell is a tiny octopus about two inches in diameter. This kind of animal can utilise the valves as a house and for protection, taking the house with it as it moves. This shot was taken during his quiet rest.
Lembeh Strait, Indonesia

Canon EOS 7D Mk II, Canon EF-S 60mm f/2.8 macro USM, 1/160, f/14, ISO 100, Sea & Sea YS-D2 strobe with Retra snoot, Easydive Leo III housing

Judges' comments:
Like a jewellery box, this shell opens to reveal a precious gem inside. Incredible textures and luminosity seem to leave the octopus bejewelled in the beautiful lighting. A fun image illustrating the cleverness of this shy cephalopod.

Osprey Fishing

Eastern osprey (*Pandion cristatus*)
John Van-Den-Broeke, New South Wales

I was in my kayak paddling upstream when I saw the osprey circling above the water ahead. I was so lucky to arrive just as the osprey was coming out of the water with the fish.
Cudgen Creek, Kingscliff, New South Wales

Canon EOS -1DX Mk 11, EF 24–105mm f4L IS USM, 1/2000, f/4, ISO 500

OVER PAGE

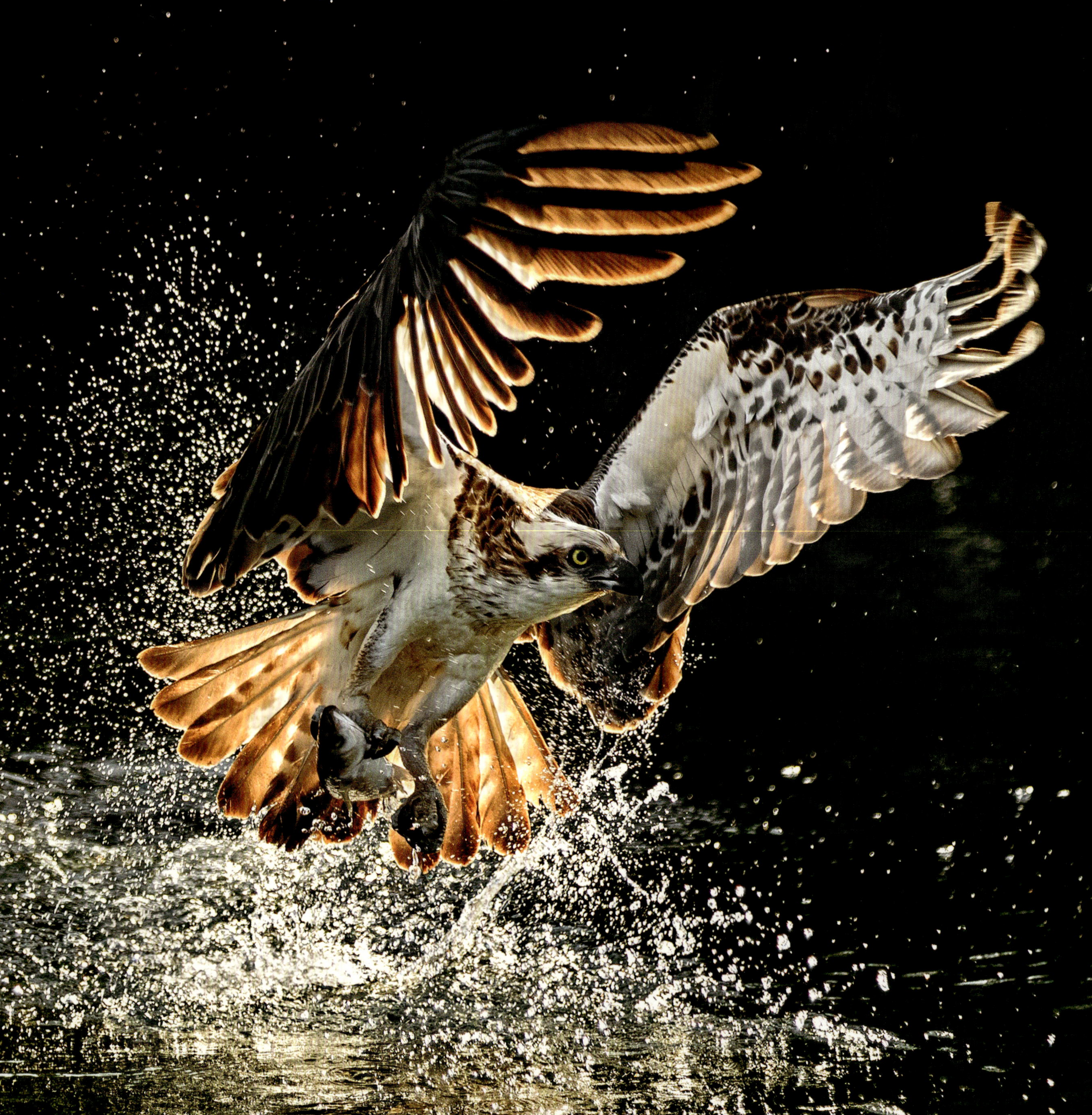

Step into my lair

Peacock spider (*Maratus speciosus*),
Flesh fly (Sarcophagidae)
Ben Clark, Western Australia

After photographing male peacock spiders dancing on the dunes of my local beach, I watched this scene of a less colourful female tackling a much larger flesh fly. It demonstrates the hunting prowess and power of these tiny jumping spiders, which reach just 5mm in length.
Woodman Point, south of Fremantle, Western Australia

Canon 5D Mk IV, Canon EF 100mm f/2.8L macro IS USM with Kenko extension tubes, 1/200, f/7, ISO 200, Yongnuo YN-24EX macro flash with homemade diffuser, handheld, 24 image stitch using Adobe Photoshop CC 2019

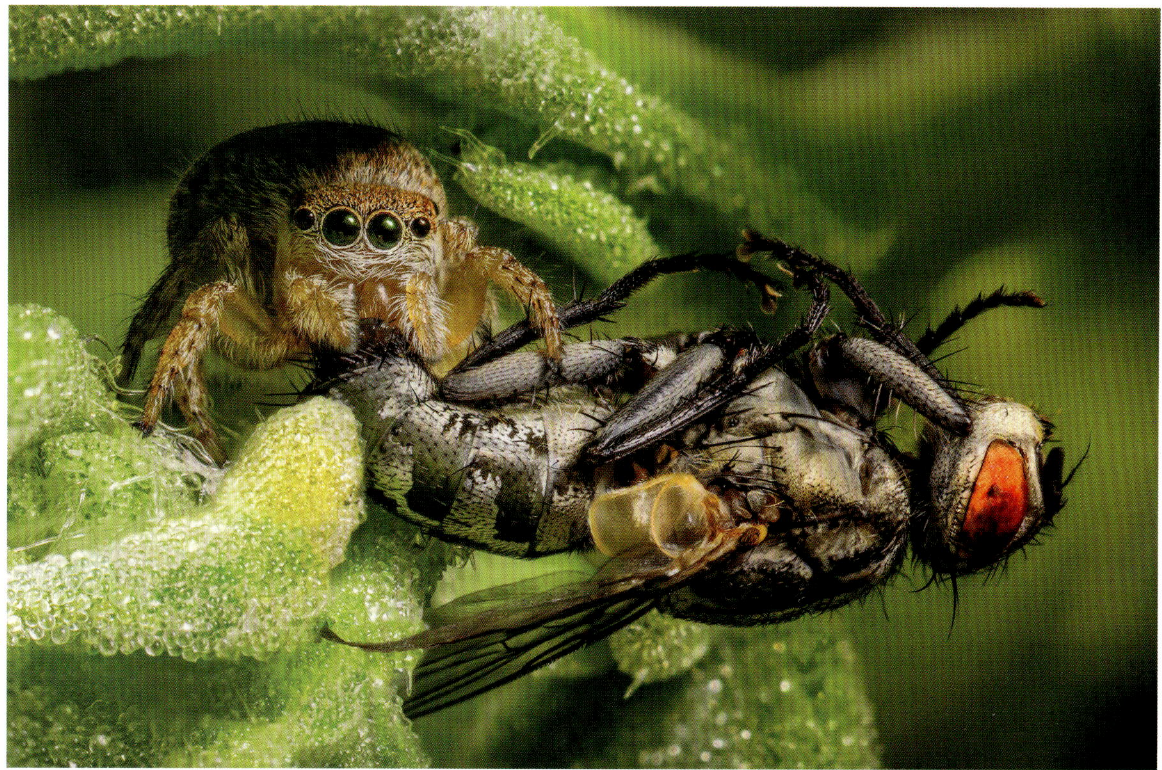

Black Ants Feeding on Broad-tailed Gecko

Broad-tailed gecko (*Phyllurus platurus*)
Ken Griffiths, New South Wales

Broad-tailed geckos are essentially found in Sydney Basin sandstone areas and are nocturnal. It was a most unusual find, especially as there are many bird species that would have made a quick meal of it. How it died is a mystery, but a feral deer or wallaby may have stepped on it the previous night.
Royal National Park, New South Wales

Canon 6D Mk II, Canon EF100–400 ISL, 1/125, f/8, ISO 400, handheld

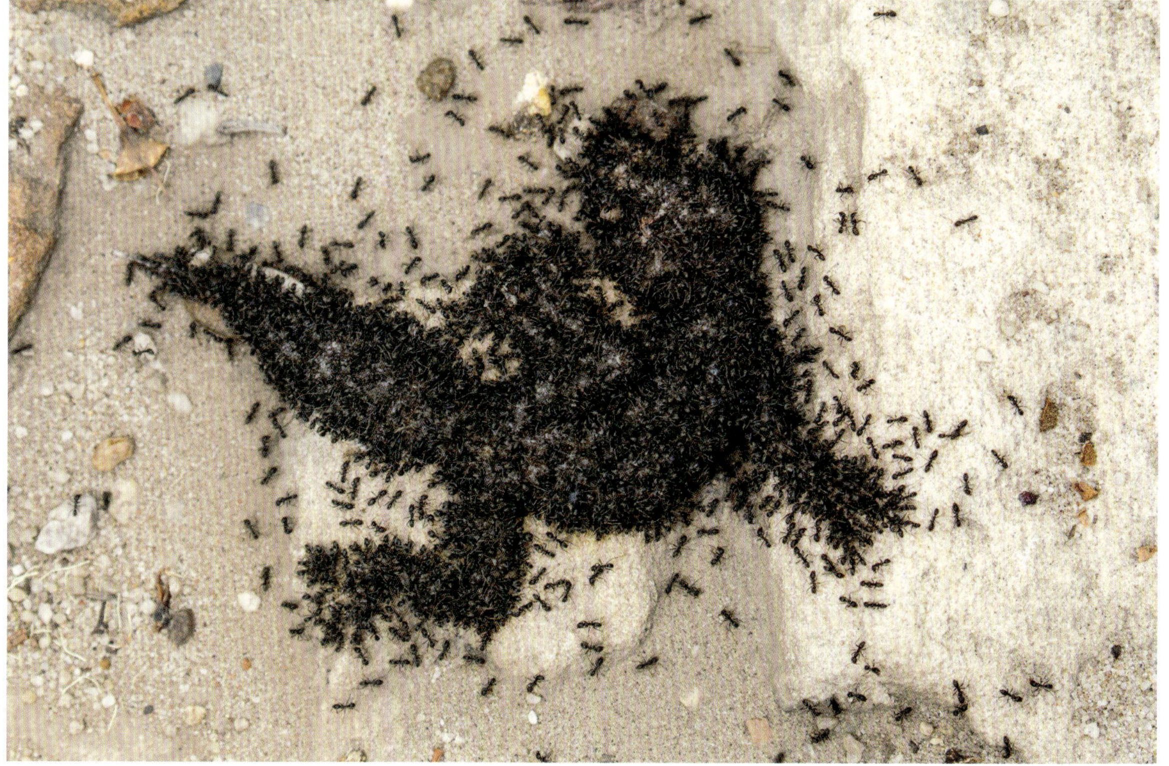

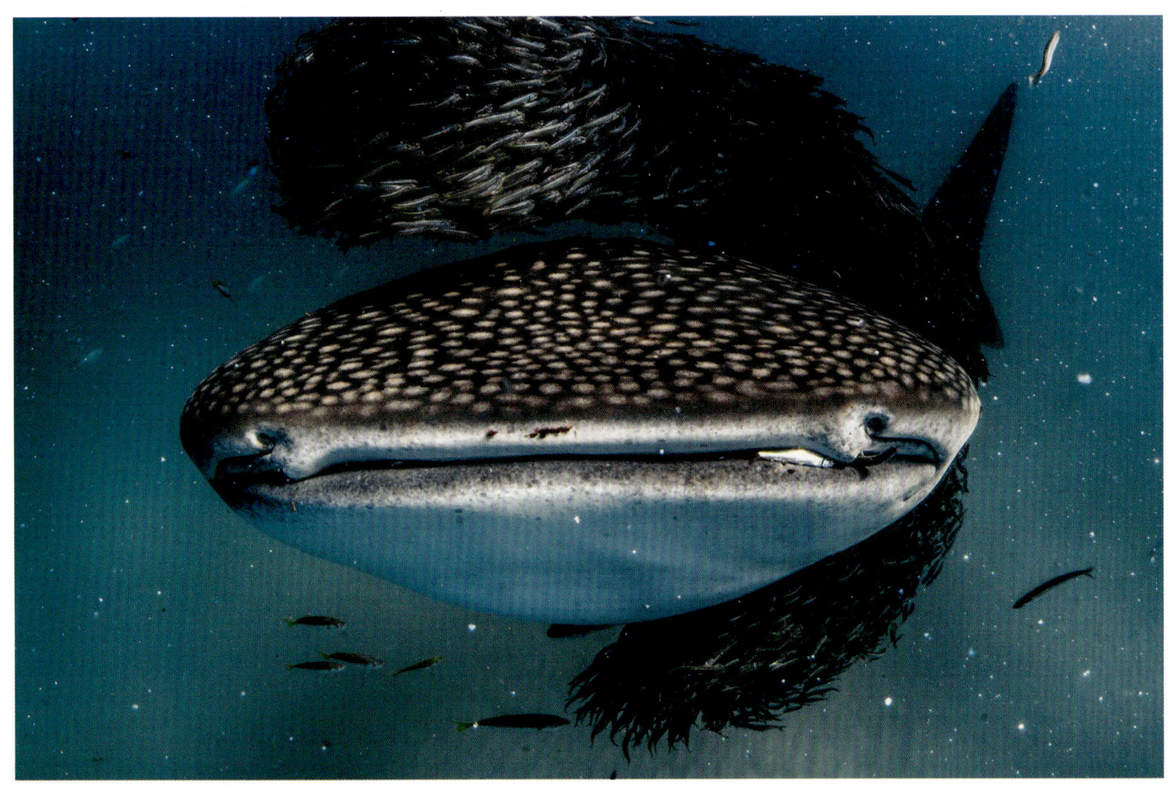

Whale Shark Feast

Whale shark (*Rhincodon typus*)
Alex Kydd, Western Australia

A rare sighting of a whale shark feeding on a large school of baitfish. Whale sharks are not often documented feeding on schools of baitfish as they're most commonly seen filter feeding. This is the first time I have seen this behaviour after five years of photographing these animals on the reef.
Ningaloo Reef, Western Australia

Nikon D810, Sigma 15mm f2.8 EX DG diagonal fisheye, 1/250, f/11, ISO 250, freediving

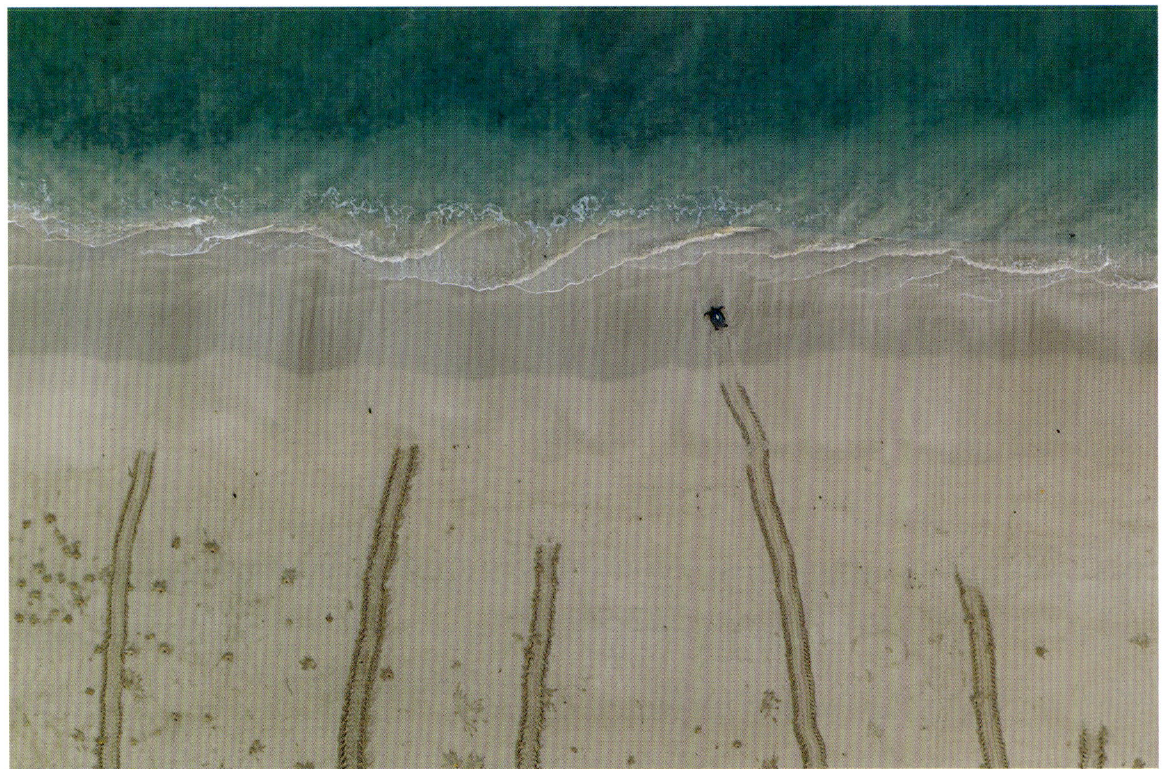

Turtle Tracks

Green sea turtle (*Chelonia mydas*)
Brett Monroe Garner, Western Australia

A large female green sea turtle returns to the ocean at dawn, after laying eggs overnight. She leaves behind a track in the sand like those who finished before her.
Ningaloo Reef, Western Australia

DJI Mavic Pro 2, Hasselblad L1D-20c 28 mm f/2.8, 1/30, f/4.0, ISO 100, PolarPro circular polarizer

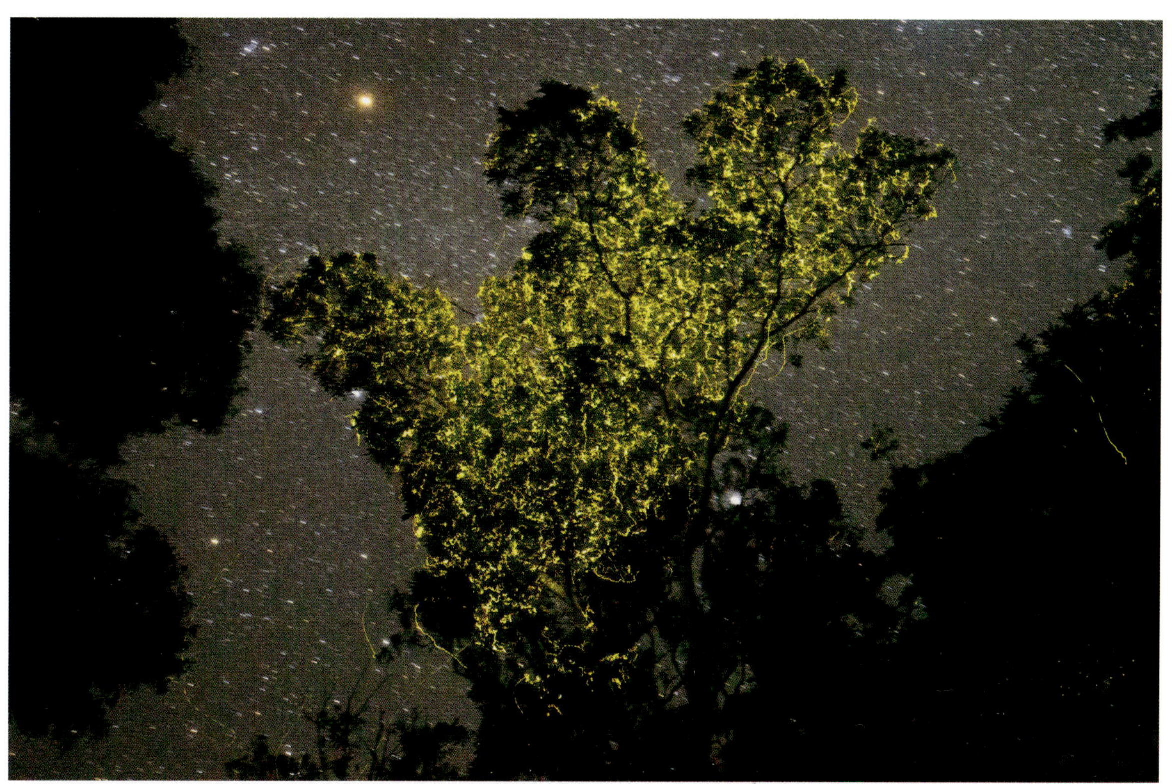

Tree of Life

Firefly (Lampyridae)
Matt Wright, Queensland

Whilst driving down a road late at night, I noticed dozens of fireflies were slowly falling to the ground. I looked up to see a single tree, illuminated by tens of thousands of fireflies. I noticed they were mating and had gathered together in unison for one giant breeding event.
Cape York, Queensland

Canon 5D Mk IV, Canon 16–35mm f4L IS, 30, f/4, ISO 16000, tripod

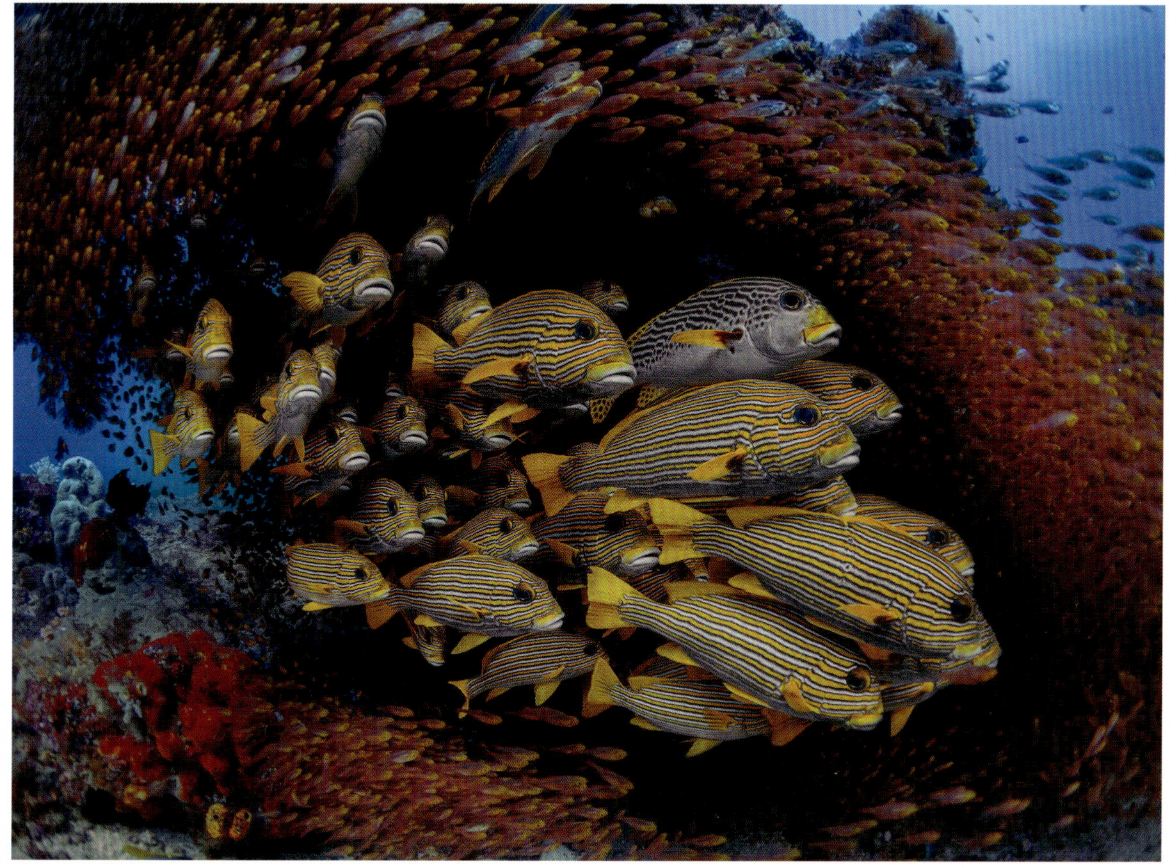

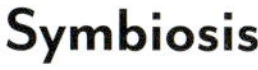

Symbiosis

Ribbon sweetlips (*Plectorhinchus polytaenia*), oblique-banded sweetlips (*Plectorhinchus lineatus*), golden bullseye (*Parapriacanthus ransonneti*)
Kevin De Vree, Belgium

Cooperation plays a vital part in some of nature's most fascinating interactions. These different species of fish are working together towards a common goal; protection against predators. They form a perfect dynamic symbiosis. This harmonic arrangement is mesmerising and provides the dynamic composition I was looking for.
Dampier Strait, Indonesia

Olympus OM-D E-M5, Olympus 8mm f/1.8 fisheye Pro, 1/180, f/2.5, ISO 200, Sea & Sea ys-01, handheld

Dance at Dawn

Wallaby (Macropodidae)

Michael Eastwell, United Kingdom

Apart from its beauty, Cape Hillsborough is renowned for its resident kangaroos and wallabies. I visited the area for three consecutive sunrises, but it was on my final morning that I captured this beautiful spectacle, two wallabies playing on the beach as the sun burst through the surrounding clouds.

Cape Hillsborough National Park, Queensland

Sony A7RIV, Sony 24–105 G OSS, 1/1600, f/9, ISO 100, handheld

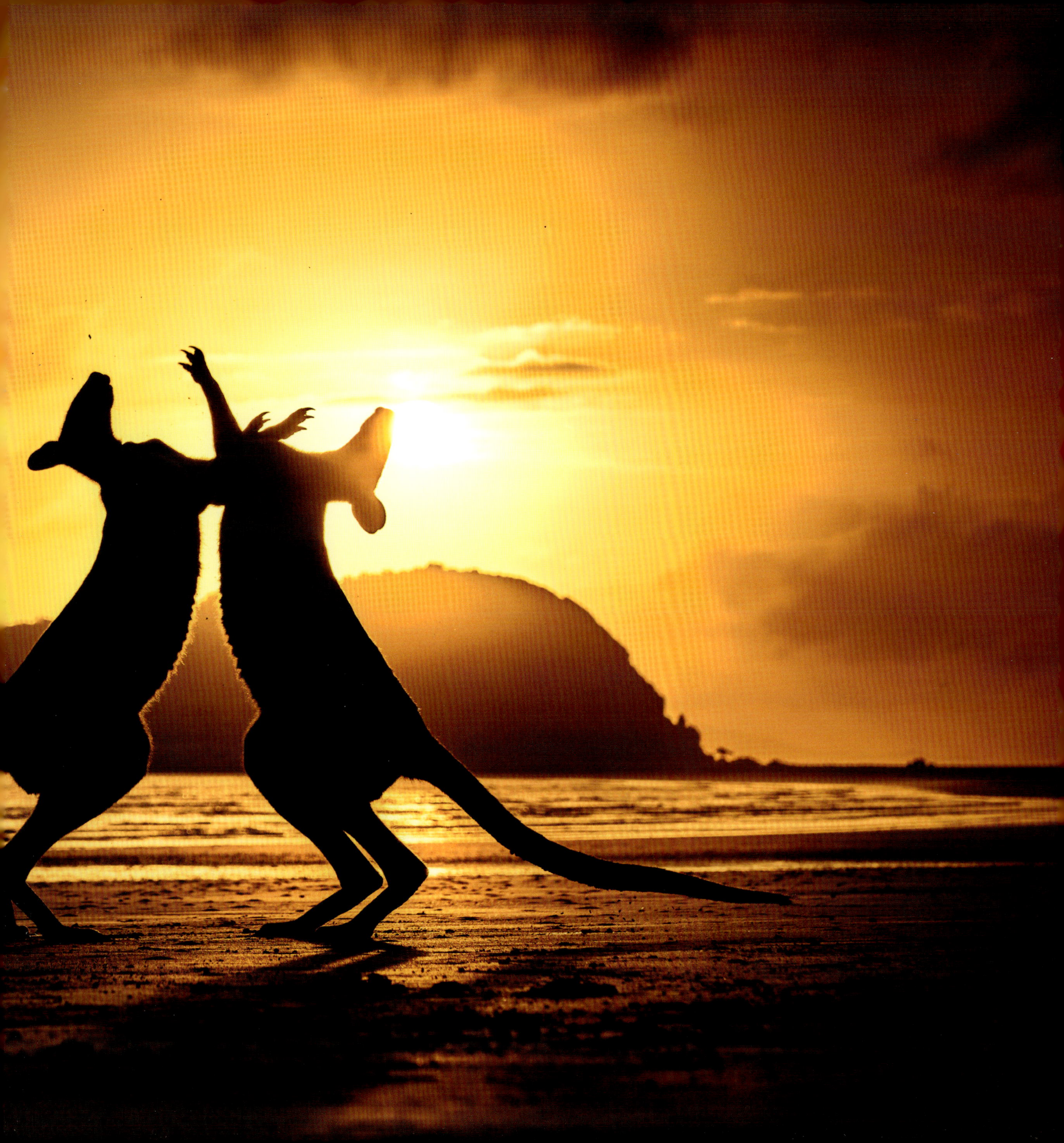

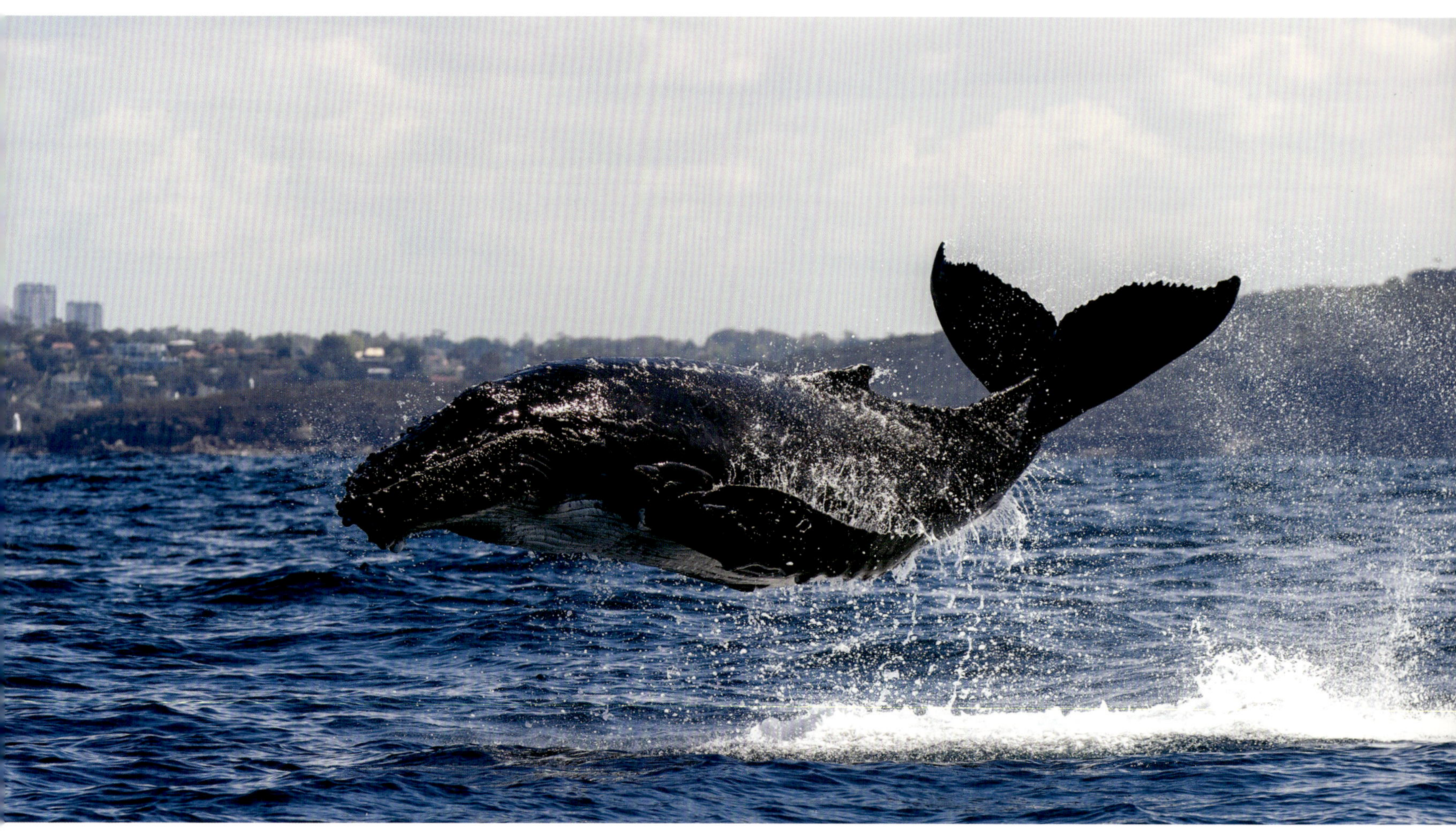

Inflight Entertainment
Humpback whale
(*Megaptera novaeangliae*)
Rachelle Mackintosh, New South Wales

This humpback calf was chilling with its mum between Sydney Heads when it suddenly took flight. The calf speedily reached its cruising altitude then crash-landed with uncoordinated grace. Calves pull some wacky shapes when they're learning to breach, but this pocket rocket's hilarious moves were next level!
Between Sydney Heads, Sydney Harbour, New South Wales

Canon EOS-1D X Mk II, Canon f/4.5–5.6L IS II USM 100–400mm 220mm, 1/2500, f/7.1, ISO 400, handheld from a boat

Better Together

Kookaburra (*Dacelo novaeguineae*)
Charles Davis, New South Wales

Not many kookaburras live high enough to get snowed on. This small family are an exception. They can often be found in a blizzard huddled together for warmth, the parents on the outside and last year's young squished in between.
Kosciuszko National Park, New South Wales

Nikon D850, Nikon 500mm PF f5.6, 1/640, f/5.6, ISO 4000

The Blowtorch

Humpback whale
(*Megaptera novaeangliae*)
Rachelle Mackintosh, New South Wales

Humpbacks are jaw-droppers, especially when they jump. But just seeing this whale exhale against North Head's cliffs – its blows ablaze in the setting sun – was enough to make me hold my own breath, completely awe-struck. If you squint you might even see a woman's profile in the blow... maybe.
North Head, entrance to Sydney Harbour, New South Wales

Canon EOS-1D X, Canon f/4.5–5.6L IS II USM 100–400mm 300mm, 1/1250, f/7.1, ISO 500, handheld from a boat

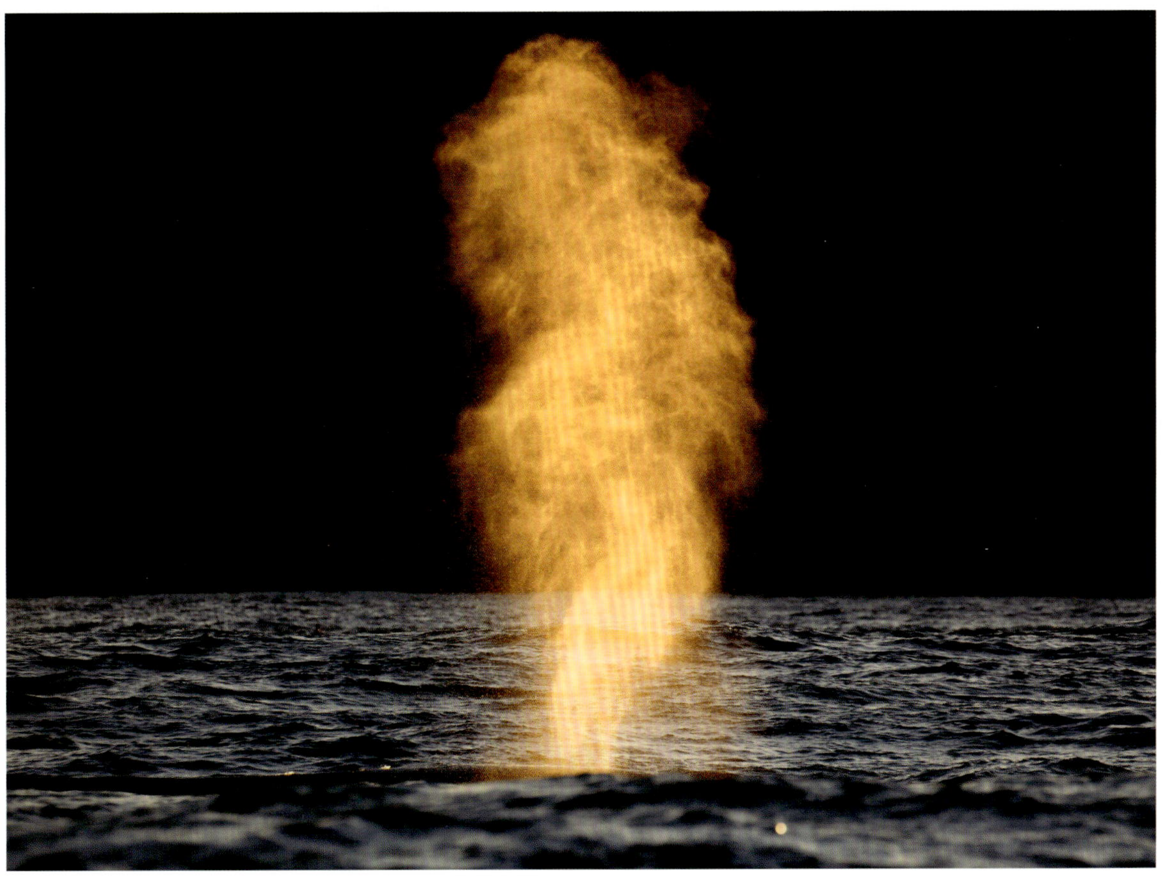

Mudskipper

Mudskipper (Oxudercidae)
Scott Portelli, Sydney Australia

Mudskippers are amphibious fish with unique adaptations that allow them to inhabit the rich, muddy intertidal zones of tropical estuaries. As the tide recedes the mudflats are exposed and the mudskippers emerge from their underwater burrows. Leaping into the air, males strive to attract females with the most impressive acrobatics.
Broome, Western Australia

Olympus OMD EM1X, 300mm, 1/4000, f/7.1, ISO 400

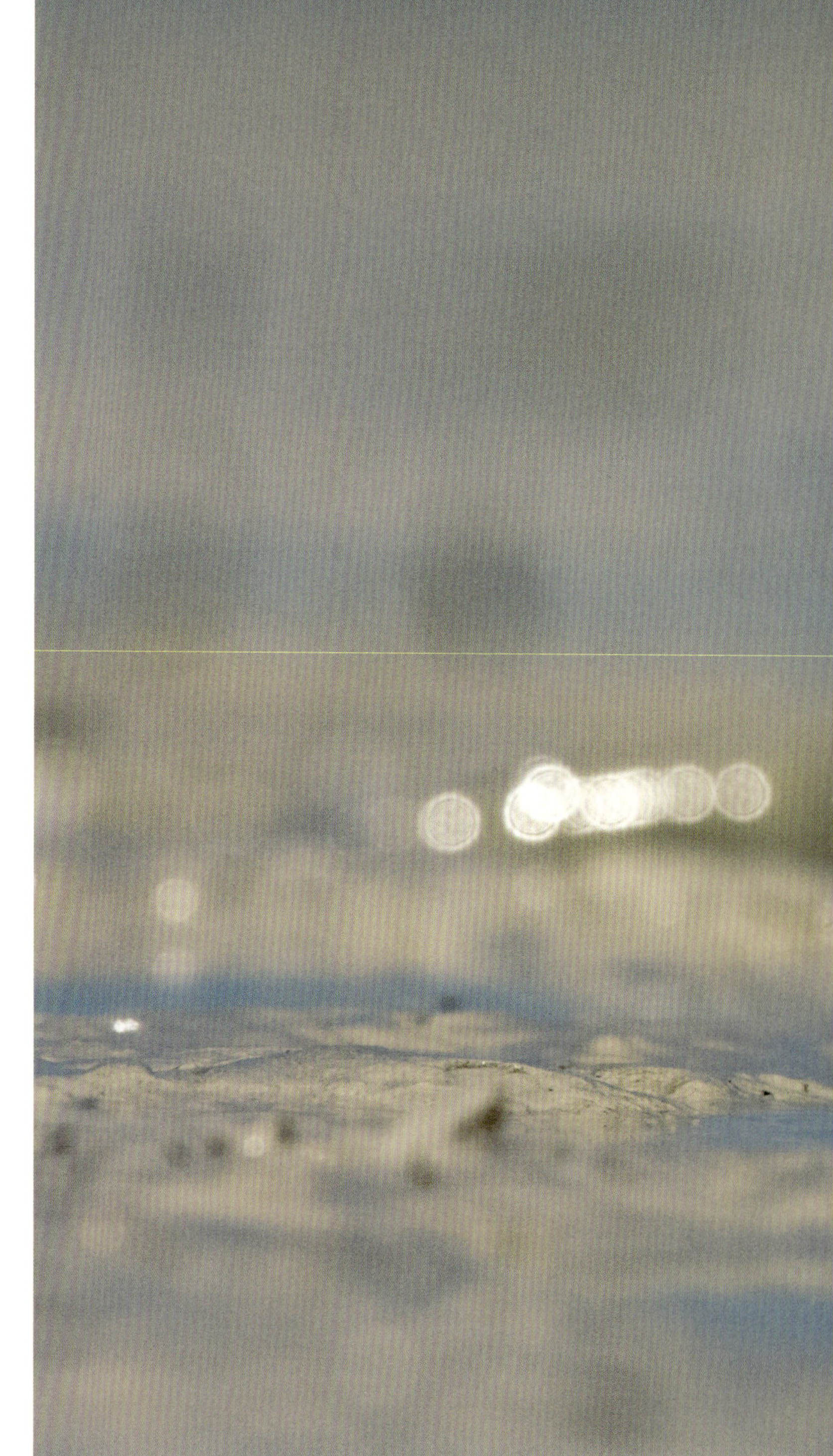

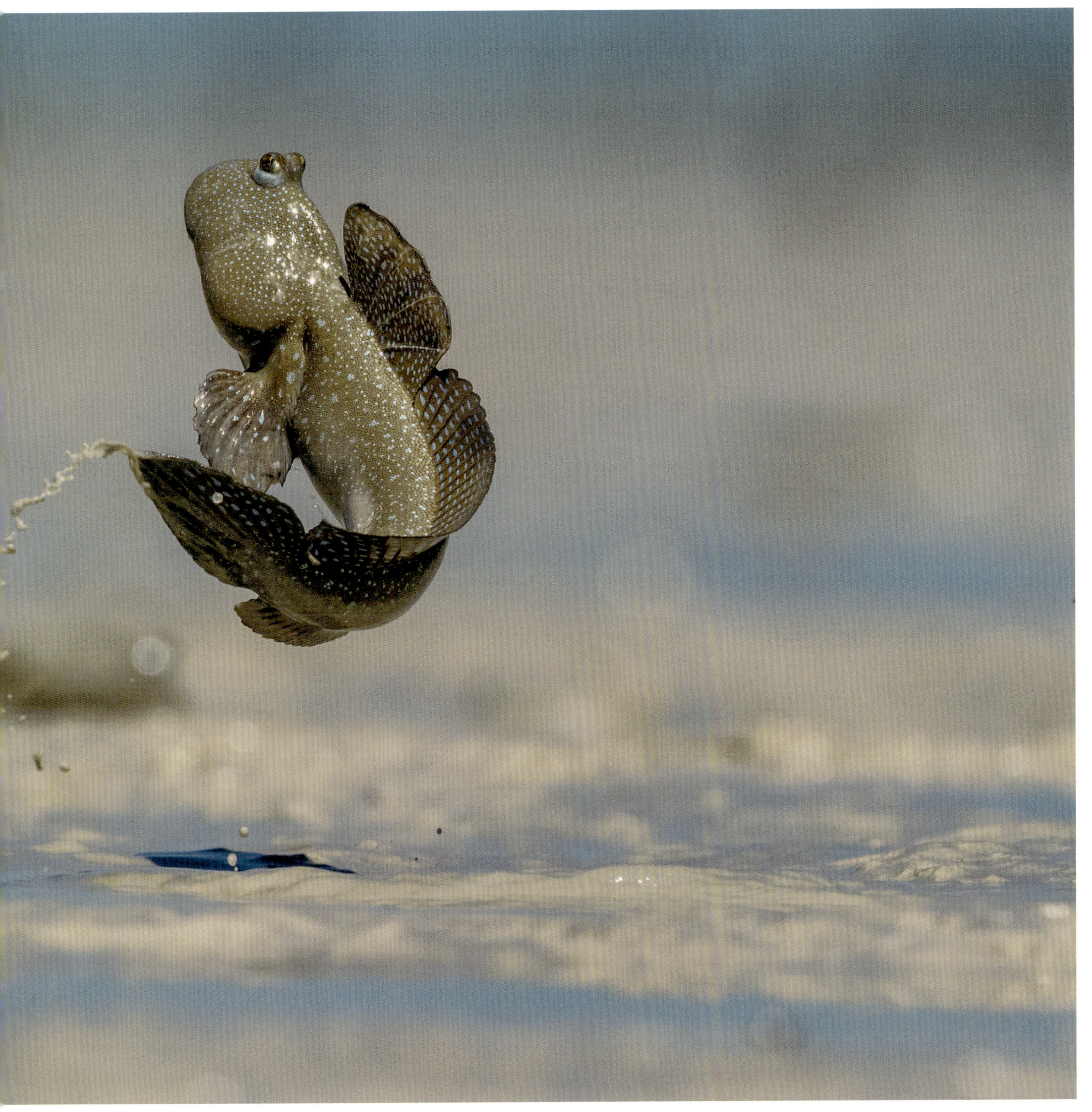

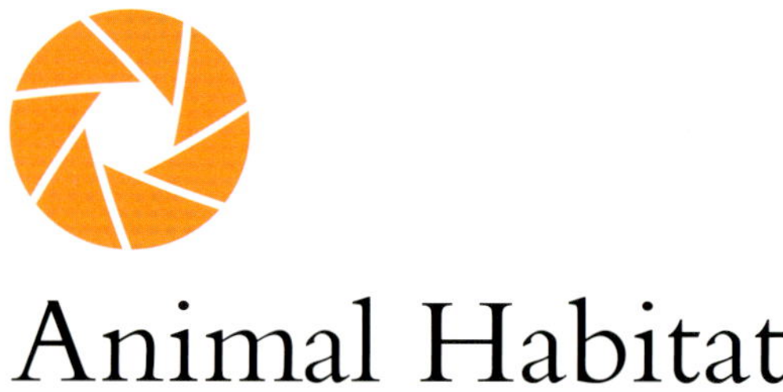

Animal Habitat

Animal Habitat Winner

A Tree Dreaming

Galah (*Eolophus roseicapillus*)
Christian Spencer, Victoria

In the Strzelecki Desert of Australia, a flock of galahs replenish on the only water available at the base of this lonely tree. It's a rare photo opportunity to get such a clear and symmetrical shot of these beautiful birds in flight, in the middle of the desert.
Strzelecki Desert, South Australia

Canon T4i, Canon 135mm, 1/250, f/10, ISO 200

Judges' comments:
Australia's unique arid outback has been beautifully depicted, highlighting the importance of a lifegiving puddle. A simple strong composition that has come to life with the flight of the galahs revealing a mirroring effect...the blue sky reflected in the water and the warmth of the land echoed in the flying birds.

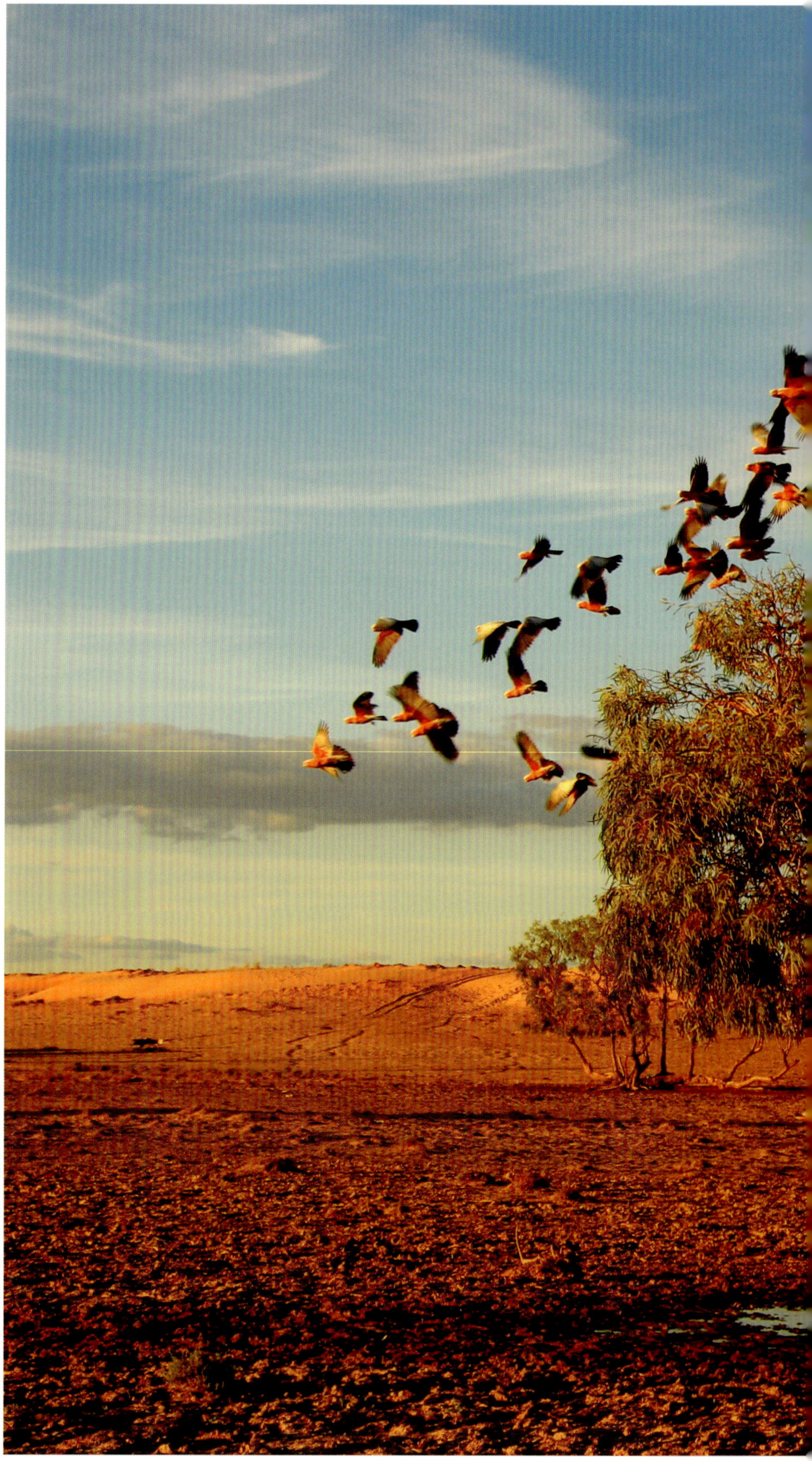

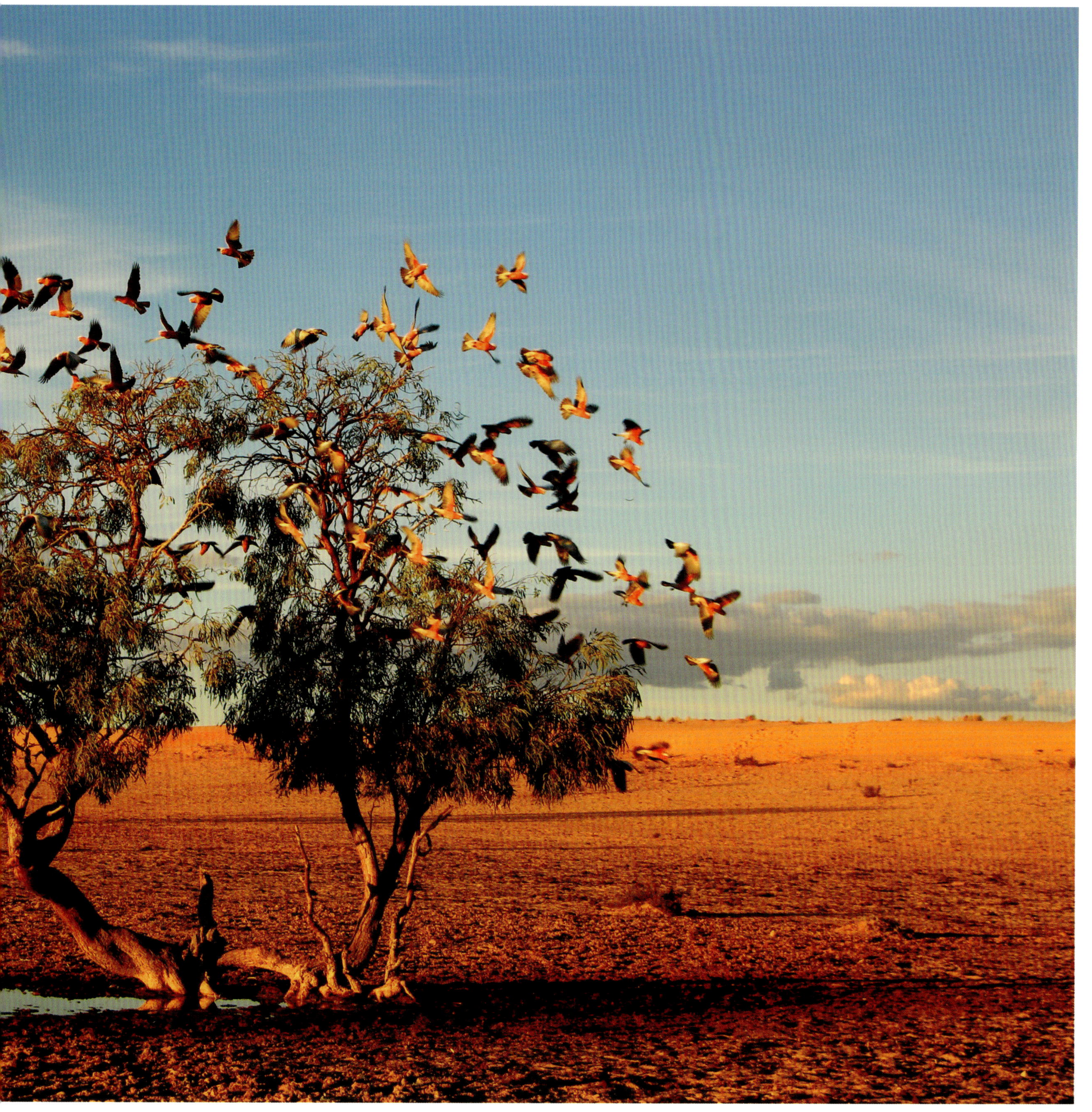

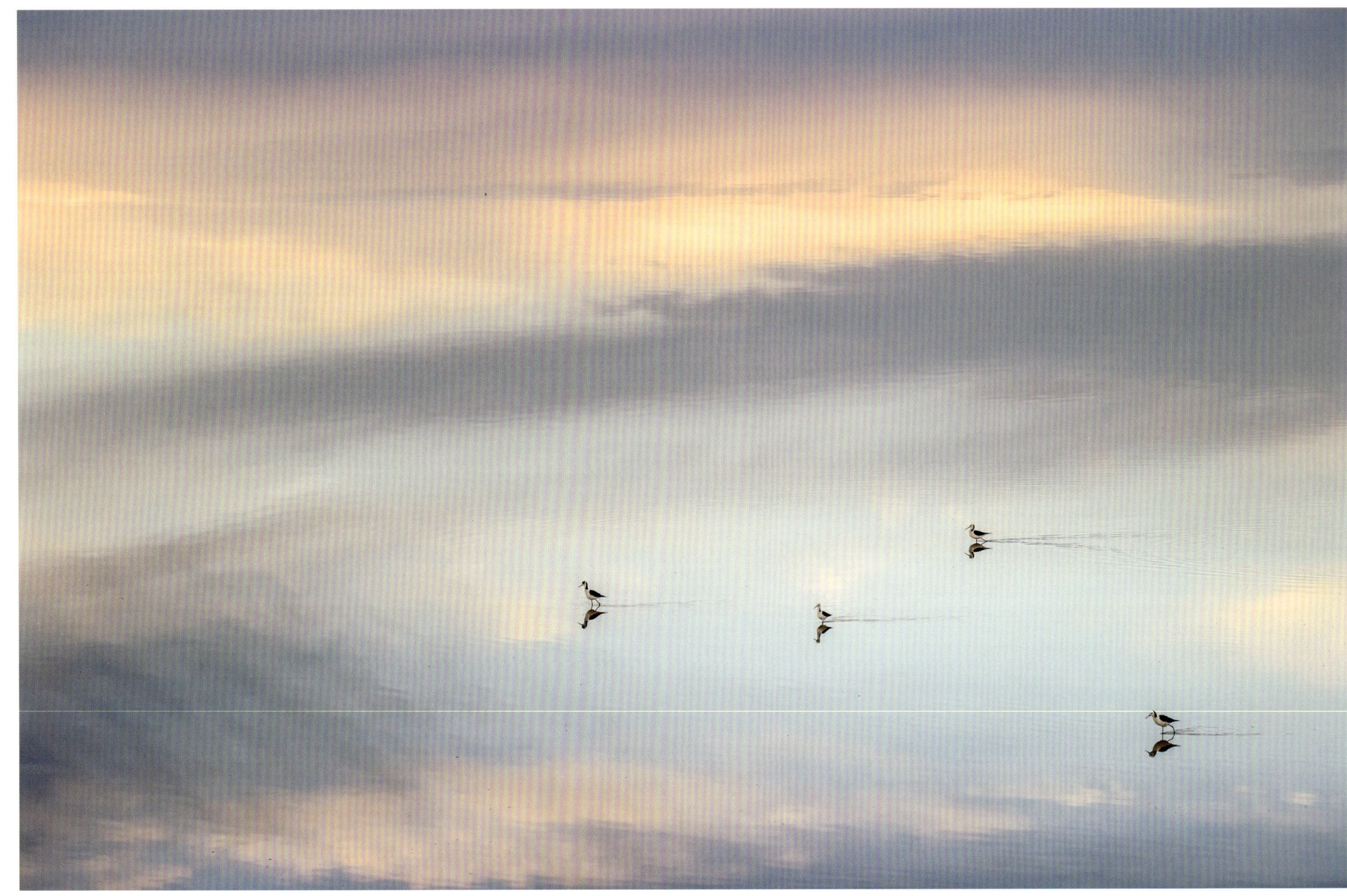

Animal Habitat Runner-Up

Stilted Reflections

Pied stilt (*Himantopus leucocephalus*)
Georgina Steytler, Western Australia

I was at a location overlooking these pied stilts feeding in shallow waters when the wind died and the sunset cast incredible reflections. I changed to a 100–400mm lens and zoomed out to capture as much of the stilts 'walking in the clouds' as I could.
Bremer Bay, Western Australia

Canon EOS-1D X Mk III, Canon EF 100–400mm f/4.5–5.6L IS II USM, 1/1000, f/8, ISO 1600, handheld

Judges' comments:
Like walking in an otherworldly sky, a surreal moment has been captured with beautiful soft, pastel colours. This is a dreamscape with beautiful placement of the stilts among the clouds.

Family Portrait

Daddy-long-legs spider
(*Pholcus phalangioides*)
Peter Baxter, Victoria

Daddy-long-legs spiders are found across Australia, successfully spinning their webs in our homes, garages and sheds. This family caught my eye when I was looking for something in the garage. I halted my search and grabbed my camera to take a family portrait.
Beaumaris, Victoria

Nikon D7100, Nikon AF Nikkor 24–120mm 1:3.5–5.6D, 1/80, f/16, ISO 800, UV filter, LED portable worklight, tripod

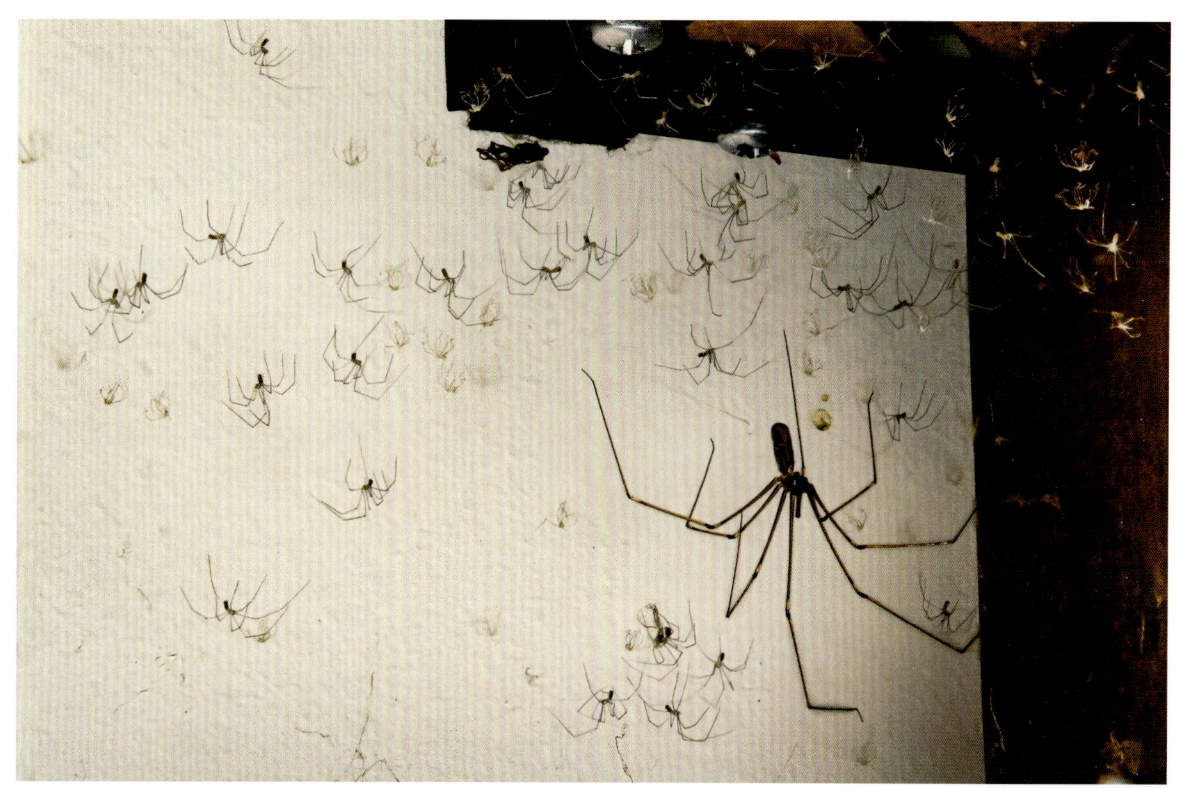

The Mythical Platypus

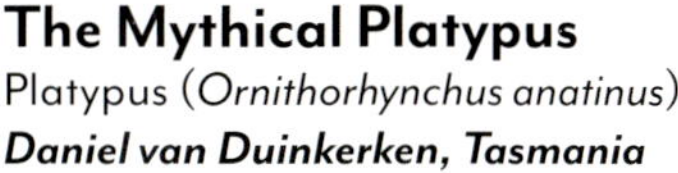

Platypus (*Ornithorhynchus anatinus*)
Daniel van Duinkerken, Tasmania

Floating early morning in my inflatable hide, I noticed these out-of-focus specular highlights lighting up while shooting into the sun. This platypus was busy foraging, repeatedly diving down and coming back up for air. I positioned myself with the platypus between me and the sun, creating this dreamy image.
Don River, Devonport, Tasmania

Sony A9, Sony 400mm f/2.8 GM, 1/1000, f/5.6, ISO100, taken from a floating hide, camera mounted onto an Fotopro E-6H Eagle Series gimbal head on the hide's inflatable raft

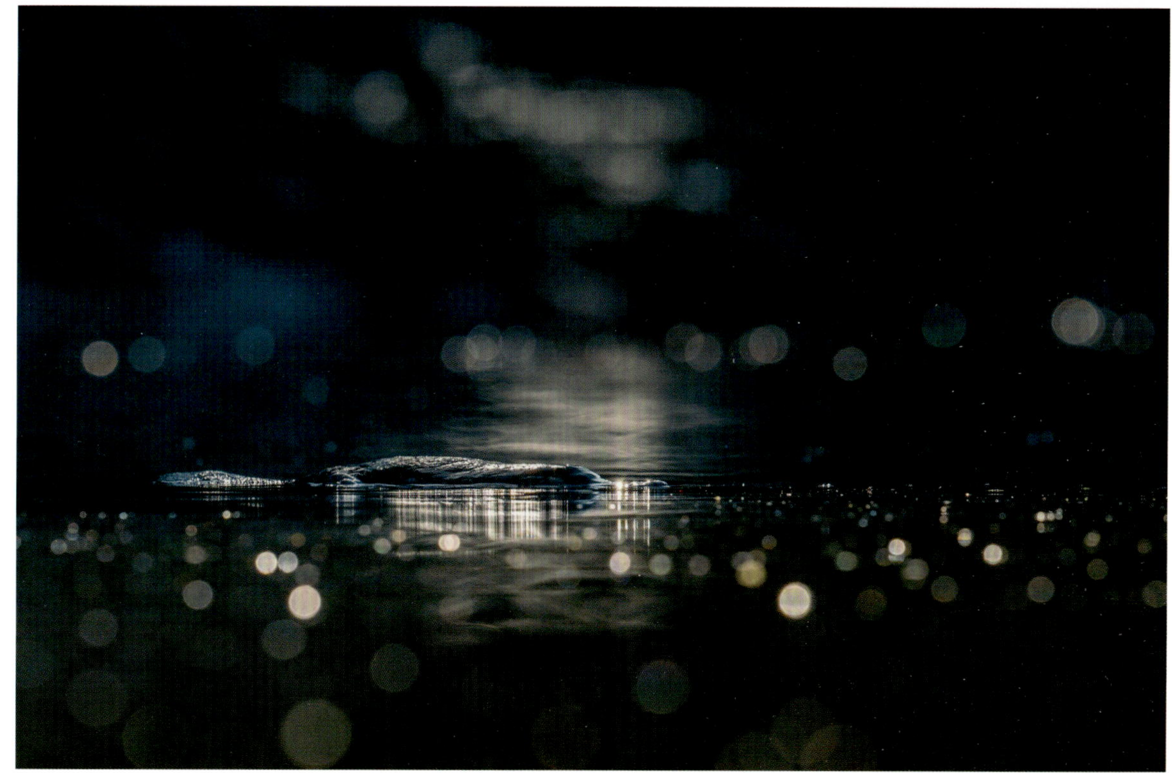

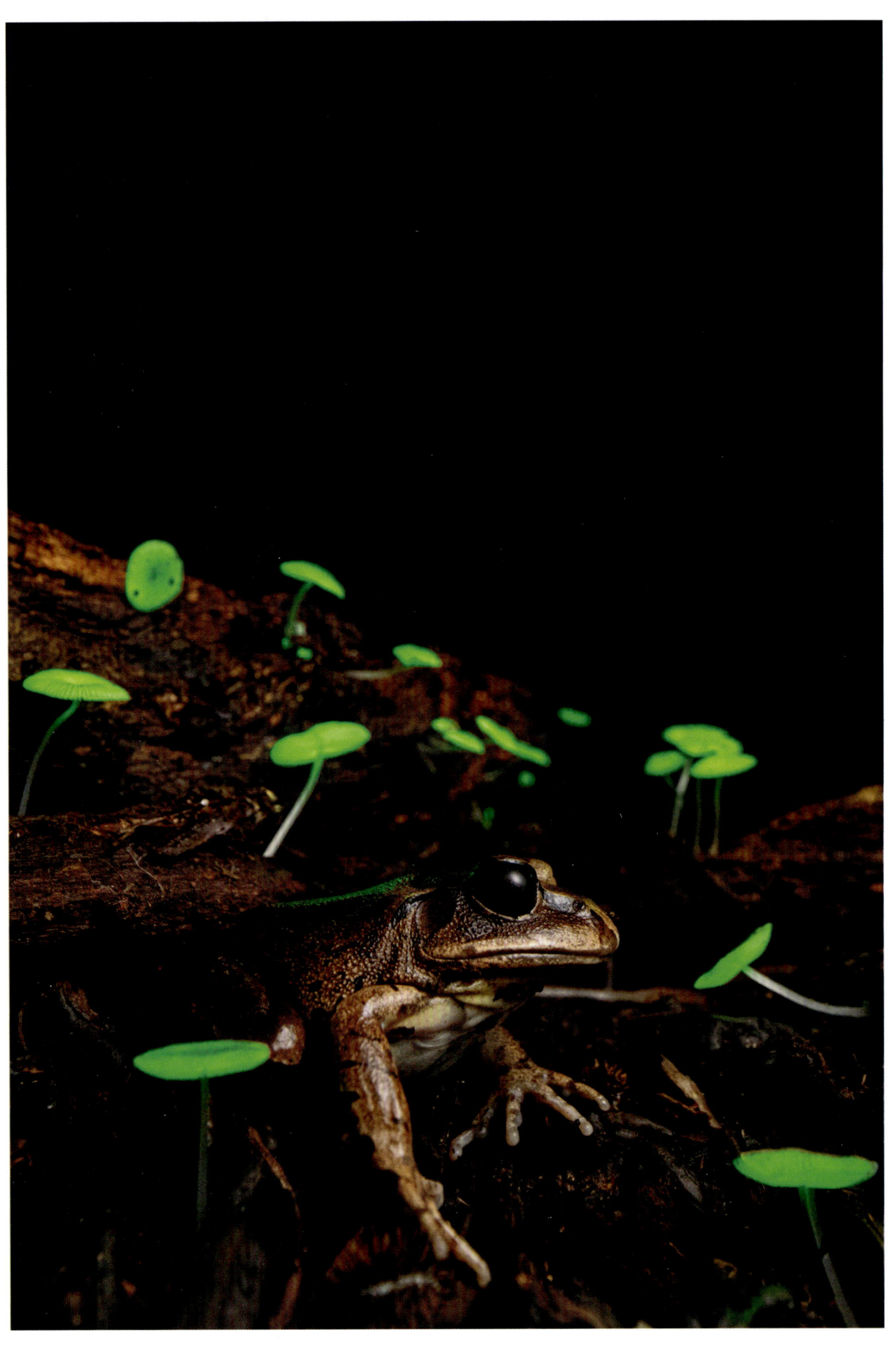

Night-light
Bioluminescent fungi (*Mycena chlorophos*), barred frog (*Mixophyes fasciolatus*)
Isaac Wishart, Queensland

My photography skills were tested by this magical scene. A long exposure with added flash was used to achieve the perfect lighting for this photo. Both the bioluminescent fungi and barred frog are lovers of rain, making the recent weather perfect for capturing this photo.
Tamborine Mountain, Queensland

Nikon D850, Tamron 15–30mm f/2.8, 30, f/9, ISO 1250, off camera flash, tripod

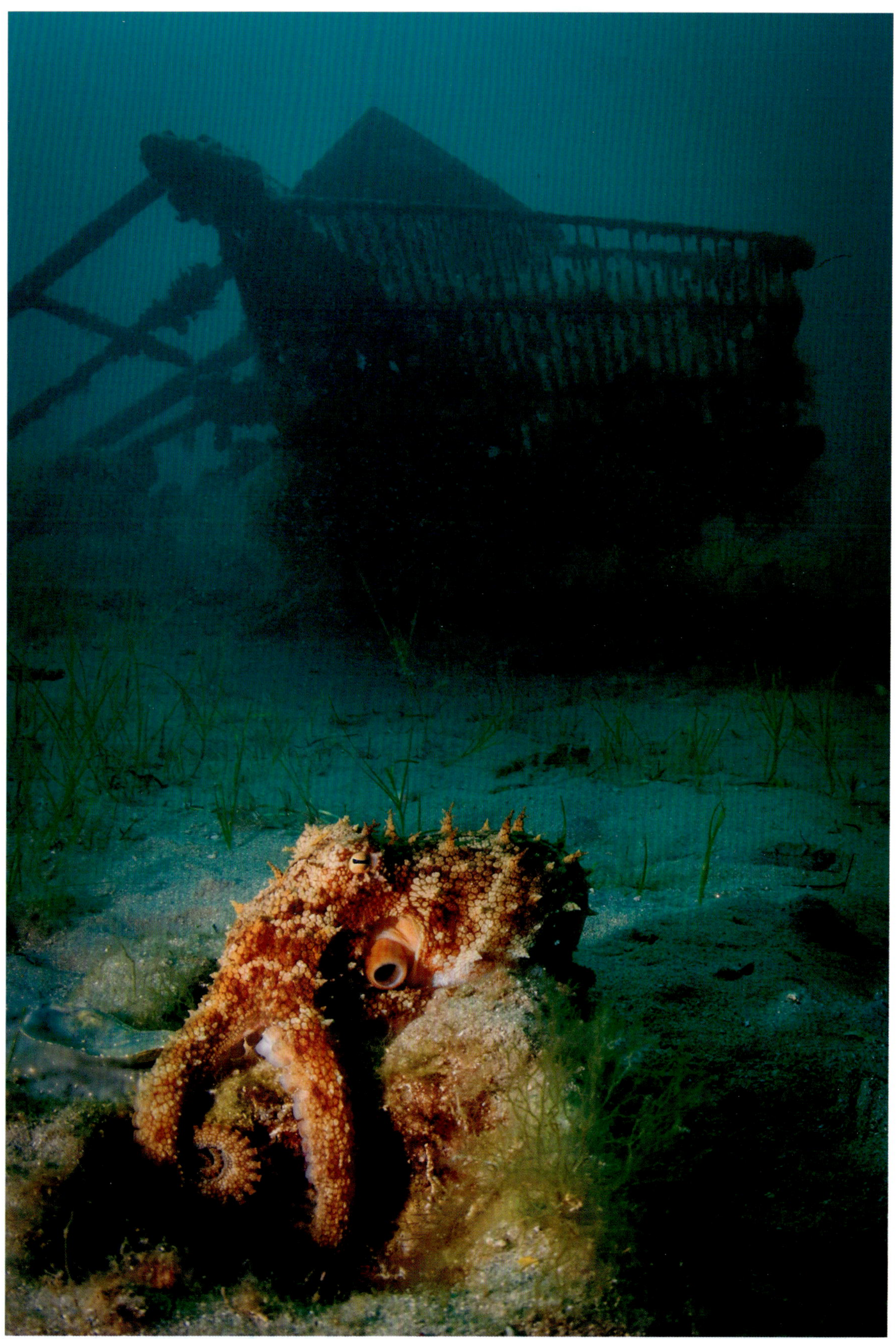

Octopus's playground
Pale octopus (*Octopus pallidus*)
Rachel Price, Victoria

Household and commercial waste is a common sight beneath the surface of Port Phillip Bay. Just metres from Rye Pier, among a landscape of discarded bicycles, metal grates, and shopping trolleys, a colony of shy but curious pale octopuses have made this artificial reef of discarded objects their home.
Elsas Reef, Port Phillip Bay, Victoria

Nikon D300, Tokina 10–17mm f3.5–4.5 17mm, 1/160, f/9.0, ISO 200, single Inon Z240 strobe, Nauticam underwater housing, handheld, shot on scuba at a depth of approximately 6m

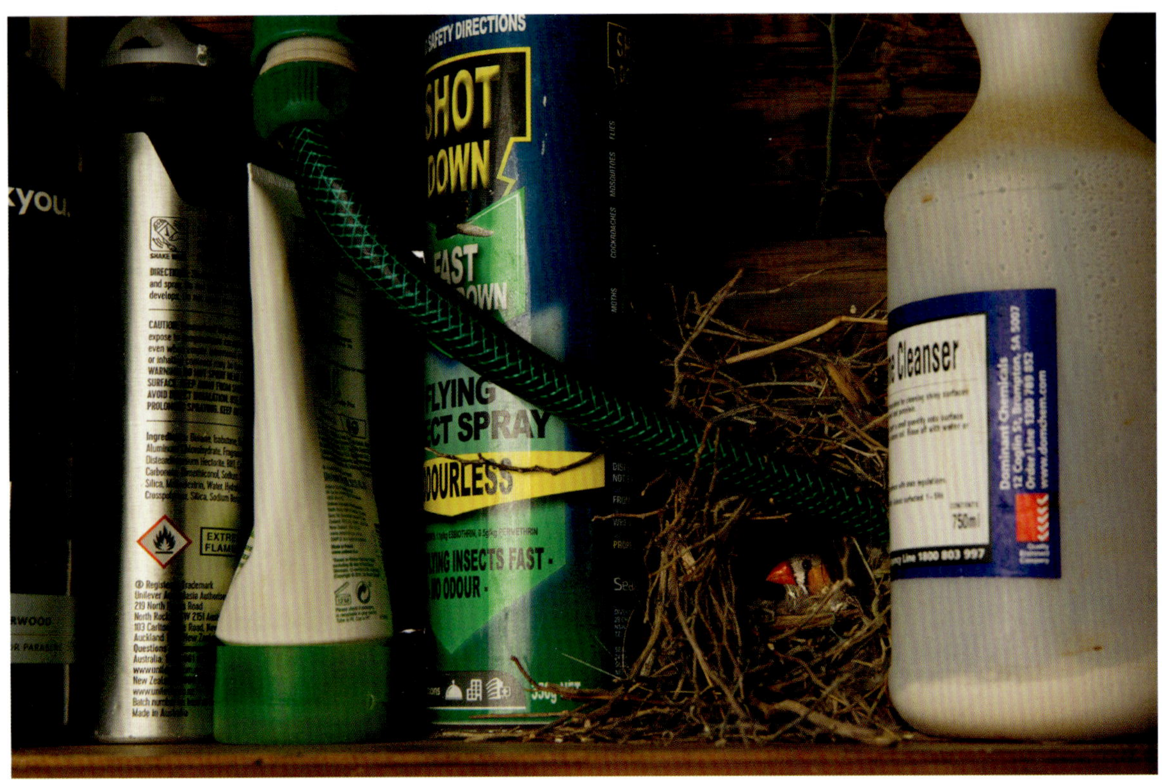

A Home Among the Toiletries

Zebra finch (*Taeniopygia guttata*)
Jasmine Vink, Queensland

A male zebra finch guards his nest while the female is out foraging. This pair of finches has made their nest on a shower bench, among an array of toiletries and cleaning products. In the desert, good nesting real estate is difficult to find!
Arid Recovery Reserve, Roxby Downs, South Australia

Canon 5D Mk IV, Canon EF 24–70mm f/2.8L II USM, 1/125, f/10, ISO 500, Canon Speedlite 600EX-RT with diffuser, handheld

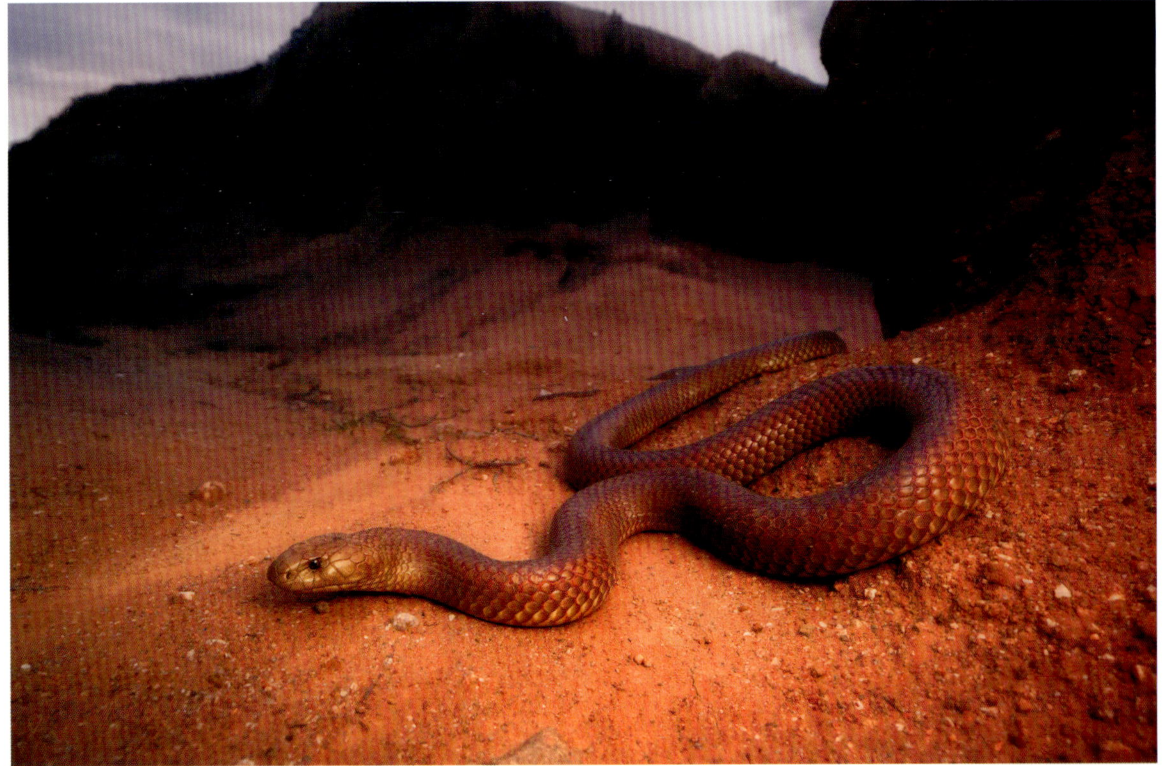

Moody Mulga

Mulga snake (*Pseudechis australis*)
Kristian Bell, Victoria

At the end of a blisteringly hot 45°C day conducting research, I visited a farm dam to see if any animals were having a drink or cooling off. Along a heavily eroded section of dam wall I stumbled across this majestic snake – an adult mulga in excellent condition.
Near Rankins Springs, New South Wales

Canon EOS 5D Mk III, Canon EF16–35mm f/4L IS USM, 1/20, f/9.5, ISO 500, single, diffused on-camera flash, handheld

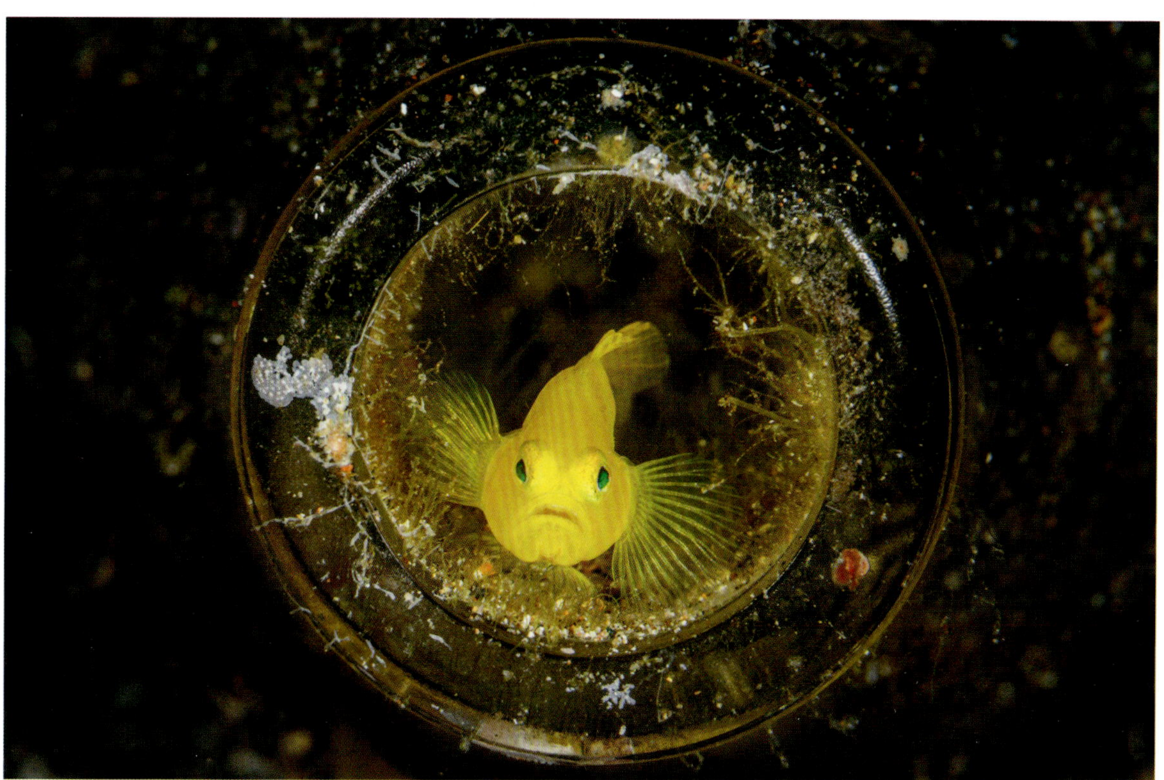

Goby in a Bottle

Yellow pygmy-goby
(*Lubricogobius exiguus*)
Mary Gudgeon, Western Australia

Rubbish lying on the bottom of the ocean is not always a bad thing, it can make good habitat for marine life. Discarded bottles have become a popular habitat for the yellow pygmy-goby. In areas such as Lembeh Strait they are more frequently found in bottles than their natural habitat.
Lembeh Strait, Indonesia

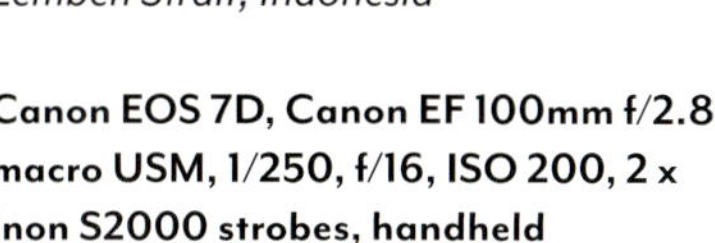

Canon EOS 7D, Canon EF 100mm f/2.8 macro USM, 1/250, f/16, ISO 200, 2 x Inon S2000 strobes, handheld

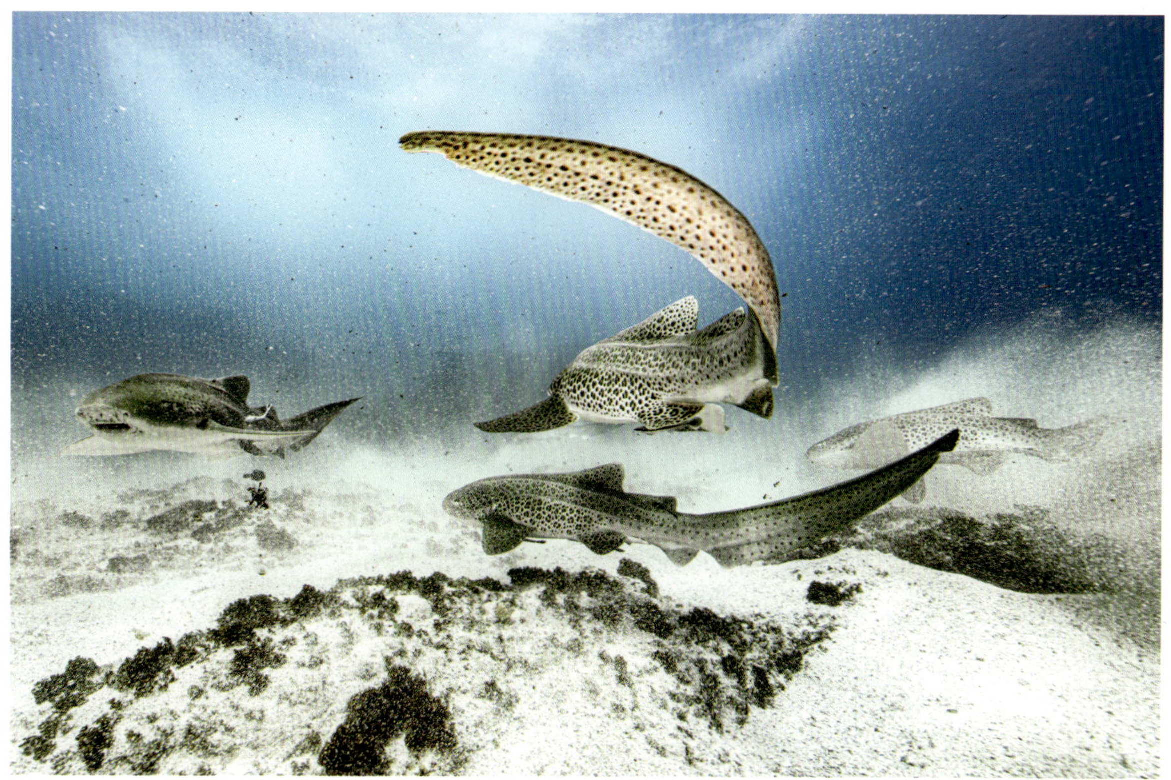

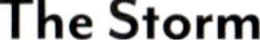

The Storm

Leopard shark (*Stegostoma fasciatum*)
David Robinson, New South Wales

I believe Julian Rocks Nguthungulli Nature Reserve to be one of the best places in the world to observe leopard sharks in the wild. That day's stormy sea made for unique photography conditions with the white sand swirling around the sharks and the sharks themselves somewhat swirling too.
Julian Rocks Nguthungulli Nature Reserve, New South Wales

Canon 5DSR, Canon EF 14mm f/2.8L II USM lens, 1/200, f/9.0, ISO 400, twin Inon Z240 strobes

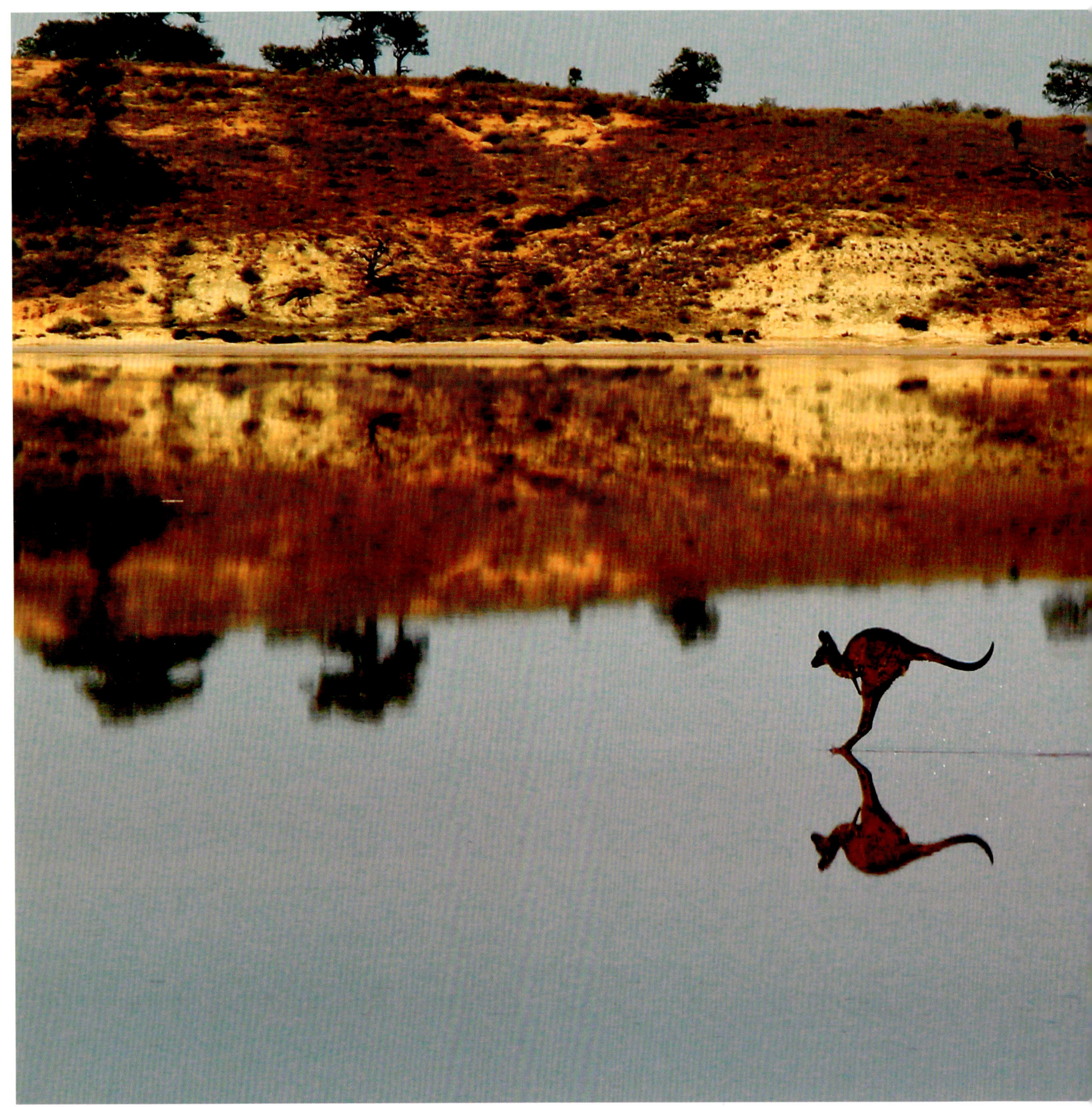

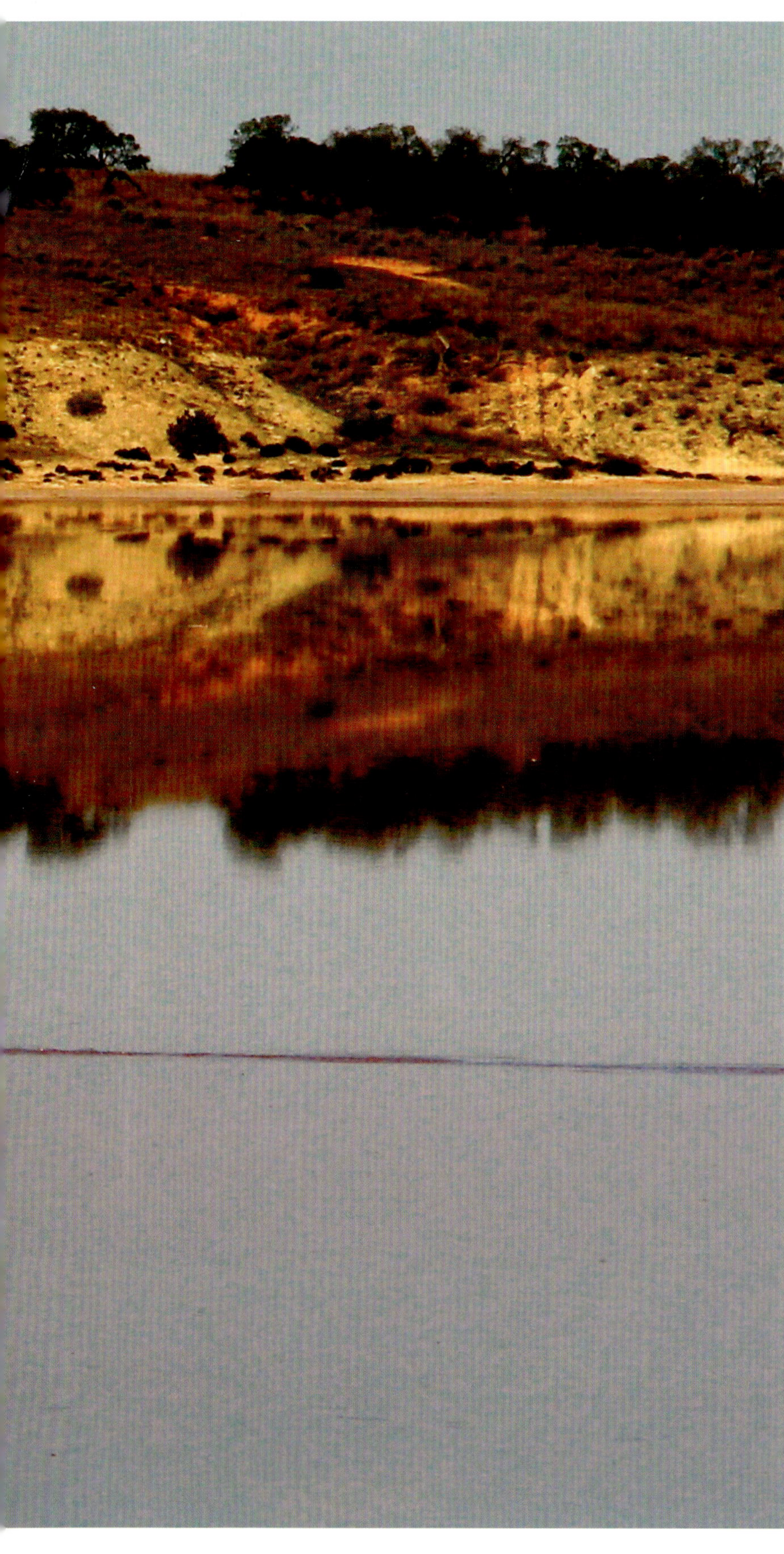

Outback Mirage

Eastern grey kangaroo
(*Macropus giganteus*)
Christian Spencer, Victoria

A surreal moment of a kangaroo magically walking on water in the pink lakes of the mallee. I saw a kangaroo in the middle of the lake and he made a run for it as I walked towards him. I managed to capture a harmonic shot of him in full flight.
Mallee region, north-western Victoria

Canon T4i, Canon 135mm, 1/1250, f/14, ISO 400

Jupiter's Spider

William Godward, South Australia

A spider hunting at night, silhouetted by the largest planet (defocused) in our Solar System, Jupiter. The distance between the spider and Jupiter is a mere 825 million kilometres. You can see a few flies for his next meal and the planet Saturn below Jupiter.
Lake Bonney, Barmera, South Australia

Sony a7iii, Sony 85mm 1.8, 2.5, f/1.8, ISO 10 000, tripod

OVER PAGE

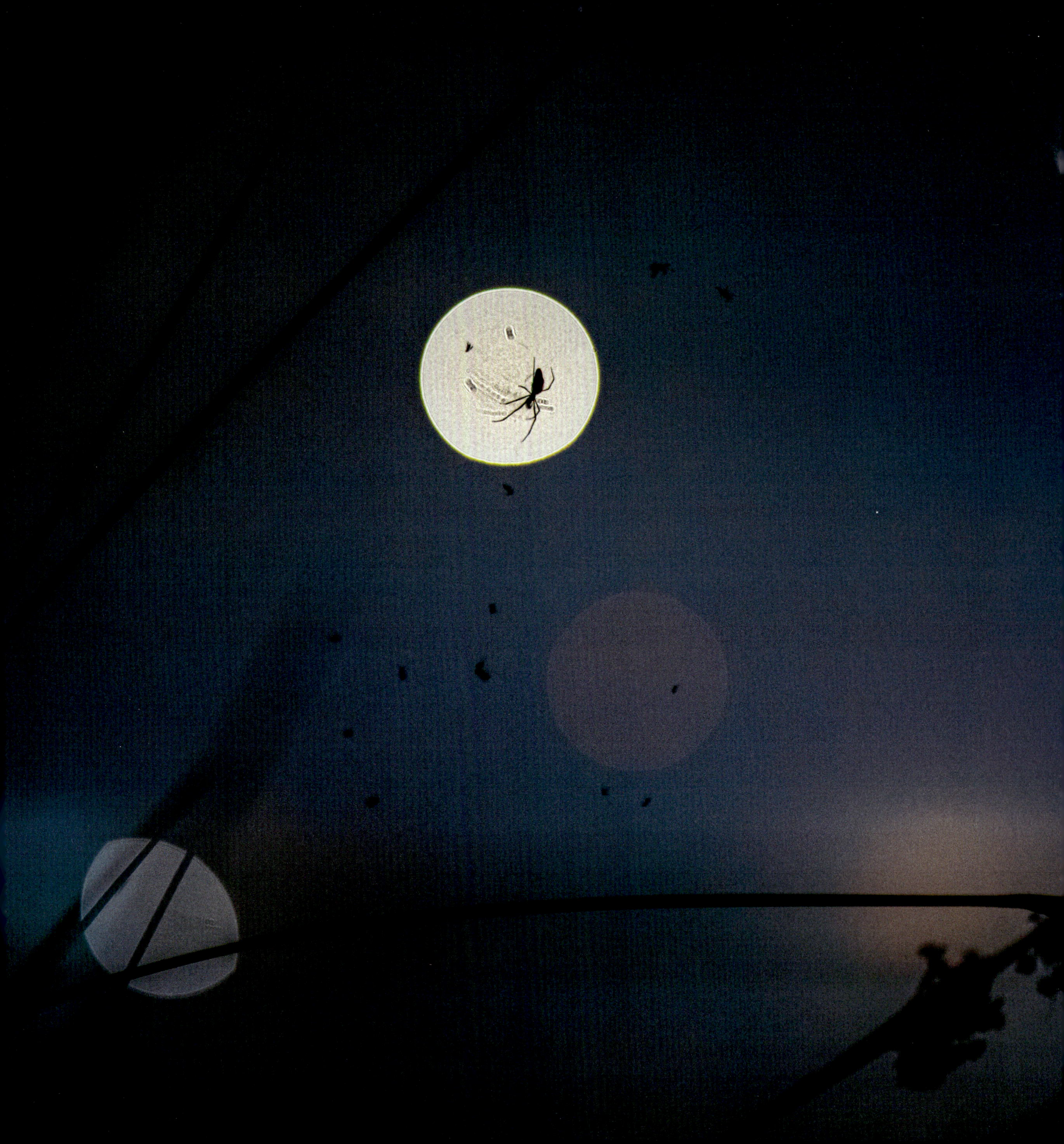

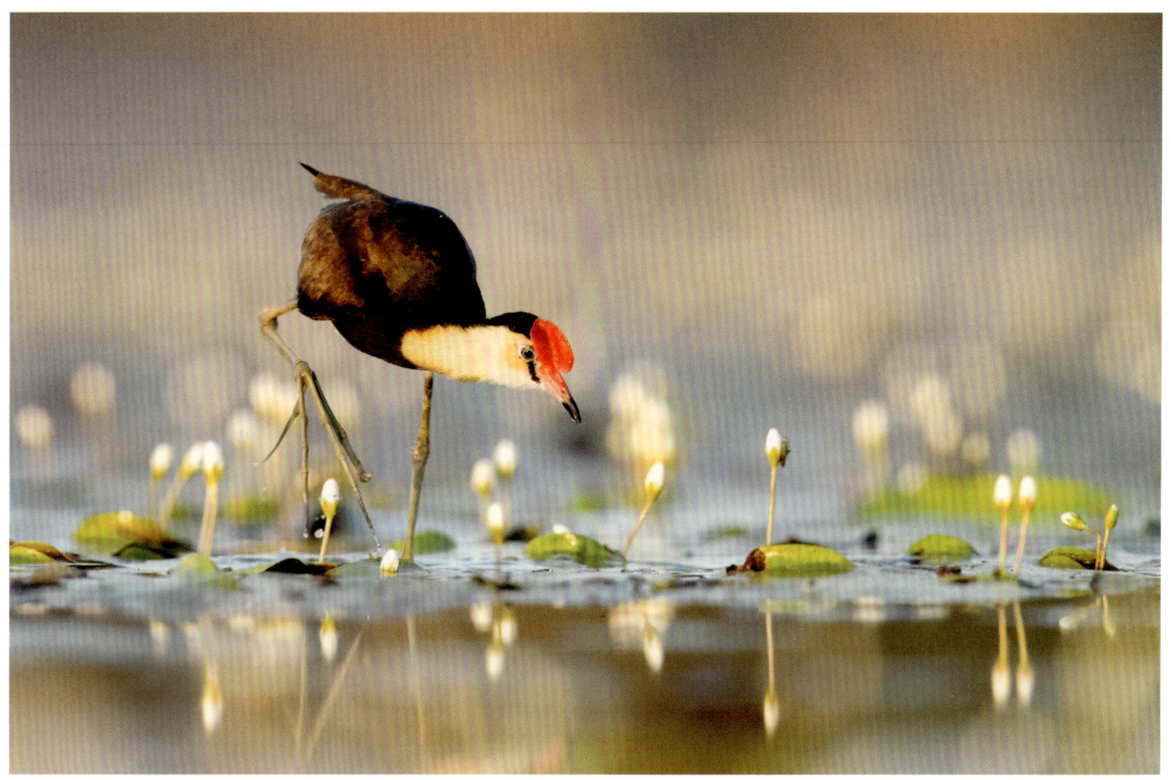

Comb-Crested Jacana

Comb-crested jacana
(Irediparra gallinacea)
James White, Victoria

A beautiful Kimberley sunrise produced soft pastel colours on Lilly Creek Lagoon. Being able to photograph these unique birds at water level whilst they walk the lily pads in search of prey was definitely a highlight of my Kimberley trip.
Lily Creek Lagoon, Kununurra, Western Australia

Canon 1DX II, EF 600mm f/4L IS II USM + EF Extender 1.4x III, 1/1600, f/7.1, ISO 3200, manual exposure, handheld

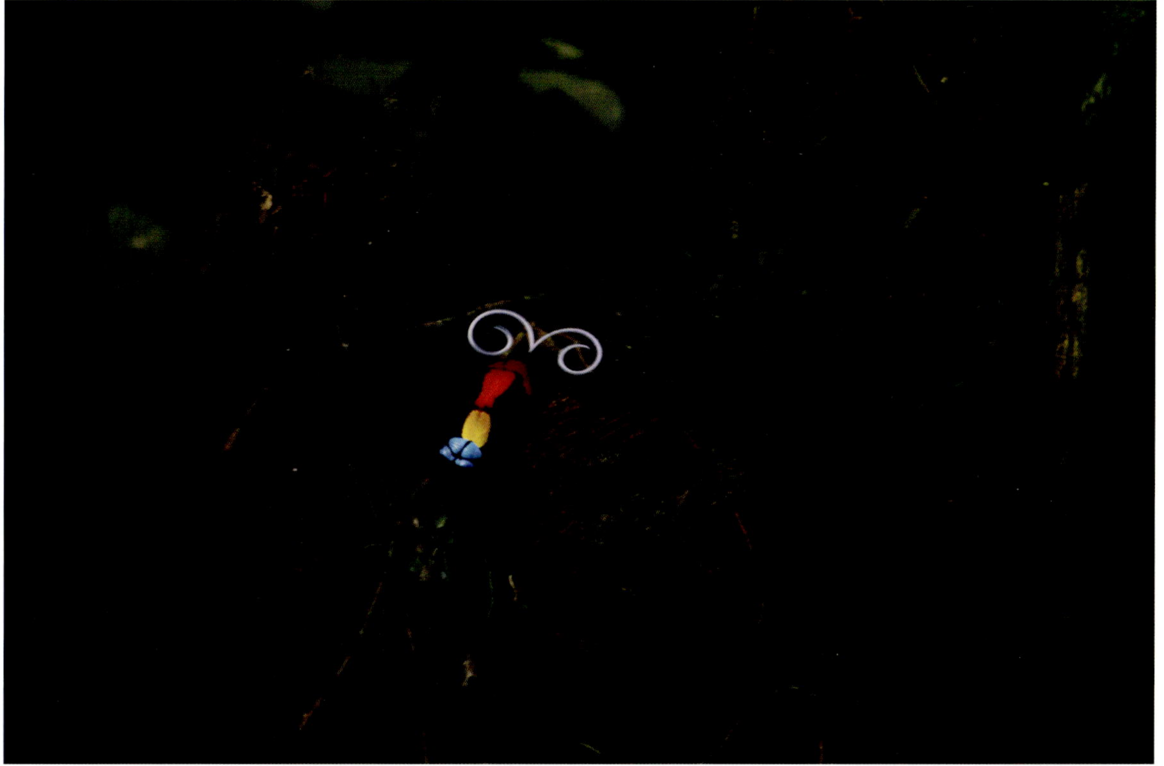

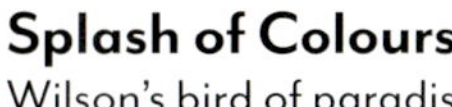

Splash of Colours

Wilson's bird of paradise
(Diphyllodes respublica)
Kevin De Vree, Belgium

As the first light travels through the rainforest's canopy, a splash of colours appear. Known for their elaborate mating dances, the Wilson's bird of paradise is one of the most colourful animals on the planet. Its quirky, handle-bar mustache-shaped tail feathers are brilliantly iridescent and reflect light that contrasts against the dark jungle.
Pulau Waigeo, Indonesia

Olympus OM-D E-M5, Panasonic 100–300mm f/4–5.6, 1/100, f/5, ISO 3200, handheld

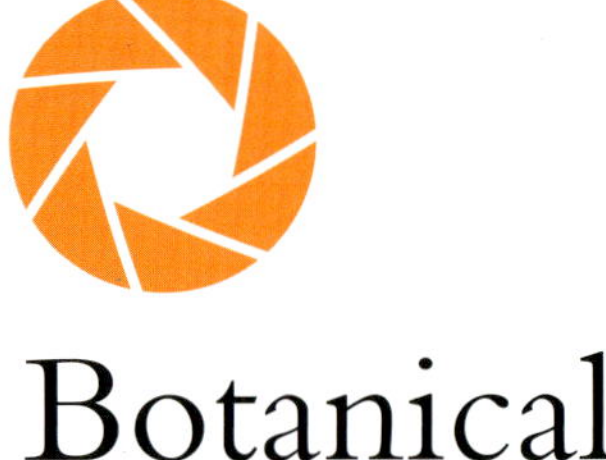

Botanical

Botanical Winner

Ghost Mushrooms
Ghost mushroom
(*Omphalotus nidiformis*)
Callie Chee, New South Wales

Nicknamed 'ghost mushrooms' due to their eerie glow, this fungi is only found in certain forests in Australia. They glow for only a few weeks in a year and are therefore quite hard to find and photograph.
Belanglo Forest, New South Wales

Canon 70D, Sigma Art, 30, f/3.2, ISO 6000

Judges' comments:
There is a magical fairy-tale feel to this image. The fungi are like glowing jewels of the forest, nestled among the trees in the mist. A cinematic quality has been given to this otherworldly scene.

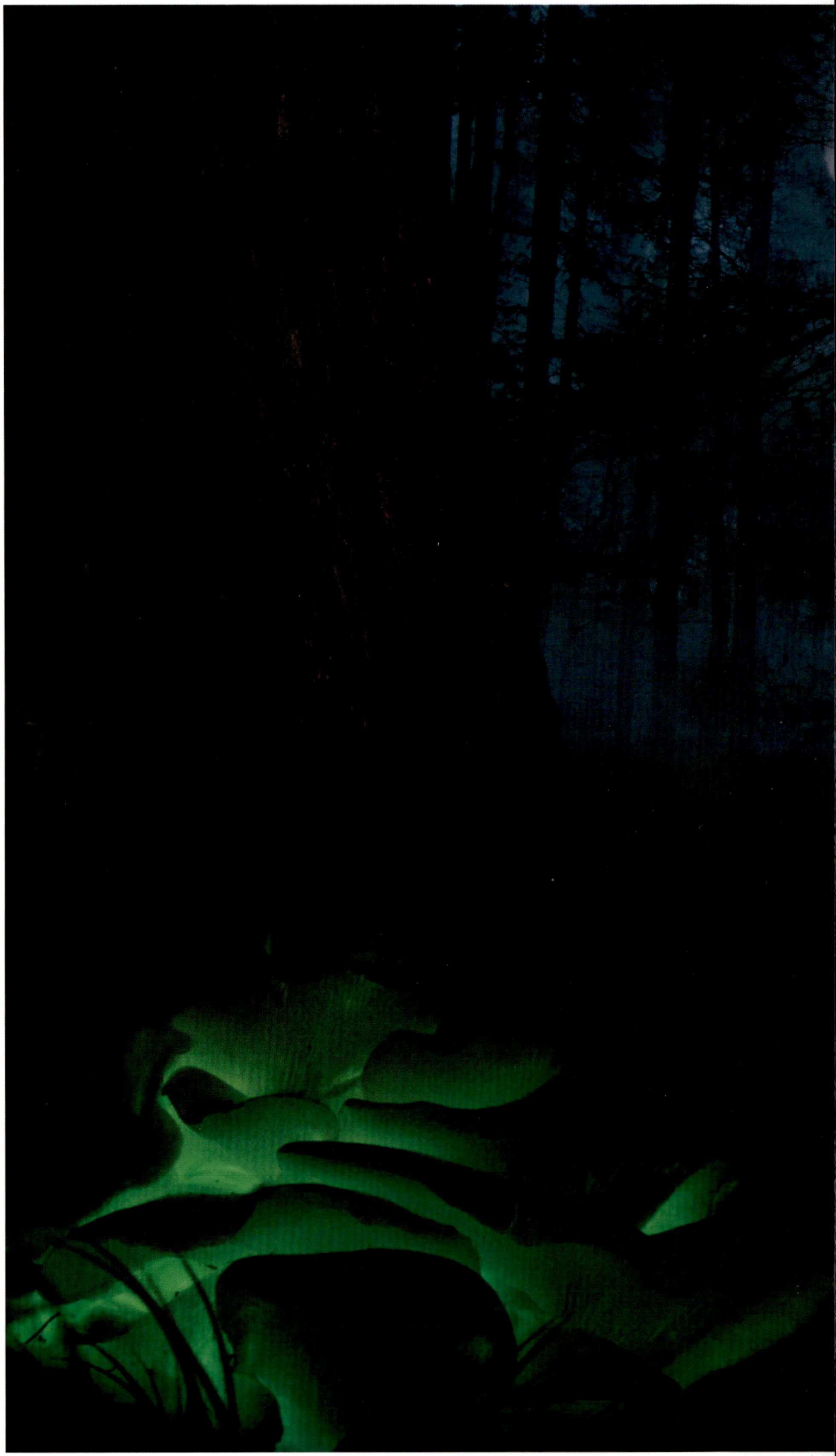

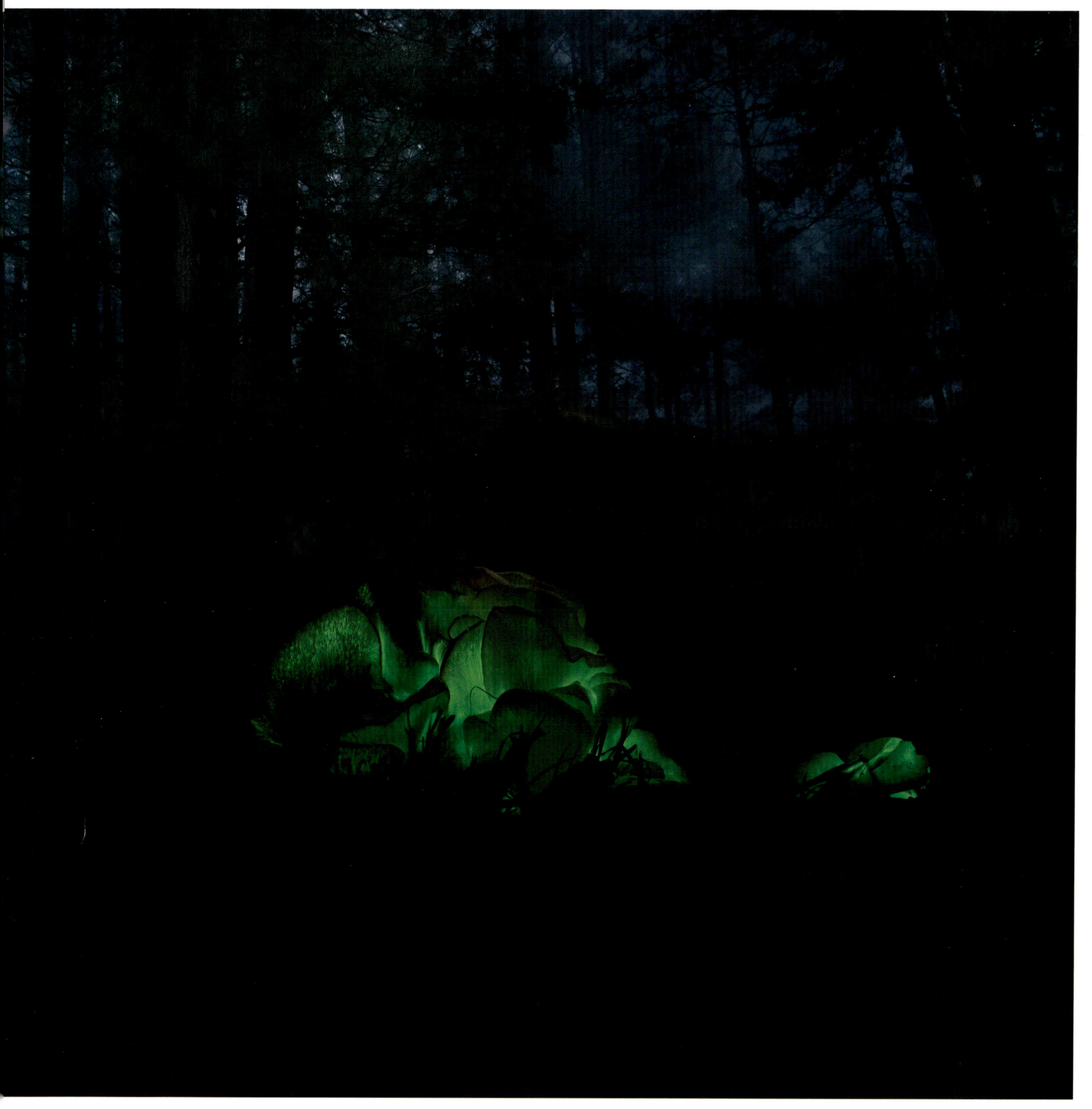

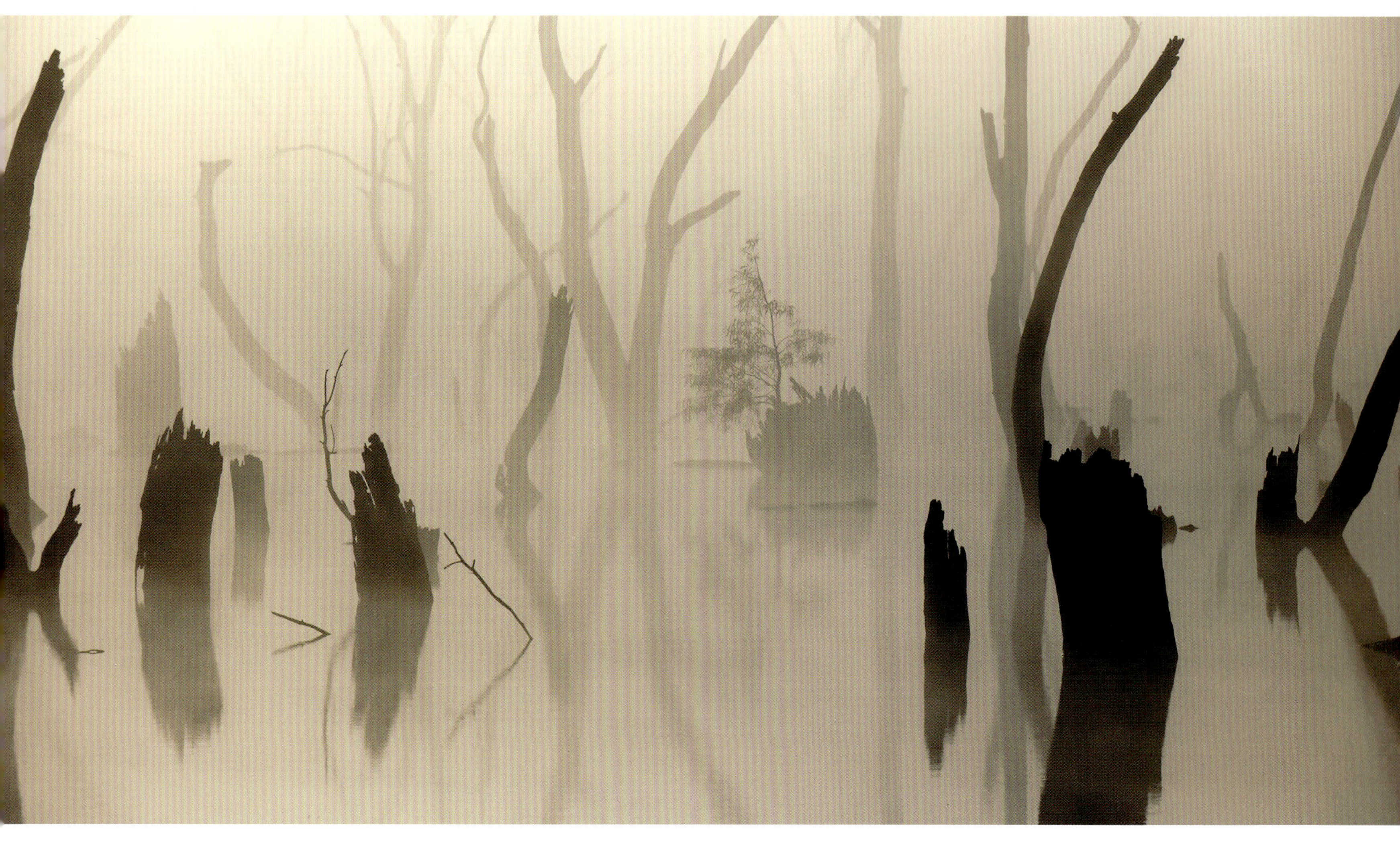

Botanical Runner-Up

Swamp Secrets

Paula McManus, South Australia

Mullinger Swamp Conservation Park is a protected area just outside of Kybybolite, on the South Australian and Victorian border. On our final day in the area, we lucked out with clear skies, still water, no wind and low-lying fog.
Mullinger Swamp Conservation Park, South Australia

Olympus OM-D E-M1, Olympus 40–150 Pro 100mm, 1/1000, f/9, ISO 200, tripod

Judges' comments:
Mood has been perfectly documented here. Monochromatic colour draws us in to a scene of stillness and quiet with an amazing tonal range. An ambiguous image, having both an apocalyptic feel and one of new beginnings.

Leafless Beauty

Rosy hyacinth orchid (*Dipodium roseum*)
Lincoln Macgregor, New South Wales

Unlike most plants that rely on the sun to produce energy in their leaves, the rosy hyacinth orchid is leafless and instead obtains its energy from decaying organic matter in the soil. To convey this unusual way of life, I photographed this species under a sunless sky.
Kangaroo Valley, New South Wales

Canon EOS R5, Canon EF 16–35mm f/2.8 III USM lens, 20, f/2.8, ISO 10 000, Canon Speedlite 580EX II with Godox XT2-C radio trigger and X1R-C radio receiver, stabilised on ground with a small sandbag, torchlight was used to light up the trees in the background

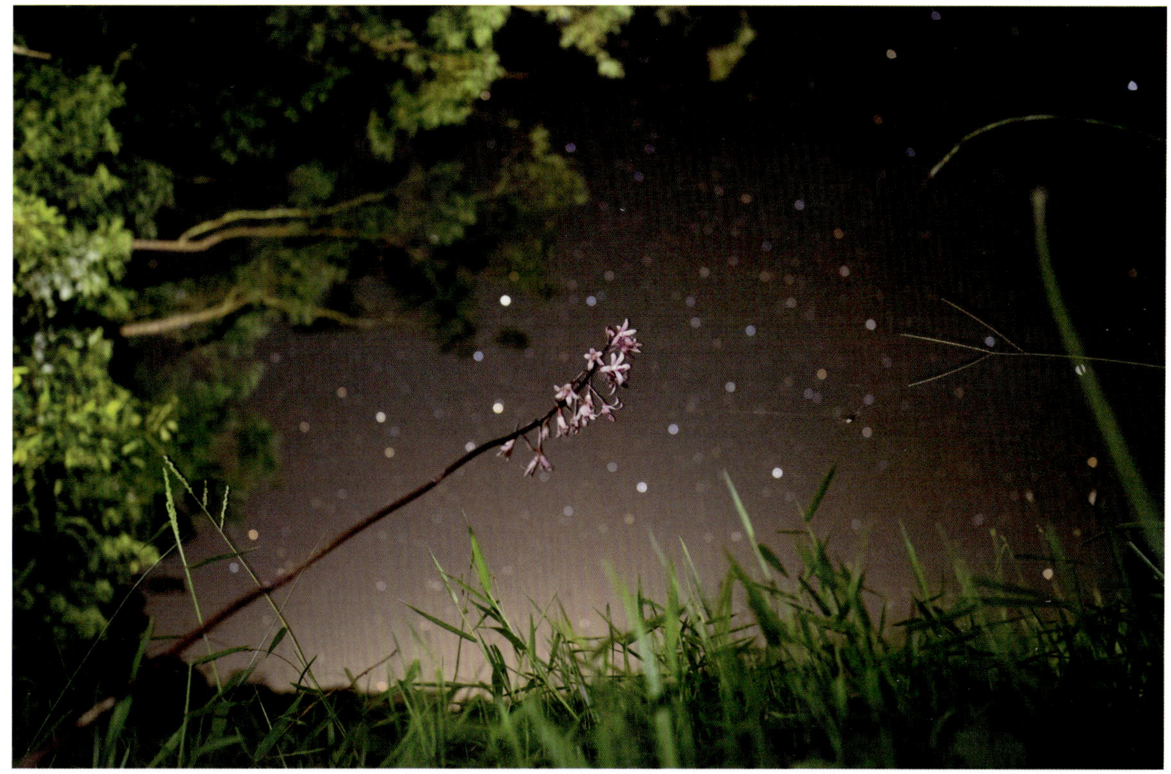

Blooming Algae

Algae (*Acetabularia peniculus*)
Georgina Steytler, Western Australia

When I first saw this little plant growing on the sides of shells I was captivated by how pretty it looked. Exposed at low tide, I used a macro lens to capture the delicate beauty. I was surprised to learn that it was actually an algae.
Shoal Bay, Albany, Western Australia

Olympus E-M1 Mk III, Olympus M.ZUIKO ED 60mm f2.8 macro, 1/320, f/8, ISO 500, handheld

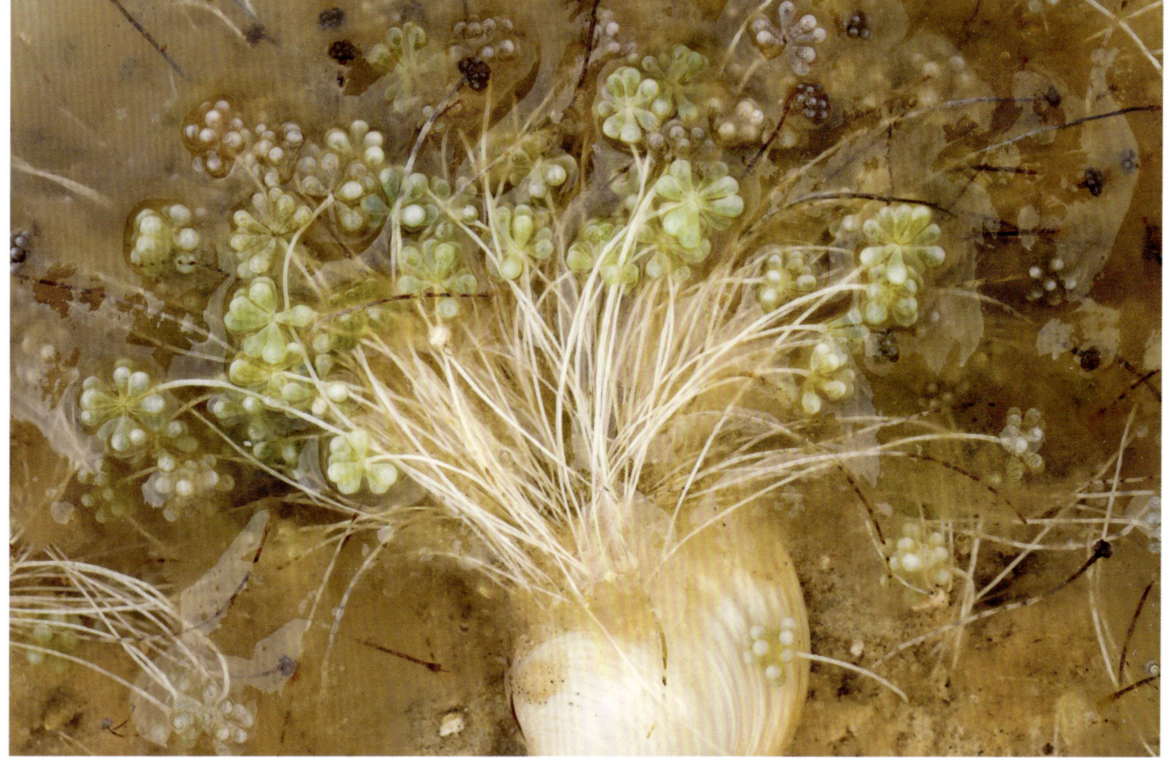

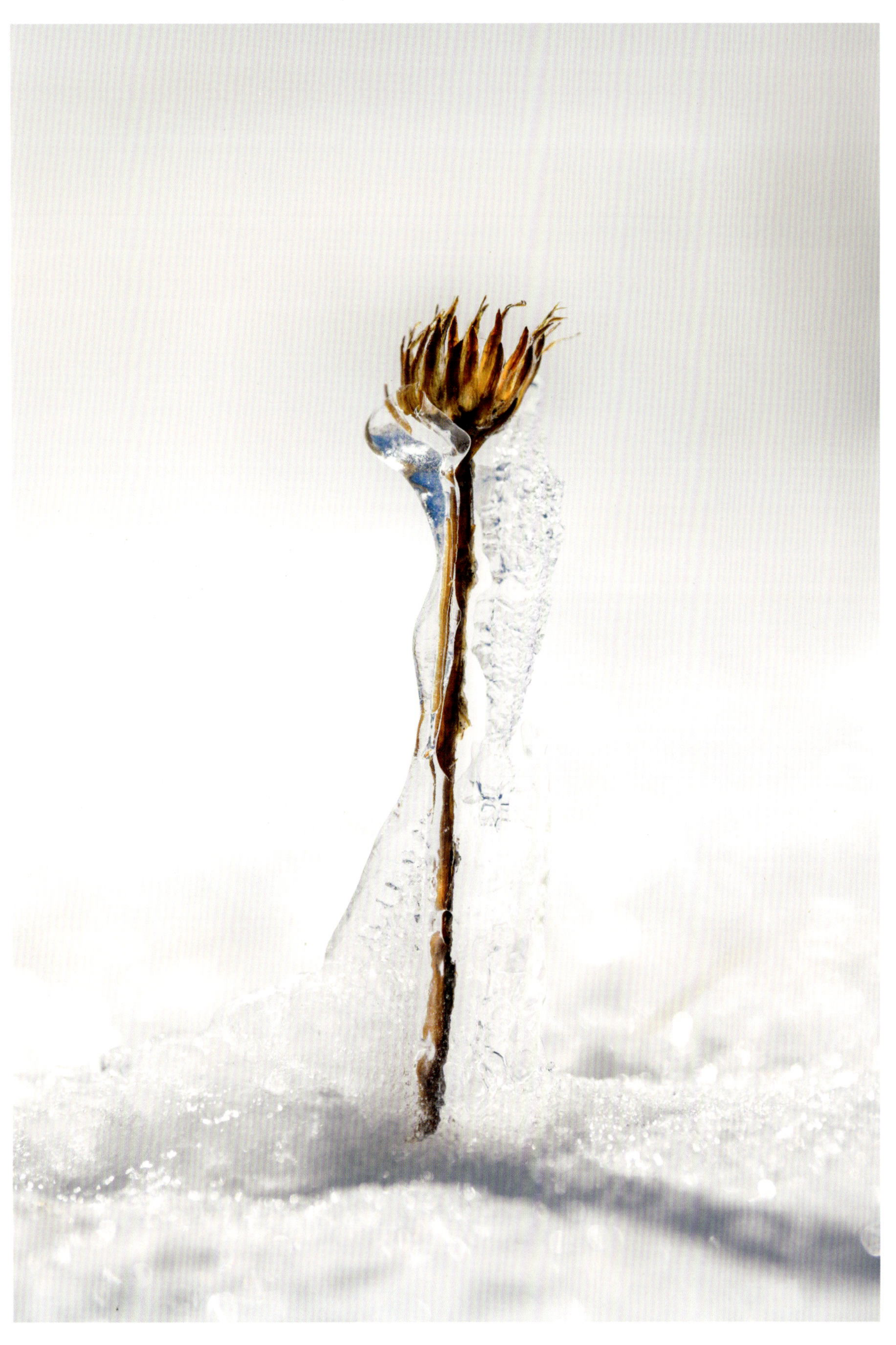

Snow Daisy

Snow daisy (*Brachyscome nivalis*)
Charles Davis, New South Wales

A lone snow daisy stands frozen in time, trapped in the ice that killed it when winter came. Normally these small flowers would be crushed under the snow, by fate it stands tall, held up by the cause of its downfall.
Kosciuszko National Park, New South Wales

Nikon D850, Nikon 70–200mm VR2 f2.8, 1/1250, f/4, ISO 31

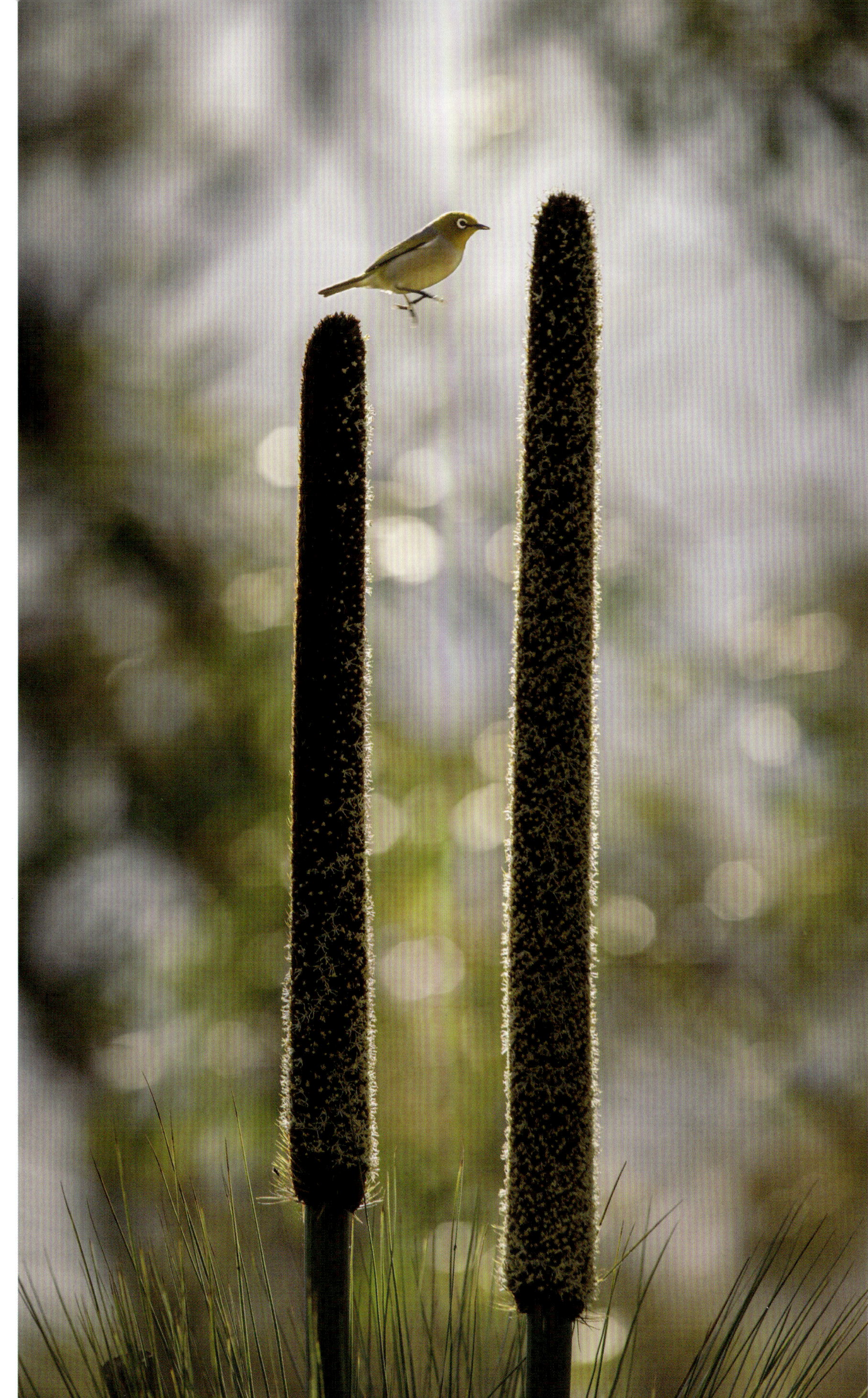

Bird on a Wire
Grass tree (*Xanthorrhoea* sp.),
silvereye (*Zosterops lateralis*)
Raoul Slater, Queensland

Over many Westcliff Lookout bushwalks, I've seen the grass trees flowering profusely only once. The birds had hundreds of flower spikes to choose from – each photo requiring a patient wait. The title references the *Man on Wire* documentary about the tight-rope crossing between the Twin Towers. *Westcliff Lookout, Bunya Mountains National Park, Queensland*

Canon 6D II, Canon 300mm f 2.8, 1/800, f/4, ISO 200, Manfrotto with Wimberly head, tripod

The Wattle Tree

Wattle tree (*Acacia* sp.)
Matt Palmer, Victoria

The Wattle Tree honours one of my favorite trees. By using off-camera flash to illuminate the tree, I was able to further subdue the background and highlight the beautiful yellows of the flowering wattle. This image can no longer be taken as the trees in the background have been harvested for timber.
Glendevie, Tasmania

Canon EOS 5D Mk III, Canon EF 70–200mm f/2.8L II IS USM lens, 1/200. f/8, ISO 400, off-camera flash used from the right-hand side, handheld

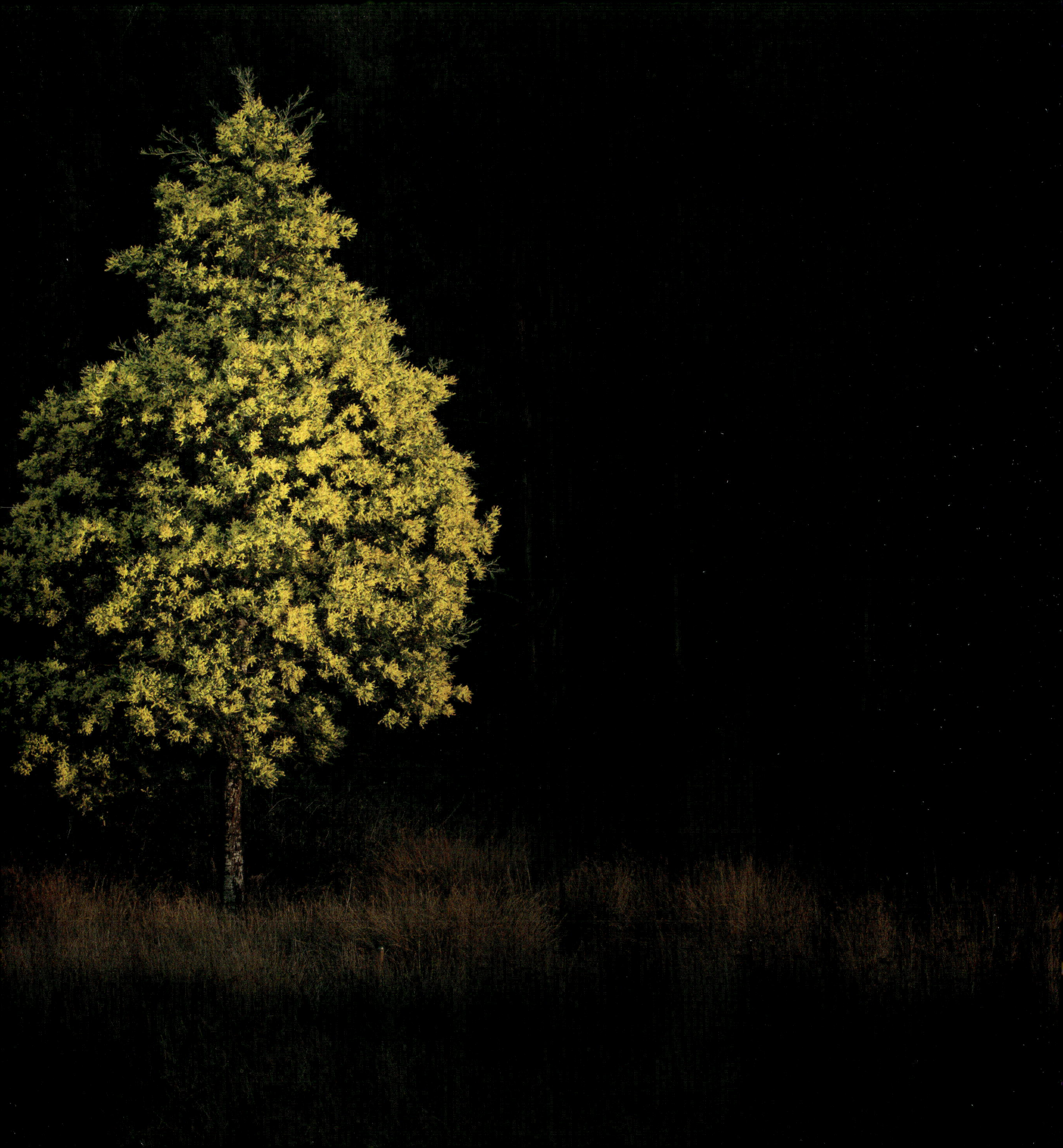

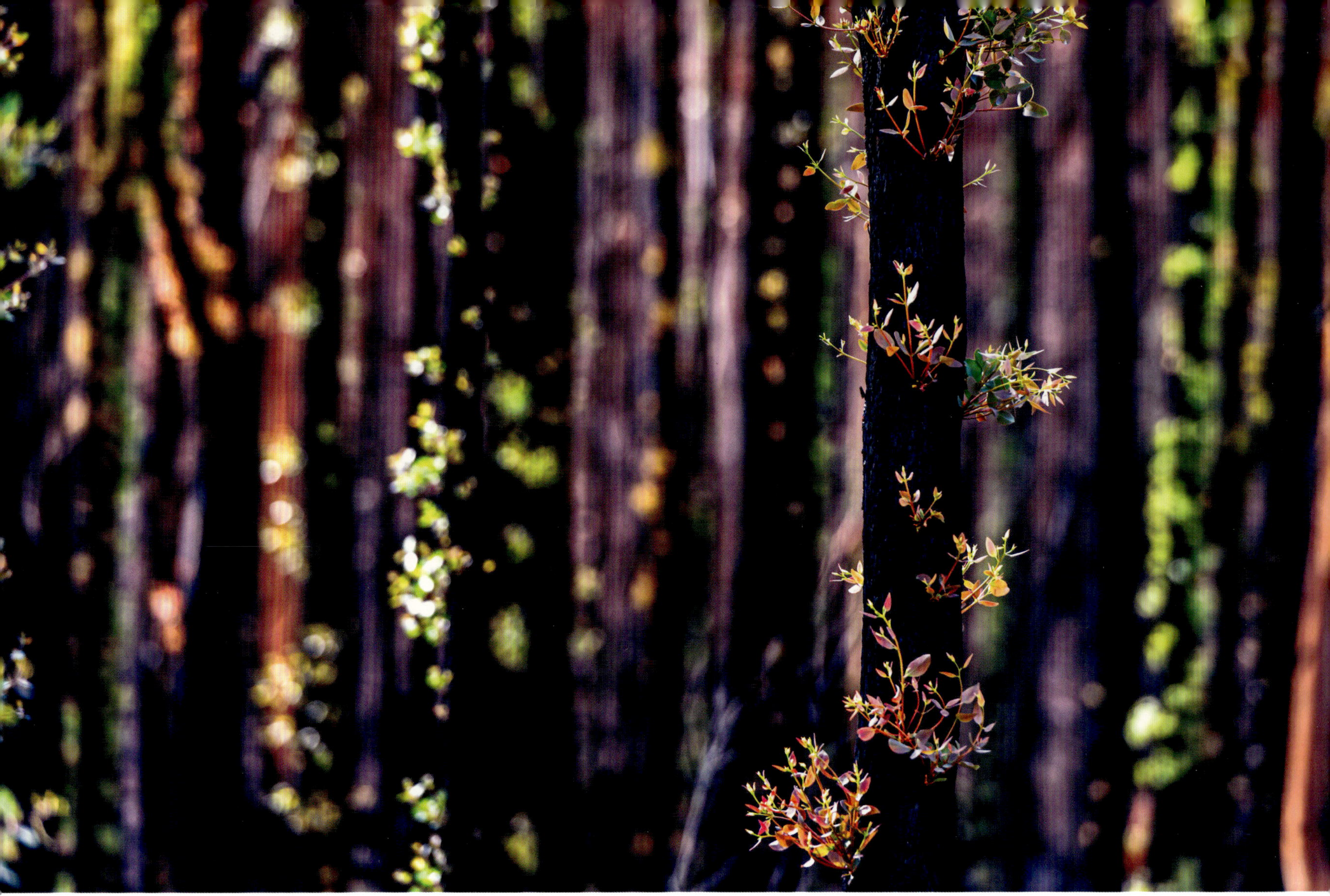

Signs of recovery

Eucalyptus (Myrtaceae)
Doug Gimesy, Victoria

Burnt eucalyptus trees start to show signs of life a few weeks after bushfires by sprouting epicormic growth/shoots from their blackened trunks. Once they sprout, all going well, the tree will begin to gradually regrow all its lost foliage, and (hopefully) recover over time. Sadly, not all trees have this capability.
Between Orbost and Goongerah, Victoria

Nikon D750, Nikon 70–200mm f/2.8, 1/320, f/4.0, ISO 160, handheld

Snow Squid
Jeff Freestone, Victoria

Captured during the peak of winter after a recent snowstorm had passed through. I was drawn to the unusual shapes of these trees scattered along the peaks of Mount Hotham. The way the trunks branch out in this unusual way give a sense of the harsh and brutal conditions faced each winter.
Alpine National Park, Victoria

Sony A7Riii, Sony 24–105mm f4 G OSS, 1/20, f/13, ISO 100, tripod

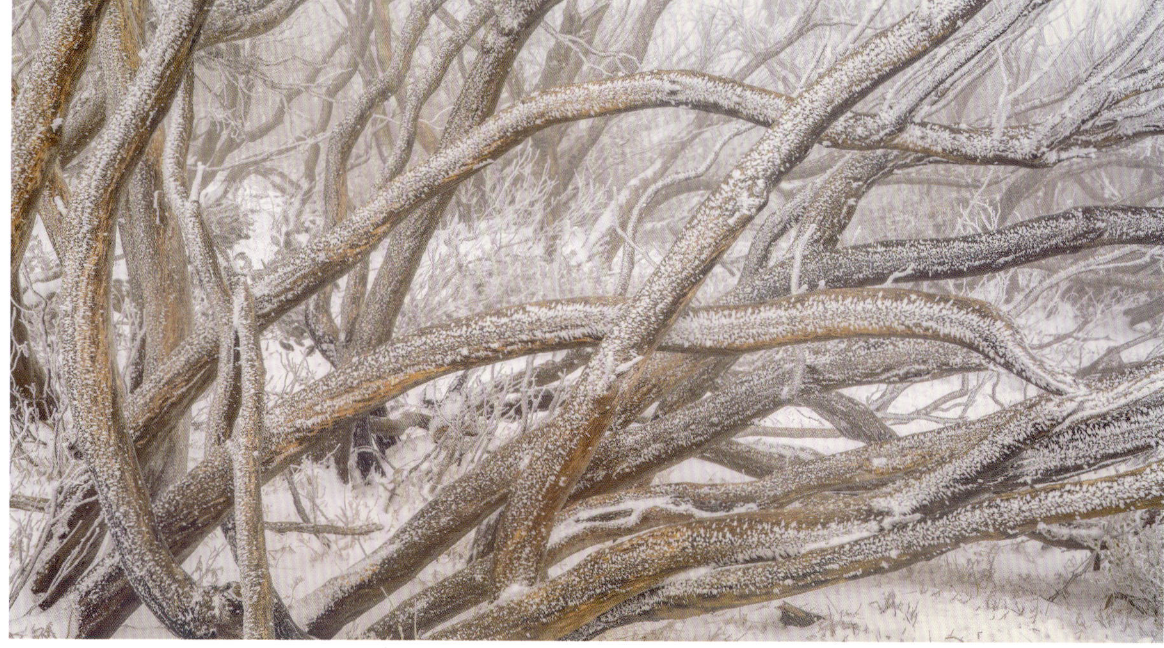

Royal Hakea
Royal hakea (*Hakea victoria*)
Andrew Peacock, Queensland

This shrub is the emblem of the Fitzgerald River National Park. Its beauty comes from brightly coloured foliage rather than its understated flowers. I found this attractive patch beside a dirt road in the park. Only when I climbed onto the roof of the vehicle could I frame this pleasing composition.
Fitzgerald River National Park, Western Australia

Canon EOS 5D Mk IV, Canon 24–105 f/4L lens, 1/640, f/11, ISO 800, digital capture, handheld

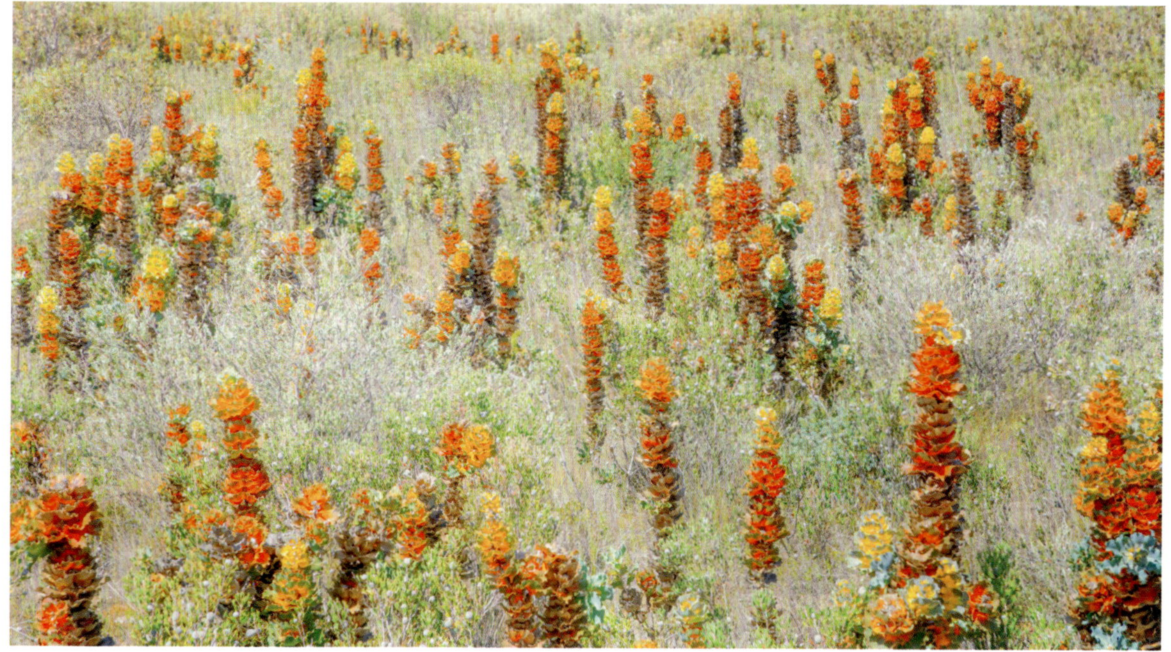

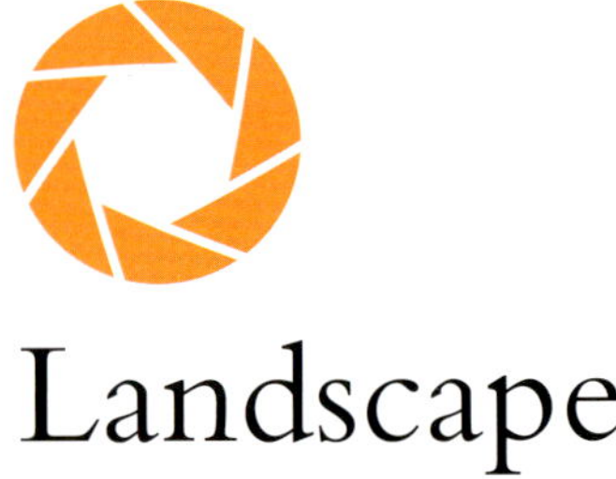

Landscape

Landscape Winner

Forest of Reflection

Hayden Cannon, Western Australia

A beautiful scene I came across one afternoon whilst scoping out a site for a photo shoot. I saw these paperbarks in the water creating stunning reflections, with some golden light emphasising the trees. I changed to my wide angle lens and took a few snaps before the light faded.
The Lakes, Dalyellup, Western Australia

Canon 7D Mk II DSLR, Canon EF 17–40mm f/4L USM, 1/80, f/4, ISO 100, handheld

Judges' comments:
There is a painterly quality in this landscape that evokes a glimpse at a lost world. The light catching on the paperbark is exquisite with the pattern of branches creating a tapestry of delicate colour.

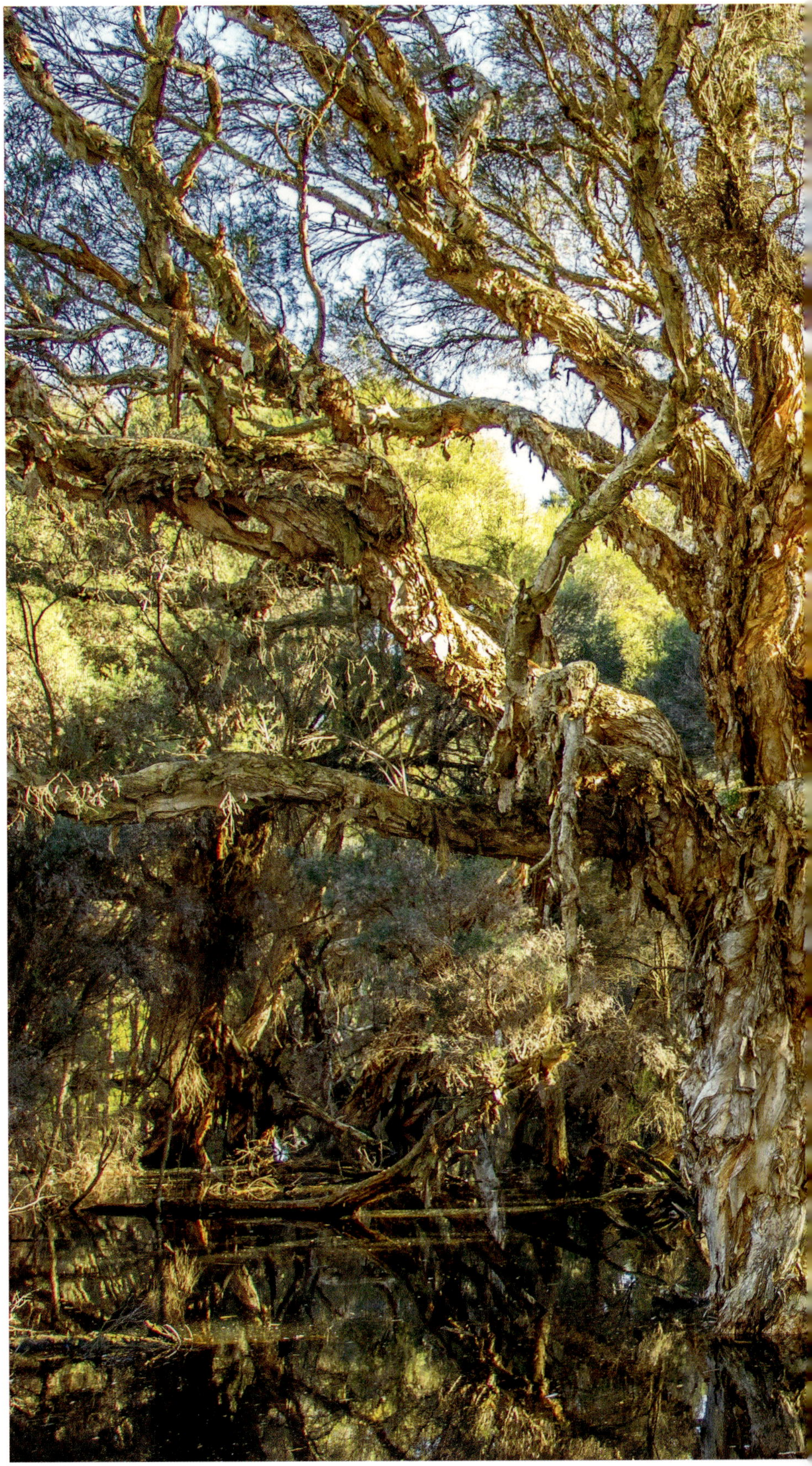

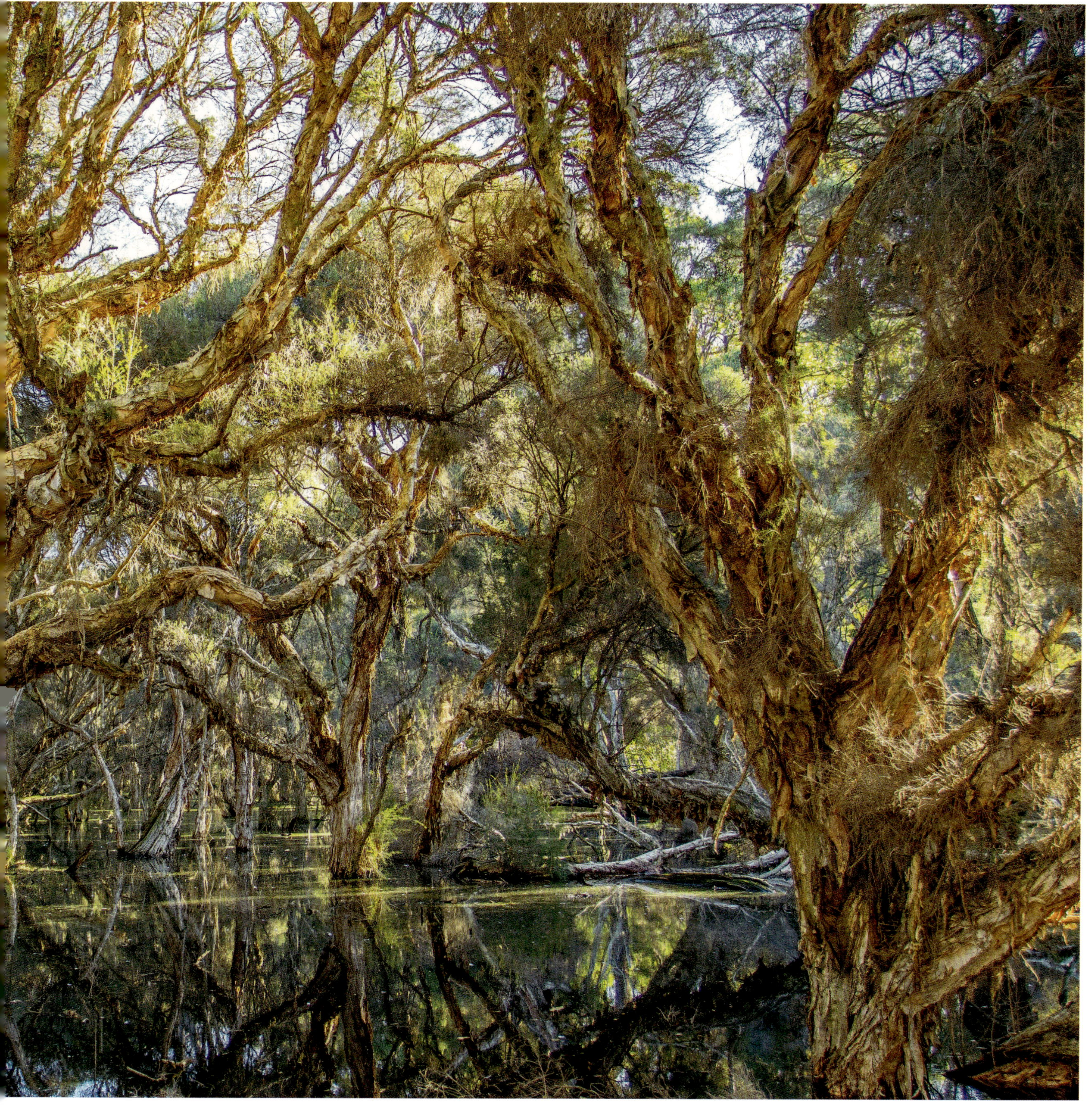

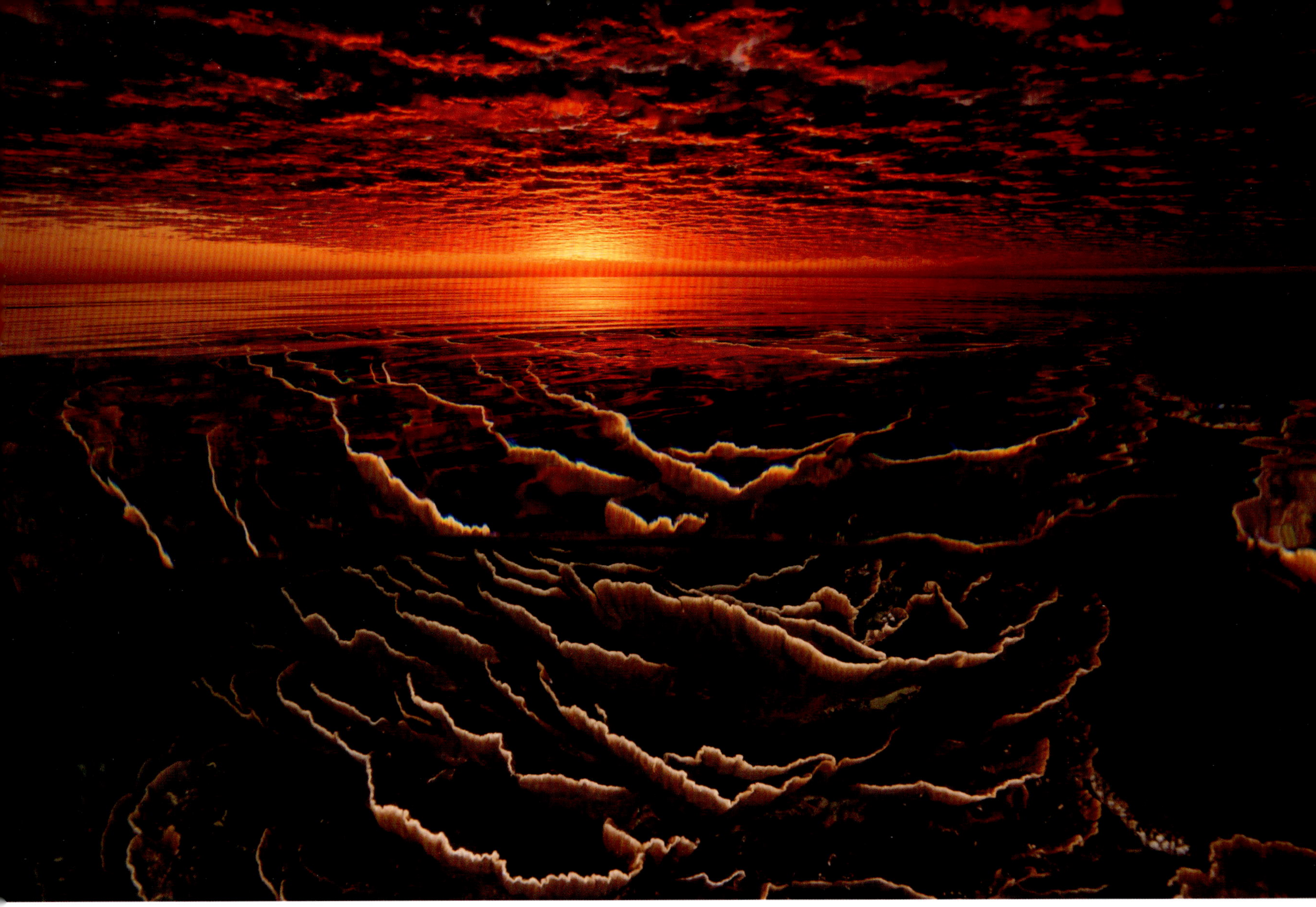

Landscape Runner-Up

Beneath the Surface

Ashlee Karas, Western Australia

For some, sunsets are a time for reflection and meditation. For me, pairing a fiery sunset with the pristine coral gardens of the Ningaloo Reef under the glassy ocean surface brings a whole new level of tranquillity. Combining two worlds to create a perfect moment.
Ningaloo Reef, Coral Bay, Western Australia

Sony A7Rii, 16–35mm f/2.8 G Master lens , 1/250, f/14, ISO 500, 2 x Inon z330 strobes, Nauticam housing

Judges' comments:
Under/over technique has been used to give a unique and abstract view of this underwater landscape. Reflecting the repetitive nature of the clouds, the coral also mimics the ripple of waves rolling into shore. Strikingly set against a dramatic sunset.

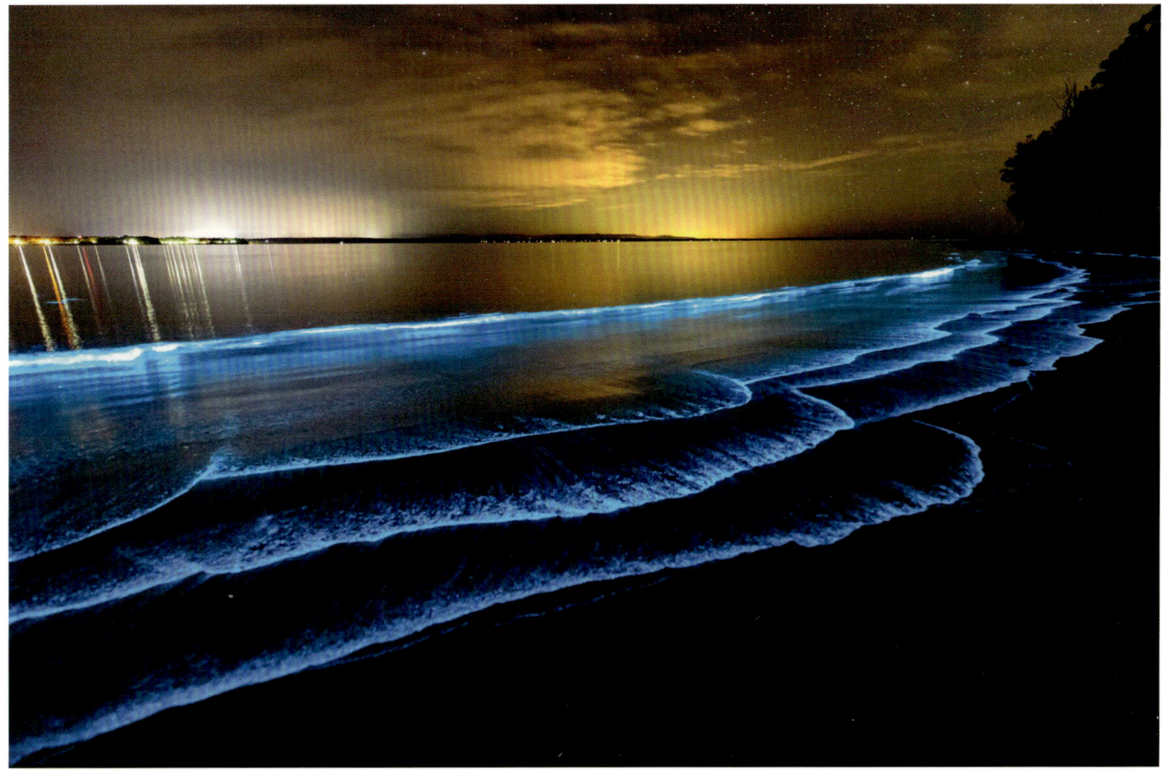

Bioluminescent Shores

Sea sparkle (*Noctiluca scintillans*)
Jordan Robins, New South Wales

Bioluminescent algae lighting up the shoreline in Jervis Bay a bright electric blue. What can be seen as a red tide during the day, the microalgae produces a bright blue glow when it is disturbed, in this case, by wind and wave action breaking on the shore.
Jervis Bay, New South Wales

Canon EOS 5D Mk IV, Canon EF 16–35mm f/4L IS USM lens, 30, f/4, ISO 4000, tripod

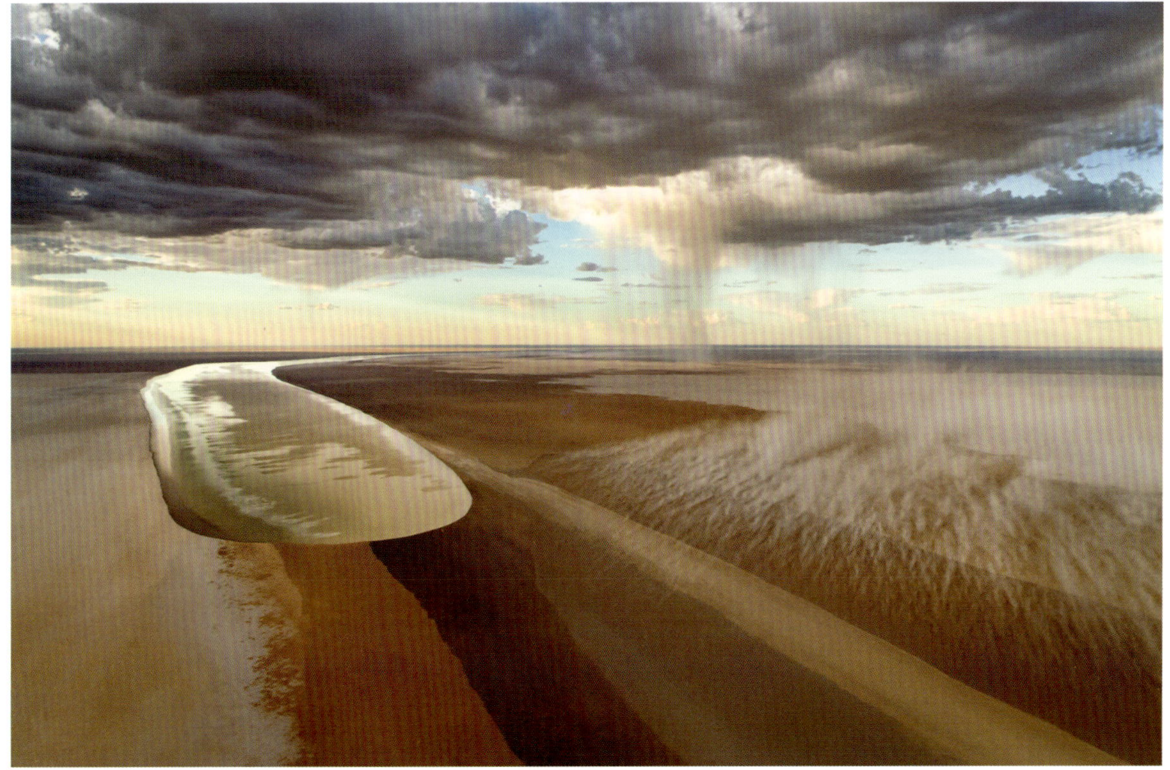

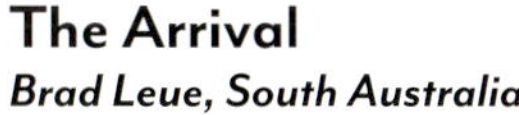

The Arrival

Brad Leue, South Australia

Water that has travelled from northern Queensland for months finally arrives at the entrance to mighty Kati Thanda–Lake Eyre. The water meandered across the Simpson and Tirari Deserts, through Australian Wildlife Conservancy's Kalamurina Wildlife Sanctuary, progressing into the Warburton Groove, bringing new life to this remarkable desert system.
Kati Thanda–Lake Eyre, South Australia

Canon 1D X Mk II, Canon EF 24–70mm f/2.8L II USM, 1/640, f/9.0, ISO 500, handheld from helicopter

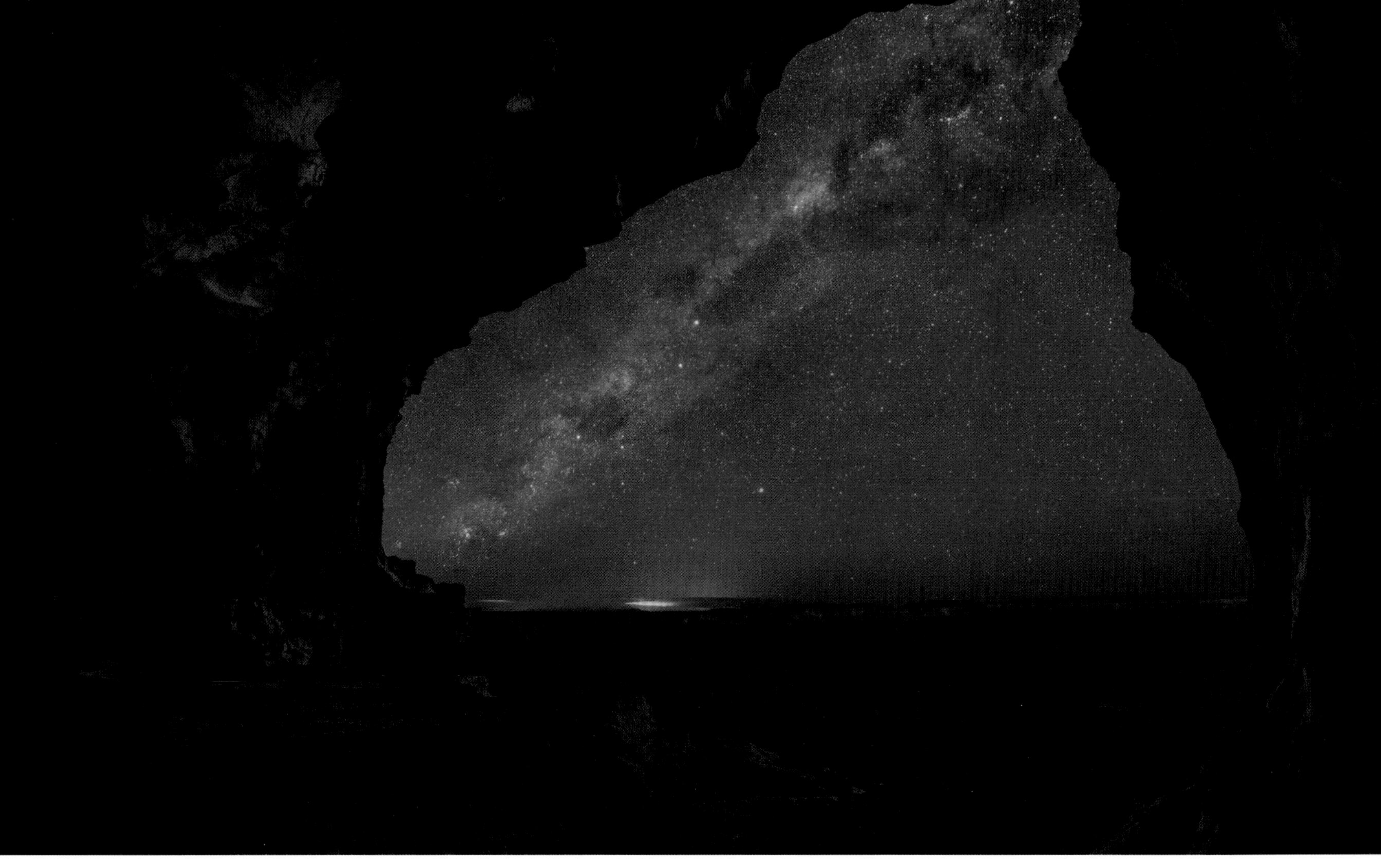

View from the Cave

Yan Zhang, New South Wales

This photo was taken in Blue Mountains. It was a clear and moonless night. I came to this tiny cave on a cliff and waited patiently till midnight. I captured this amazing moment when the Milky Way was just aligned with the cave edge. *Blue Mountains, New South Wales*

Nikon D850, Nikon 14–24mm f/2.8 14mm, 20, f/2.8, ISO 8000, Benro Tortoise TR328C, RRS Ballhead BH-55 tripod

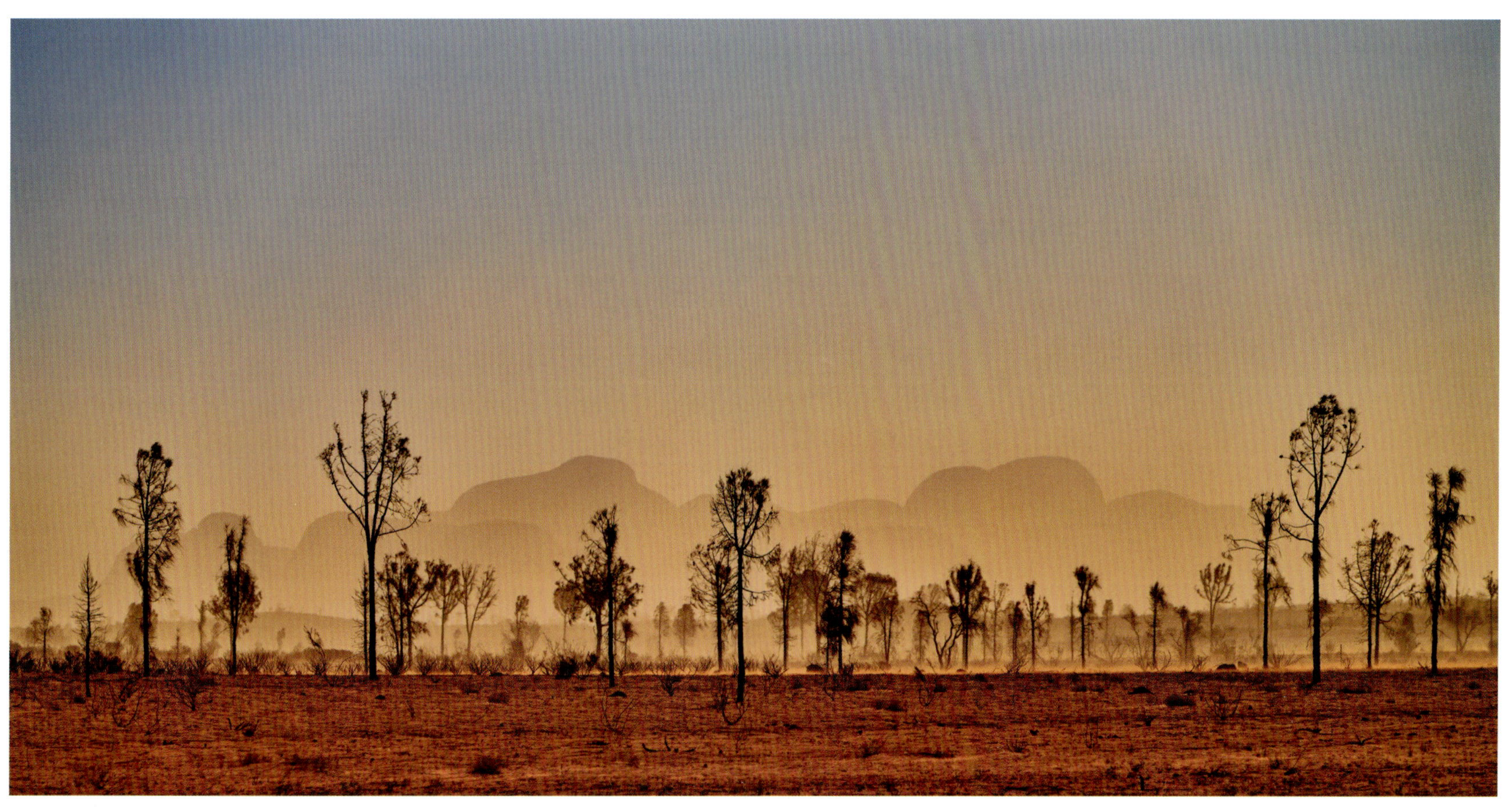

Sandstorm through Kata Tjuṯa

Michael Eastwell, United Kingdom

As I left Yulara to head towards Uluṟu, I noticed a sandstorm charging over Kata Tjuṯa (Pitjantjatjara term meaning 'many heads'). I'd never seen this occur over these iconic formations before, so I pulled over as quickly as possible to capture this dramatic scene.
Yulara, Northern Territory

Sony A7RIV, Sony 100–400 GM OSS, 1/3200, f/8, ISO 100, handheld

Lunettes

Callie Chee, New South Wales

Lake Mungo was once an icy lake, but it dried more than 10,000 years ago at the end of the Ice Age. Today its stark unearthly formations resemble a moonscape. Mungo is also a site of prime significance culturally and archaeologically, bearing evidence of the oldest civilisation on earth.
Mungo National Park, New South Wales

Canon 6D Mk II, Tokina 11–17mm, 1/320, f/7.1, ISO 500

OVER PAGE

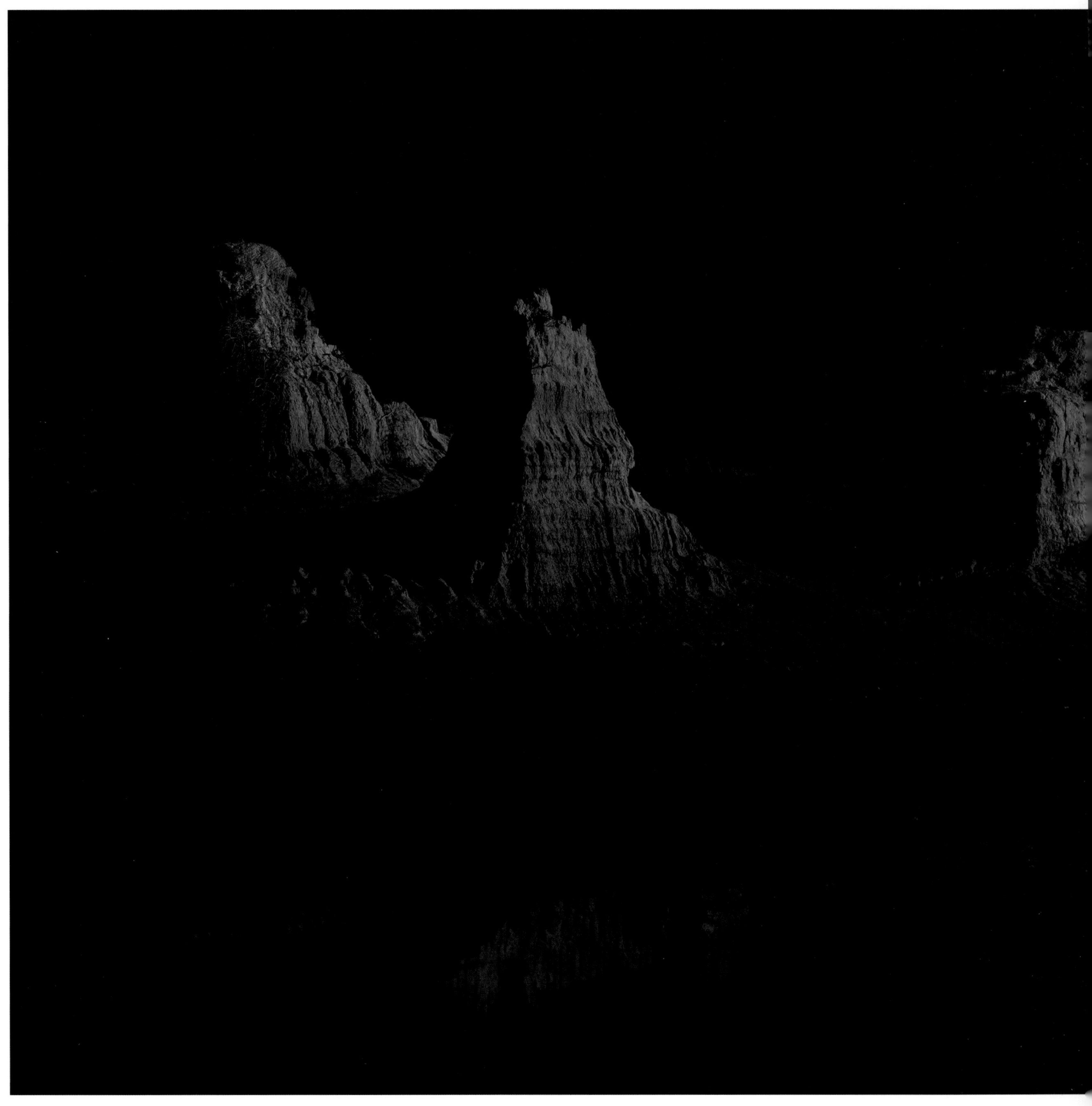

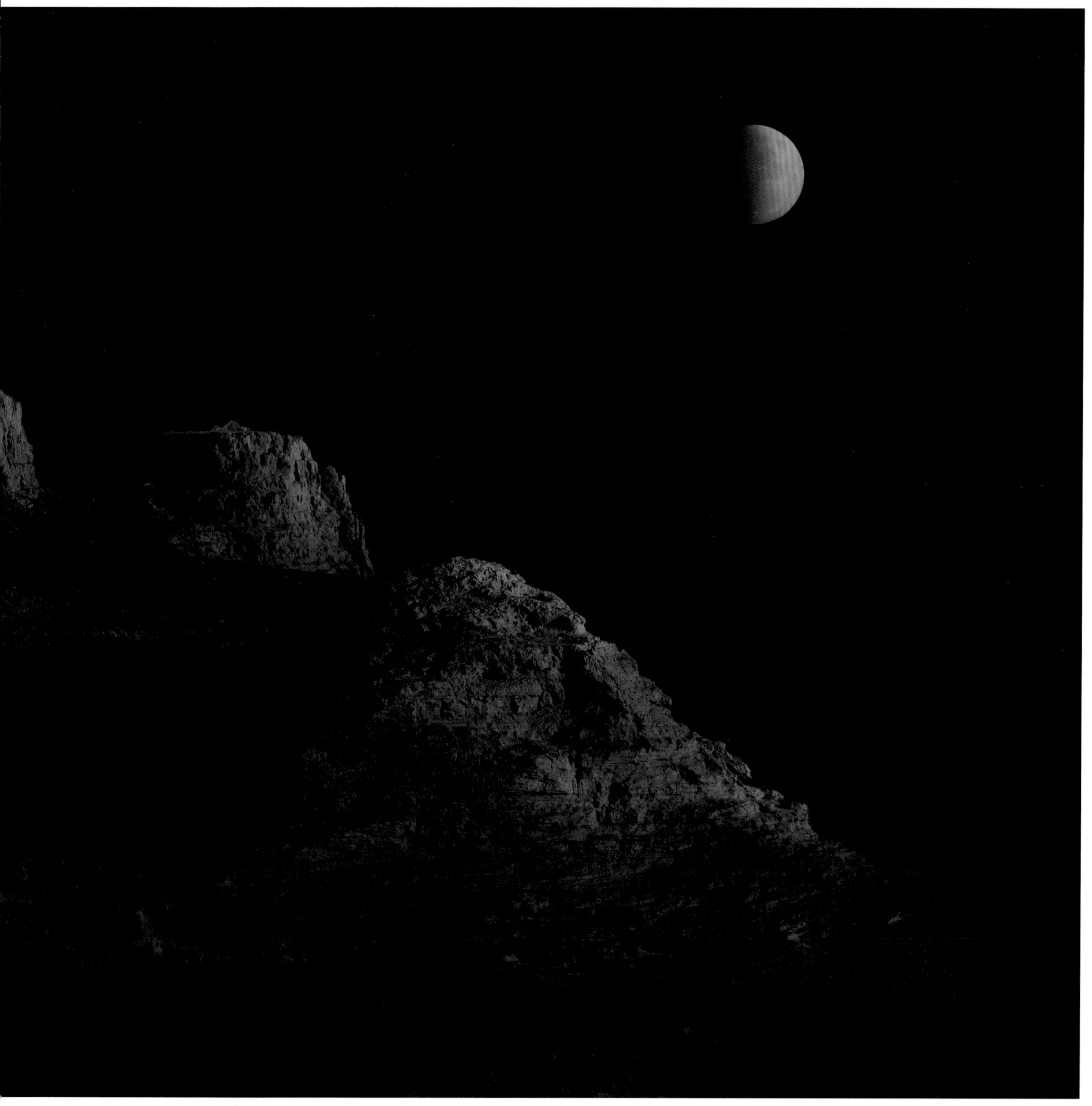

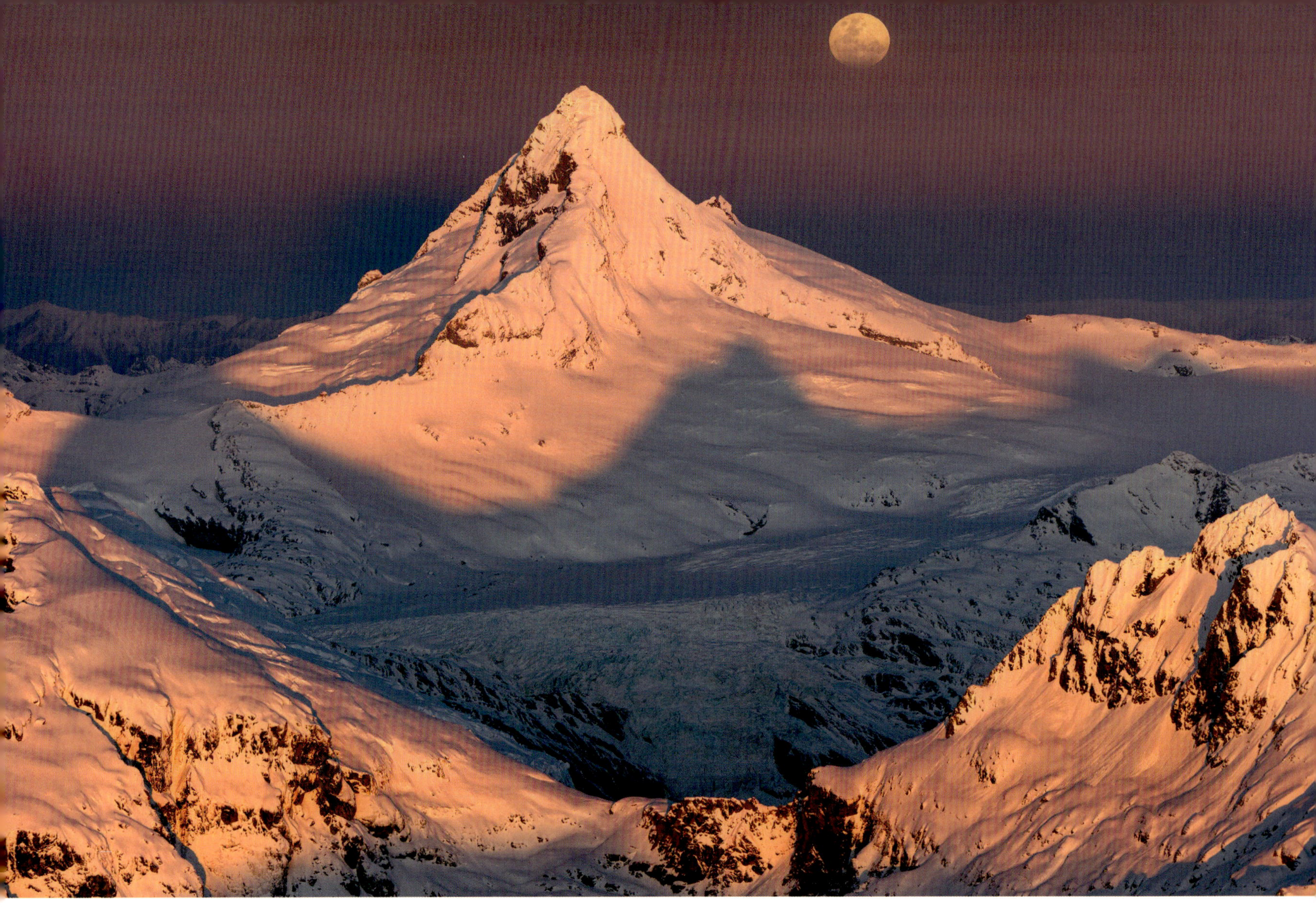

Moonrise

William Patino, New Zealand

It took almost 12 months to finally capture this aerial image of the full moonrise at dusk. With the sun sinking down to the horizon, the mountains were painted in a rosy hue as the moon began to ascend out to the east. A surreal moment to experience, drifting in the air at 9000 feet.
Mount Aspiring, New Zealand

Sony A7R III, Sony 100–400mm, 1/320, f/8.0, ISO 200

Sunset Over Lake Pedder

Cam Blake, Tasmania

This shot was taken late on a cold winter's afternoon as the sun set over Lake Pedder. The original Lake Pedder, flooded in 1972 is located just around the corner from this image. You could say it's still making its presence known with this display of natural beauty.
Lake Pedder, Tasmania

Olympus EM1 Mk II, Olympus Pro 40–150mm f2.8, 1/60, f/5.6, ISO 64, circular polarising filter, handheld

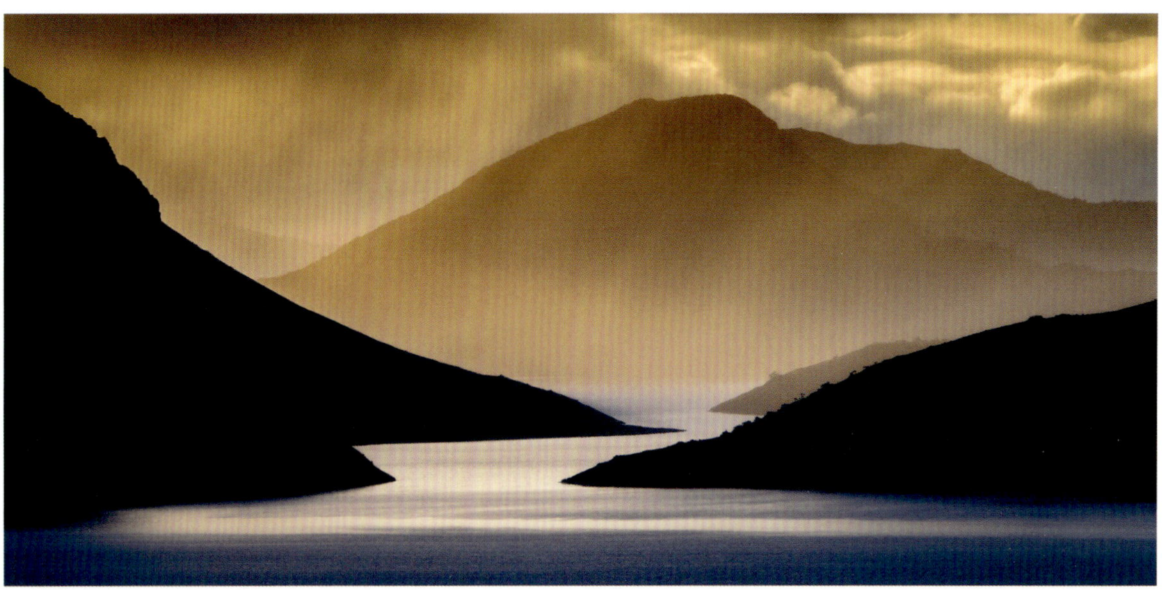

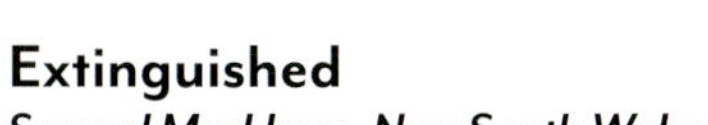

Extinguished

Samuel Markham, New South Wales

From one extreme to another. Heavy rain and large hail stones batter a fire scorched and damaged Australian landscape, bringing much needed rain and relief. Smoke, hail and rain combine after the devastating New South Wales bushfires.
Parma Creek Nature Reserve, Yerriyong, New South Wales

Canon EOS 5D Mk IV, Canon EF 100–400mm f/4.5–5.6L IS I, 1/1000, f/5.6, ISO 1000, handheld

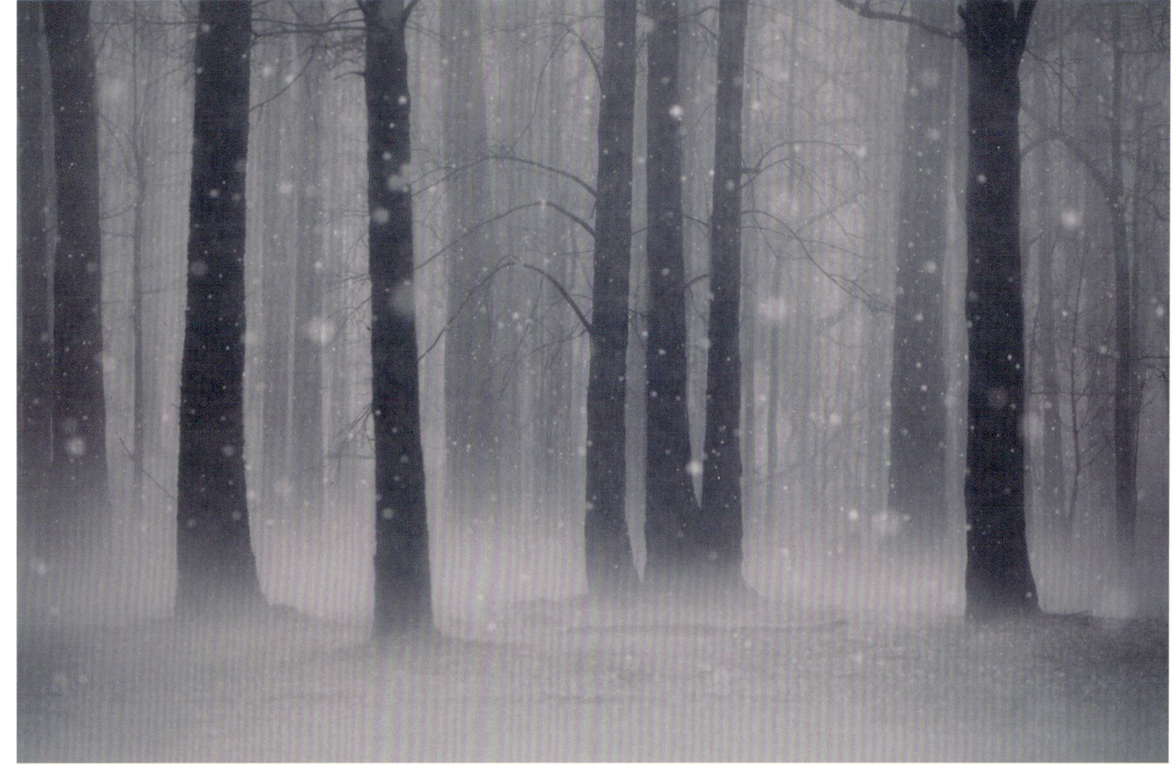

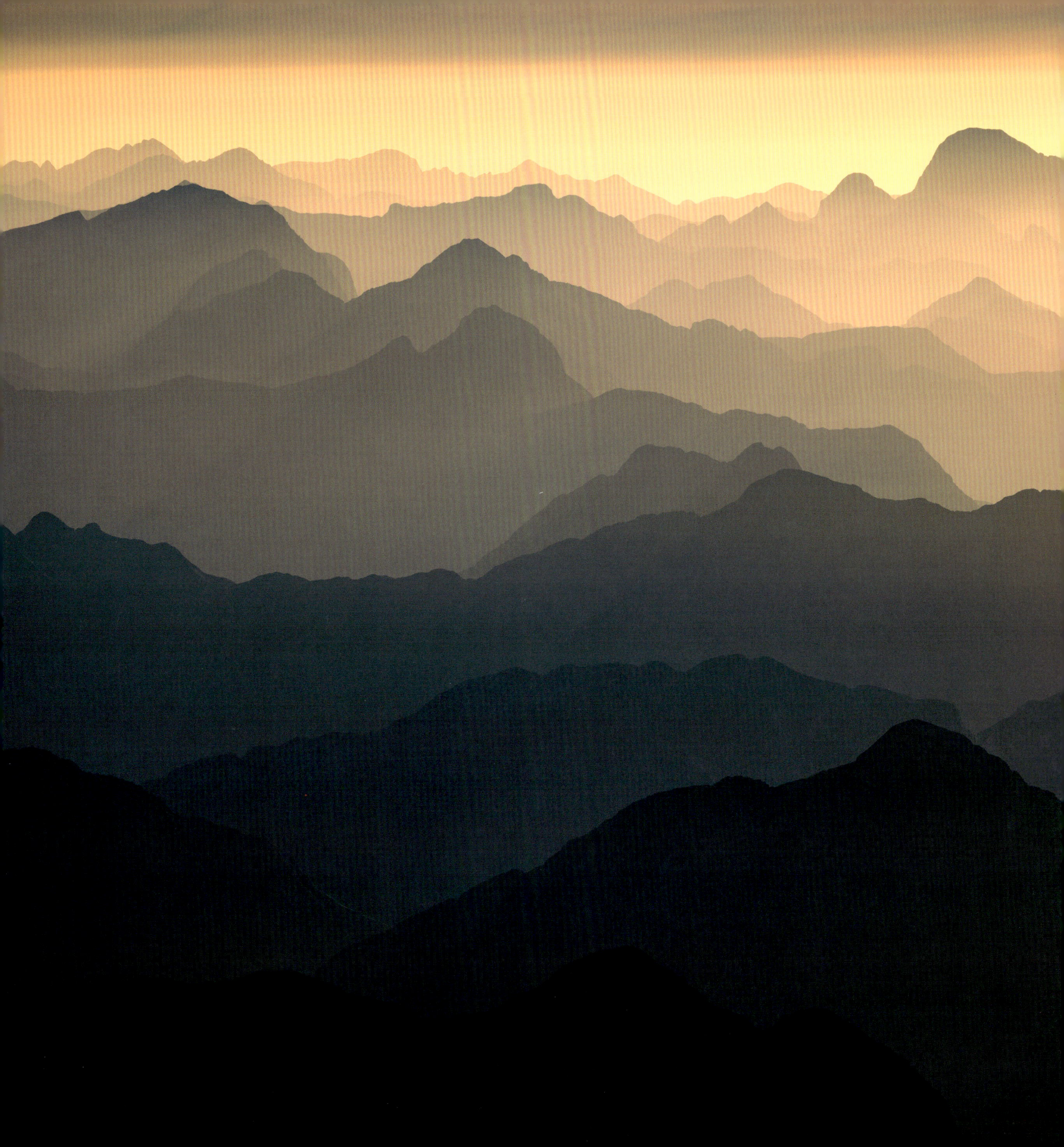

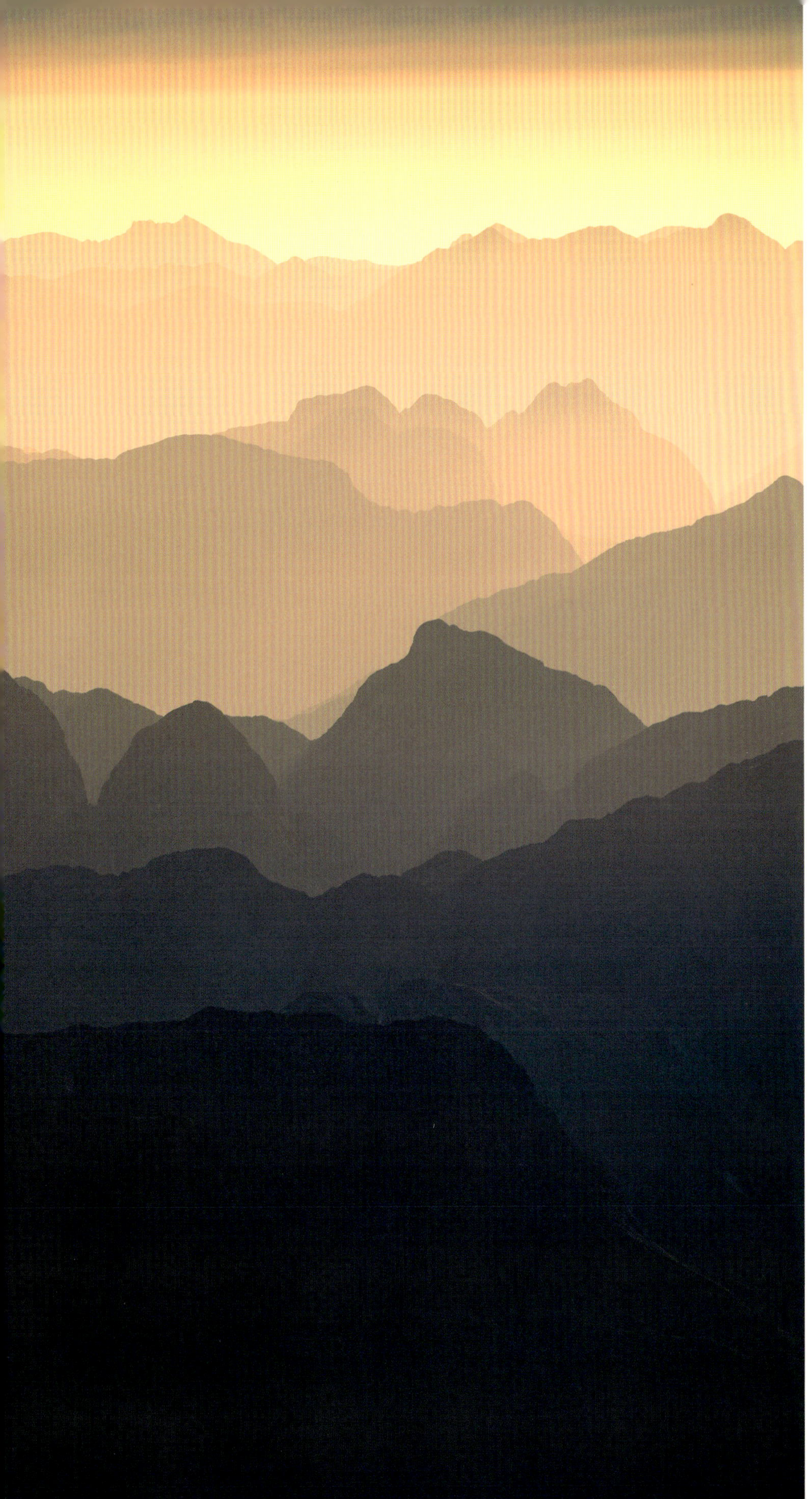

Above the Darkness

William Patino, New Zealand

Light and atmosphere, separating the steep multitude of valleys that define Fiordland. I released this image at the start of the Covid-19 pandemic, during a time of much uncertainty and concern for us all. This image and title represent resilience and, that even in life's darkest of valleys, light and hope can always be found.
Fiordland, New Zealand

Sony A7R III, Sony 100–400mm, 1/1250, f/7.1, ISO 100

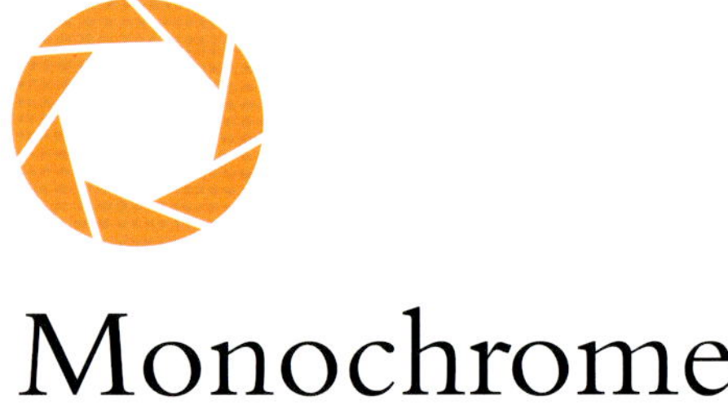

Monochrome

Monochrome Winner

Incoming

Jeff Freestone, Victoria

Captured in Omeo, Victoria, looking out towards Ensay as the 2019–20 fires in east Gippsland began to develop. The rising smoke cloud symbolised the impending doom these fires were to bring and the havoc they would cause as they ravaged this beautiful region.
Omeo, Victoria

Sony A7Riii, Sony 24–105mm f4 G OSS, 1/250, f/11, ISO 100, tripod

Judges' comments:
A classic Australian landscape that contains a contradiction of beauty and terror, with the spectacular form of what could be cumulus clouds, belying the impending destruction. The approaching fire storm dwarfs the tree as it looms over it. An ominous symbol of the over-whelming and devastating nature of a bushfire.

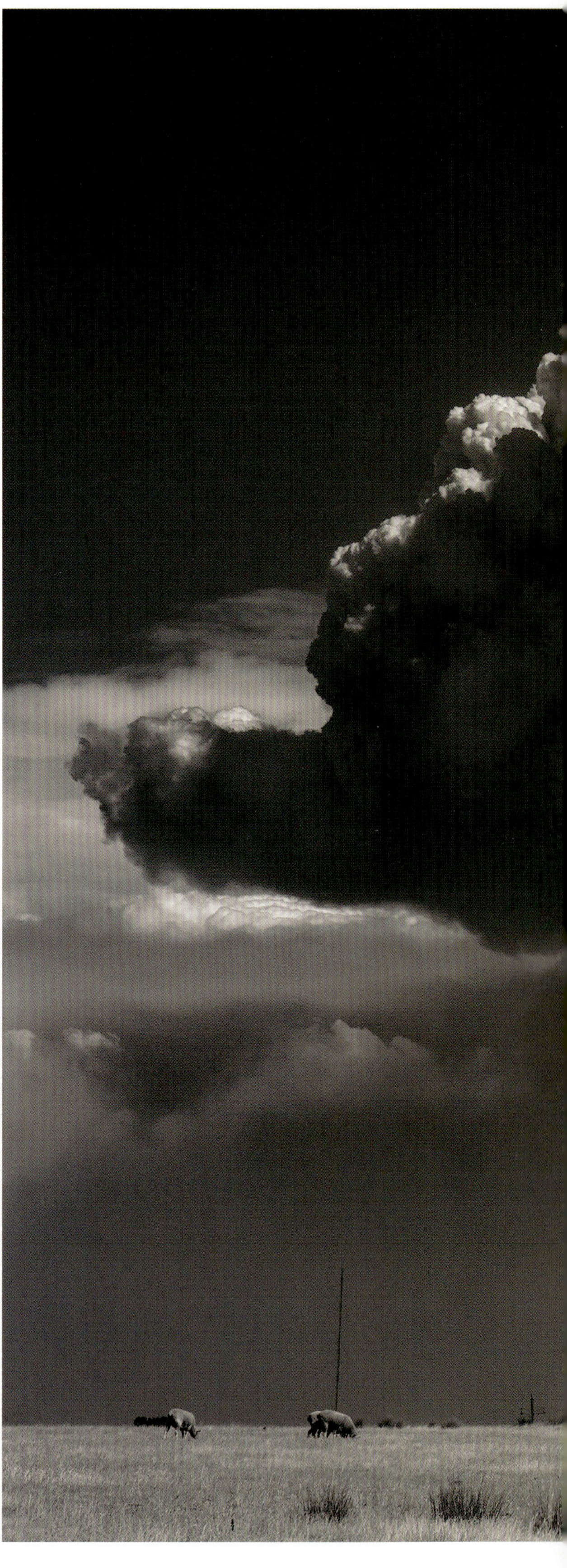

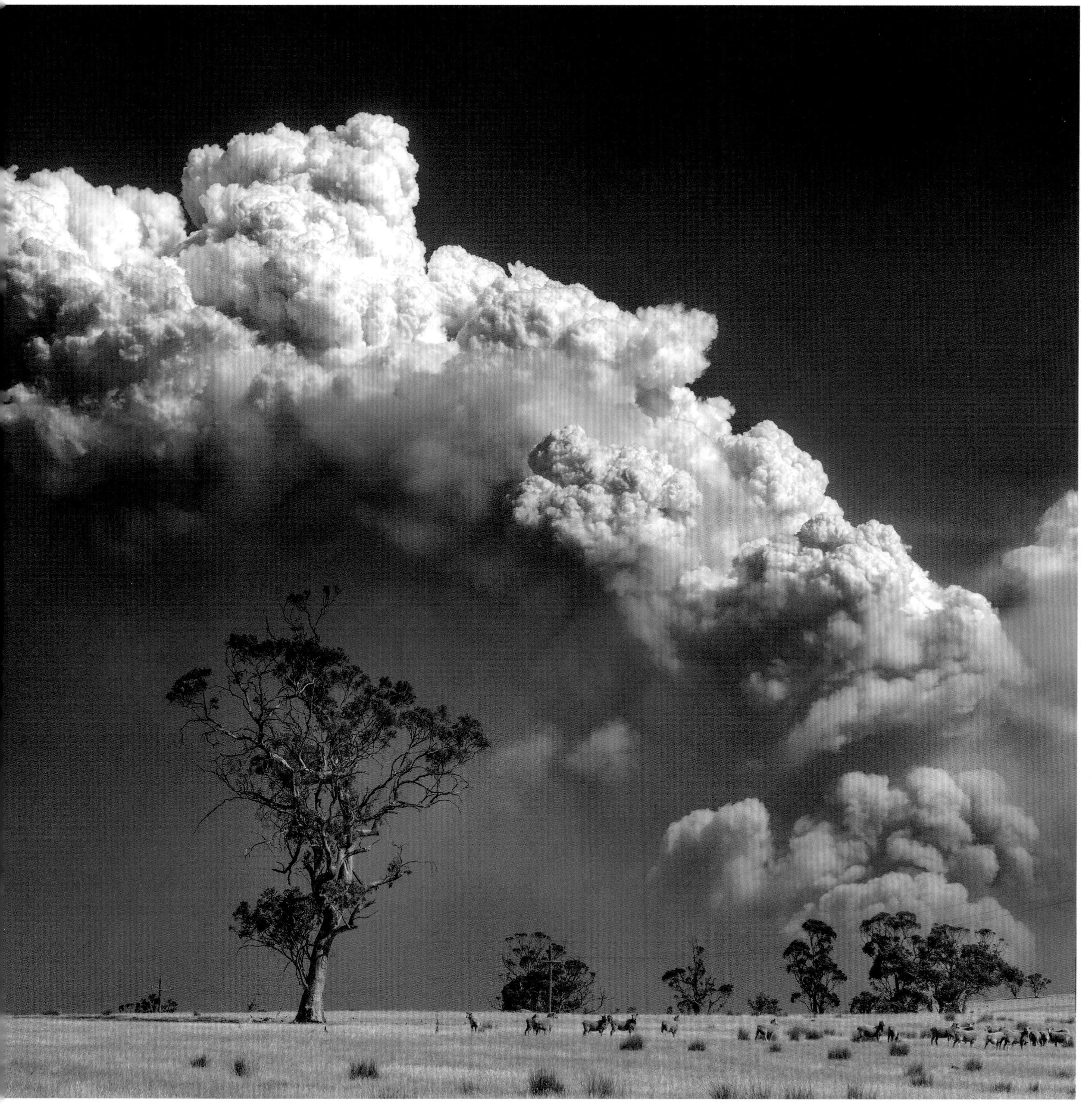

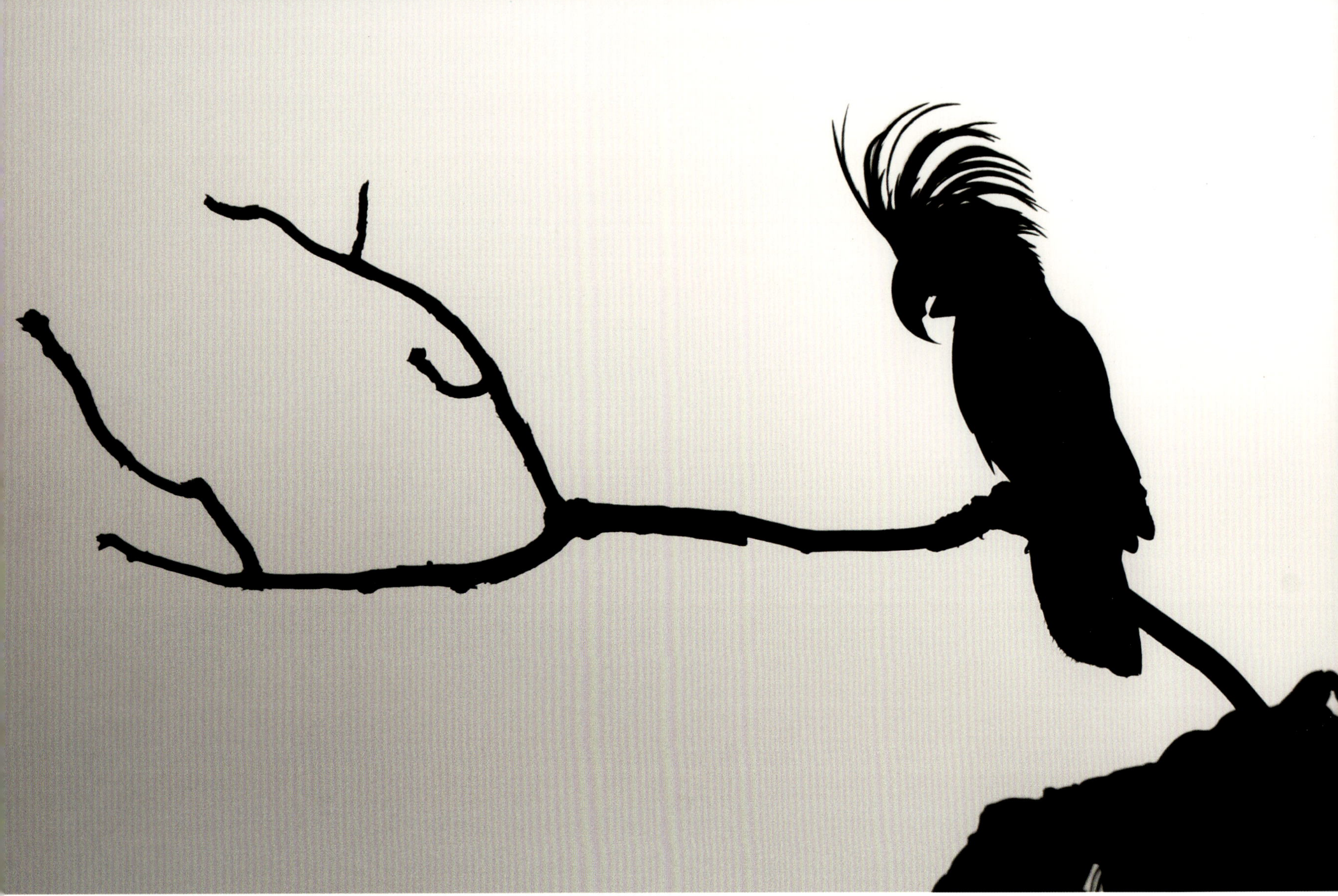

Monochrome Runner-Up

King of the Cape

Palm cockatoo (*Probosciger aterrimus*)
Matt Wright, Queensland

Palm cockatoos are undoubtedly one of the biggest drawcards for any nature lover wanting to visit Cape York. Naturally shy, to capture a glimpse of these declining birds is a magical experience. Recent fires and cyclones have destroyed valuable nesting trees but education and awareness of their plight may save them in the long run.
Cape York, Queensland

Canon 1DX Mk II, Canon 800mm f5.6L IS, 1/1250, f/6.3, ISO 2000, handheld

Judge's comments:
Stark graphic composition highlighting the unique distinctive shape of a palm cockatoo. The striking, crisp silhouette is a great capture.

Wire Coral

Wire coral (*Cirrhipathes leutkeni*)
Ross Gudgeon, Western Australia

Wire coral forms a long, single, unbranched, wire-like stalk that often twists and takes a coil shape. They may reach over 4m in length. This specimen was close to the maximum length and was slowly waving about and coiling/uncoiling in the current.
Lembeh Strait, Indonesia

Canon EOS 7D Mk II, Canon EF8–15 f/4L fisheye USM 8mm Kenko 1.4X Teleplus Pro teleconverter, 1/125, f/8, ISO 200, 2 x Retra flash, handheld

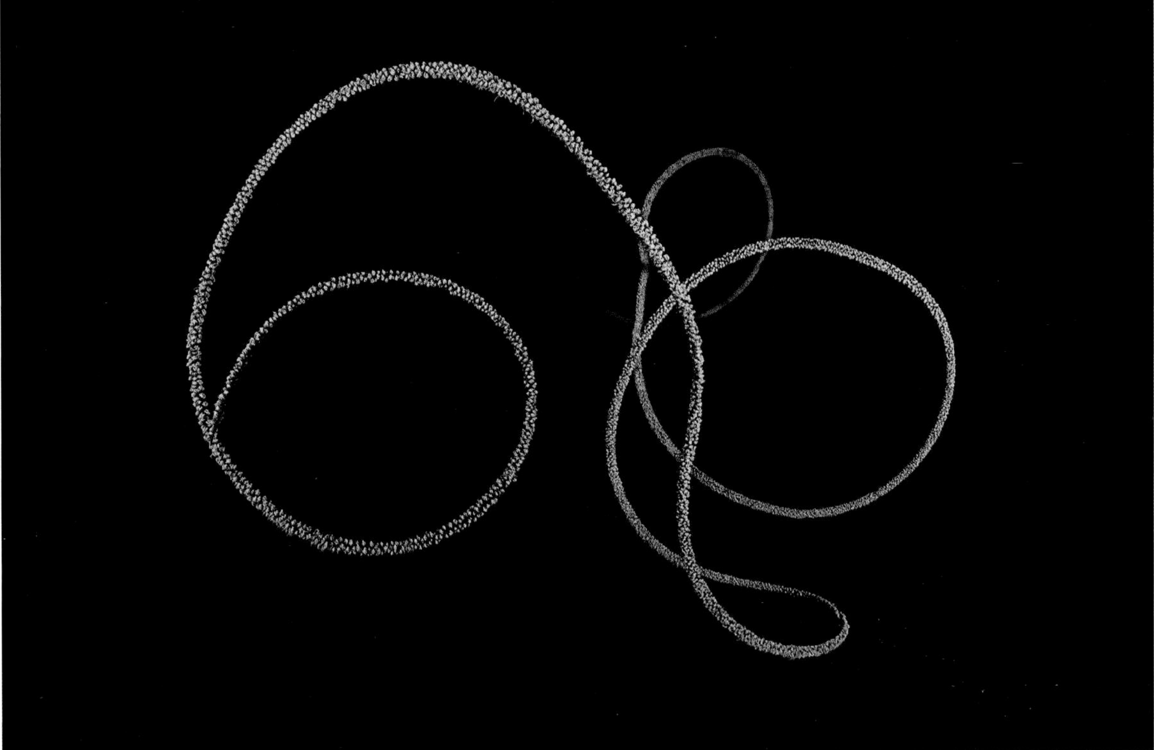

Fractal

Jeff Freestone, Victoria

It is not hard to find beautiful grand landscape vistas when we are seeking the beauty nature has to offer us. However, nature is all around us and if we pay attention and look, we can find nature's most intricate details in the most unexpected of places.
Swifts Creek, Victoria

Sony A7Riii, Sony 24–105mm f4 G OSS, 1/4, f/11, ISO 100, tripod

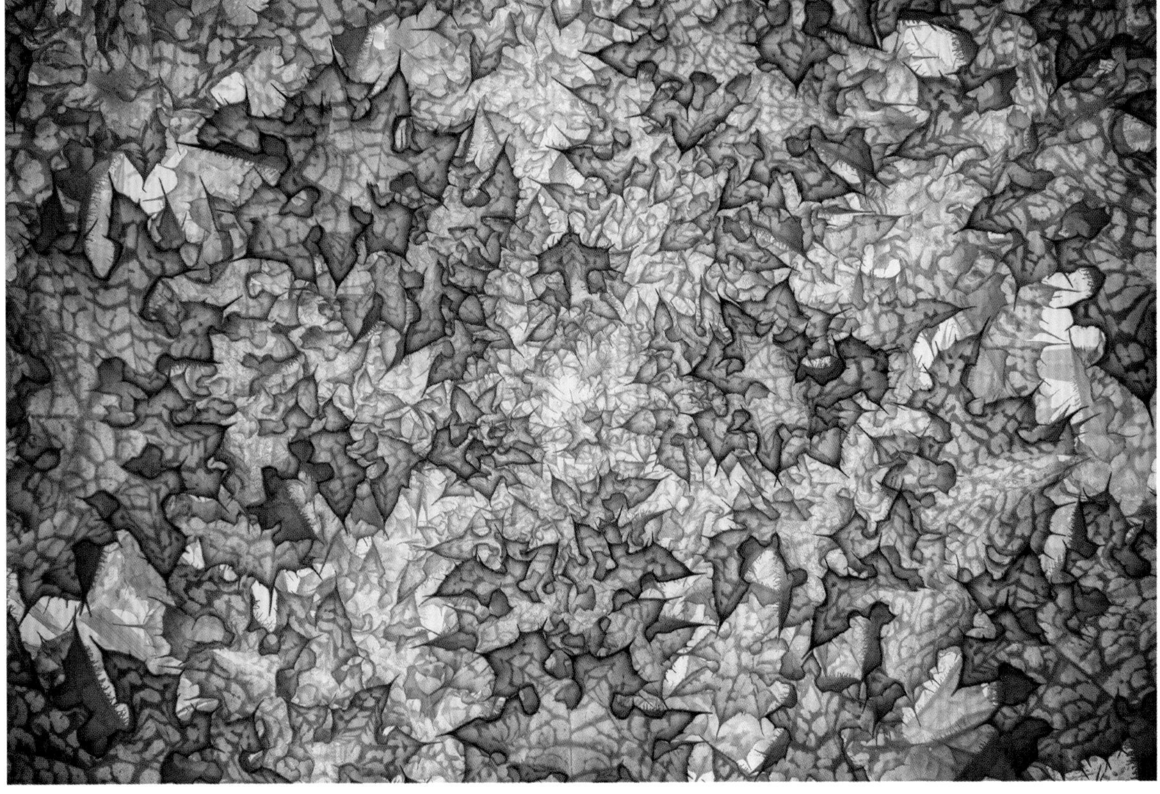

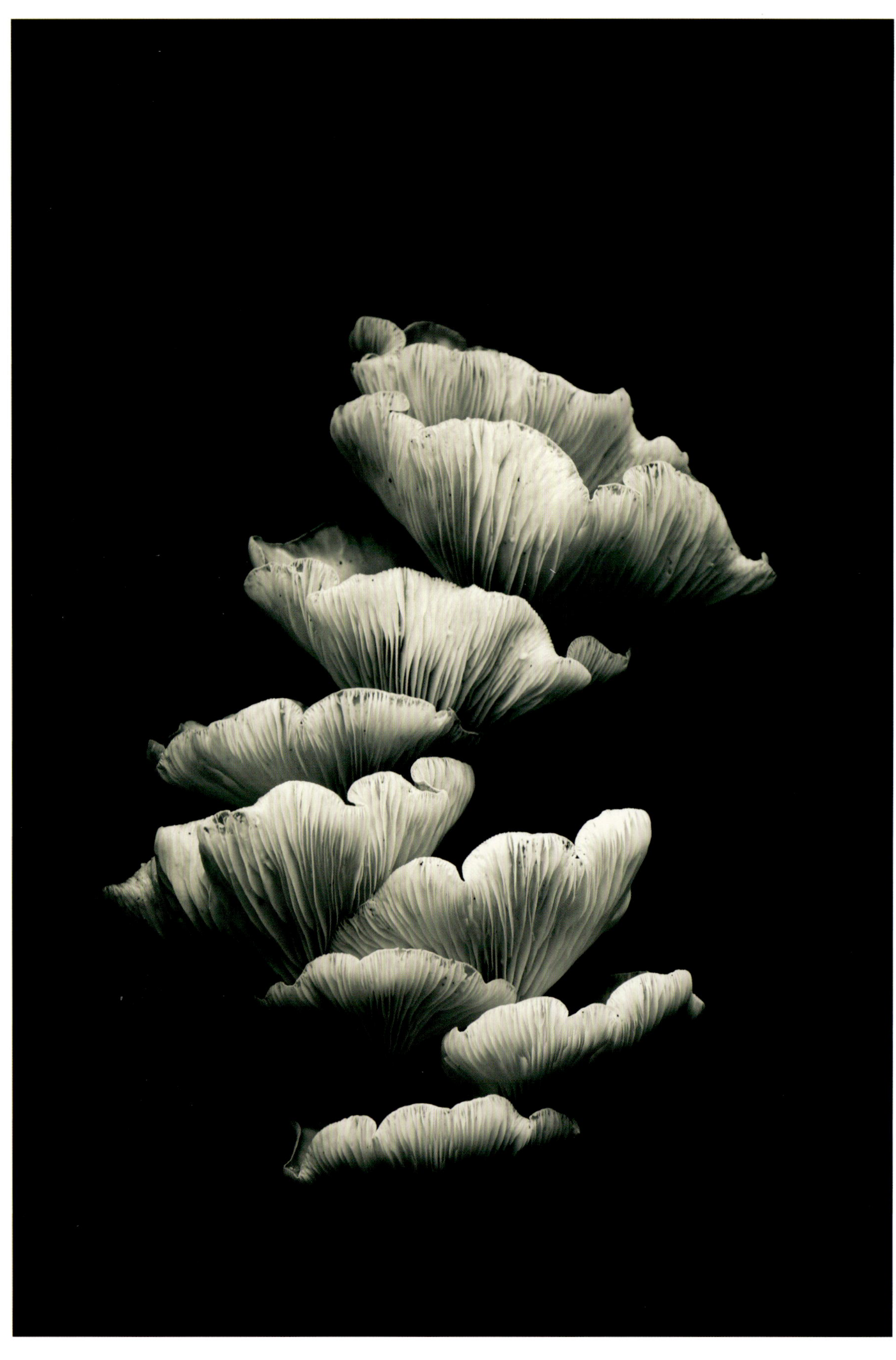

Tarkine Fungus
Craig Burns,
Australian Capital Territory

The image of fungi was taken on a very wet autumn day on the Balfour Track in Tasmania's Tarkine region. Along the track at this time of year, you are immersed in a rainforest world alive with several types of fungus.
Balfour Track, Tarkine region, Tasmania

Nikon D810, Nikon 70–200mm, f2.8 200mm, 4.0, f/10, ISO 200, Sirui tripod, raw image converted to black and white, all adjustments made in Adobe Lightroom

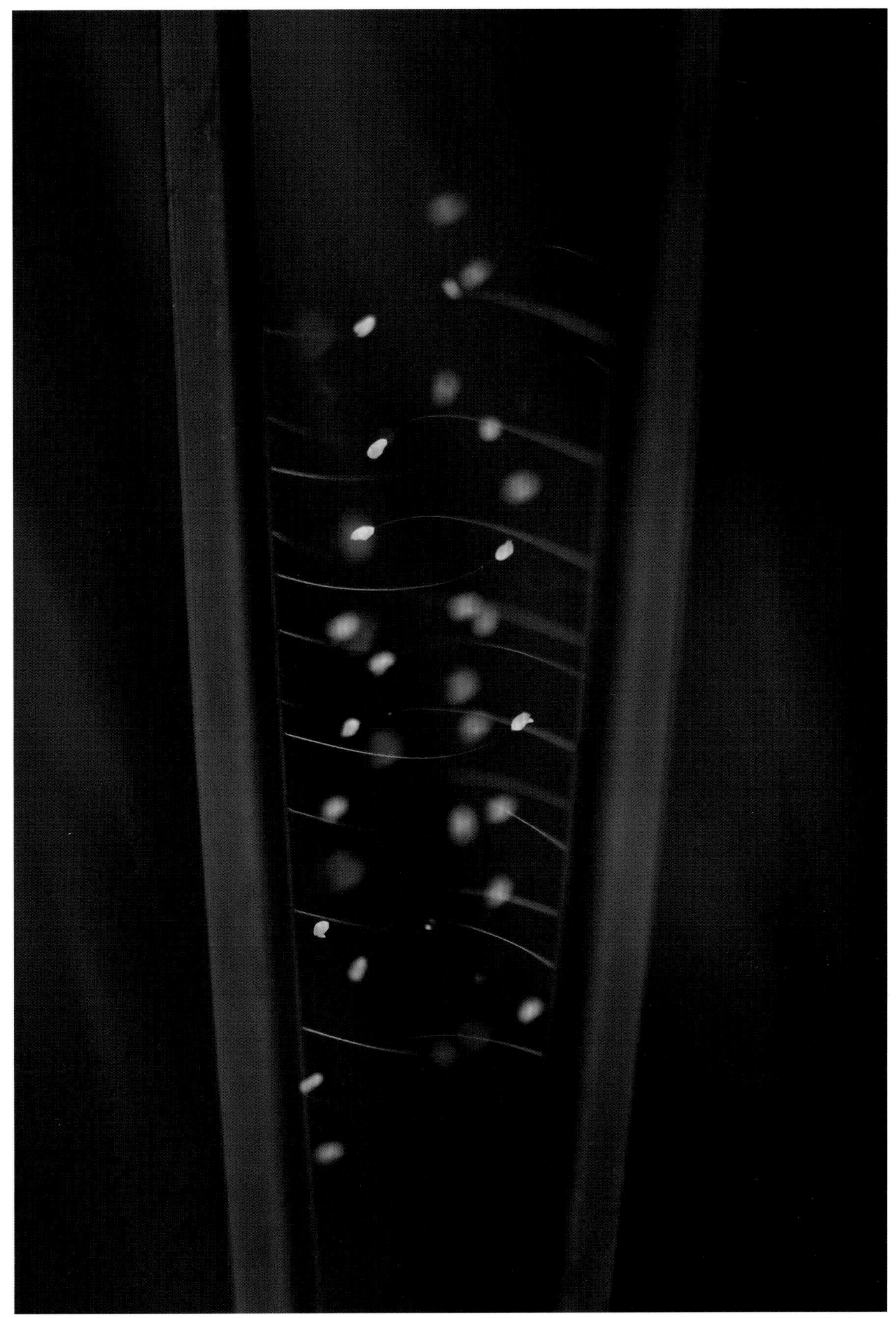

DNA Helix

Yicai Chang,
Australian Capital Territory

Lots of lacewing eggs are laid on the side of two strands of grass. The two spiral groups of eggs wind around each other like coiled pieces of DNA.
Canberra, Australian Capital Territory

Nikon D750, Nikon 105mm macro f2.8, 1/160, f/4.2, ISO 1250, handheld

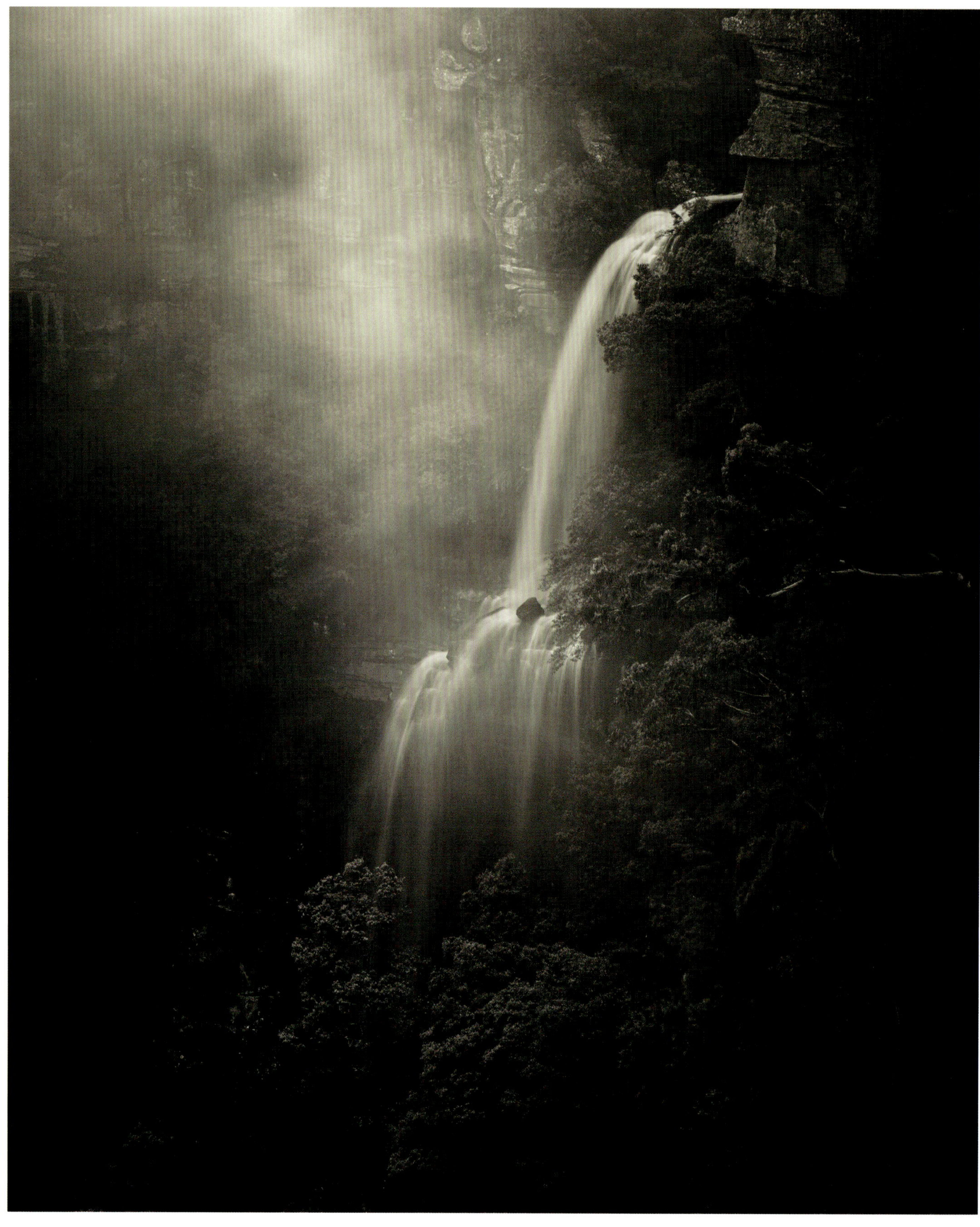

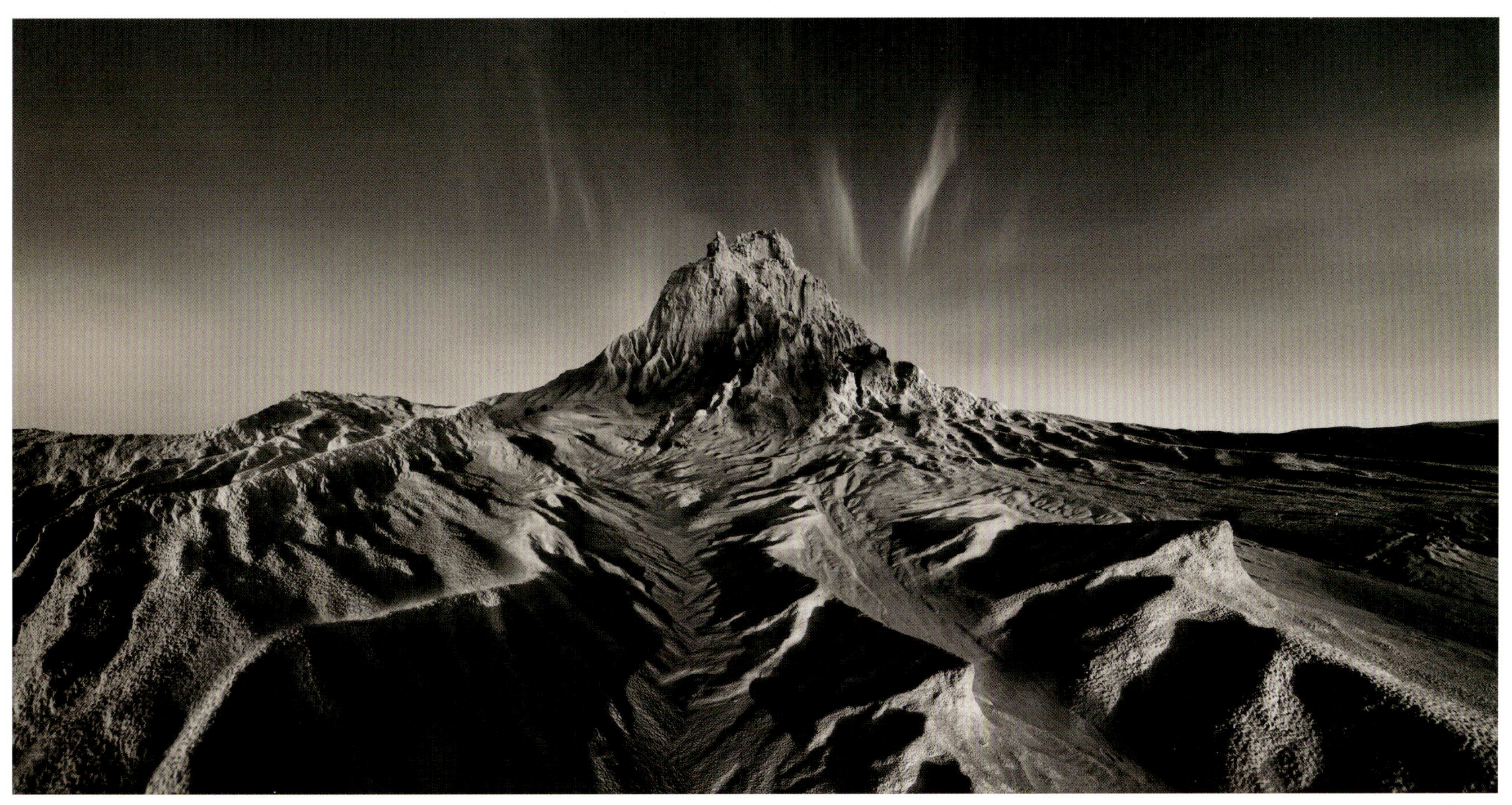

The Fall

Grant Galbraith, New South Wales

I had been to this location when it was bone-dry in the drought of 2019 and thought it might be nice when rain returns. Upon arrival, it was my great delight to see this second fall across the valley, which was full of swirling mist. A magical sight.
Twin Falls, Moreton National Park, New South Wales

Sony A7rii, Sony FE 24–105mm f4 G OSS 105 mm, 0.5, f/18, ISO 50, tripod

Tentacles

Callie Chee, New South Wales

Taken at the Mungo National Park which bears evidence of the oldest civilisation on earth, lunettes such as these, shaped by tide and weather thousands of years ago are fast disappearing under climate change and tourist's footprints. Mungo is truly spectacular with its alien-like landscapes and is culturally and historically sacred.
Mungo National Park, New South Wales

Canon 6D Mk II, Tokina 11–17 mm, 1/320, f/7.1, ISO 500

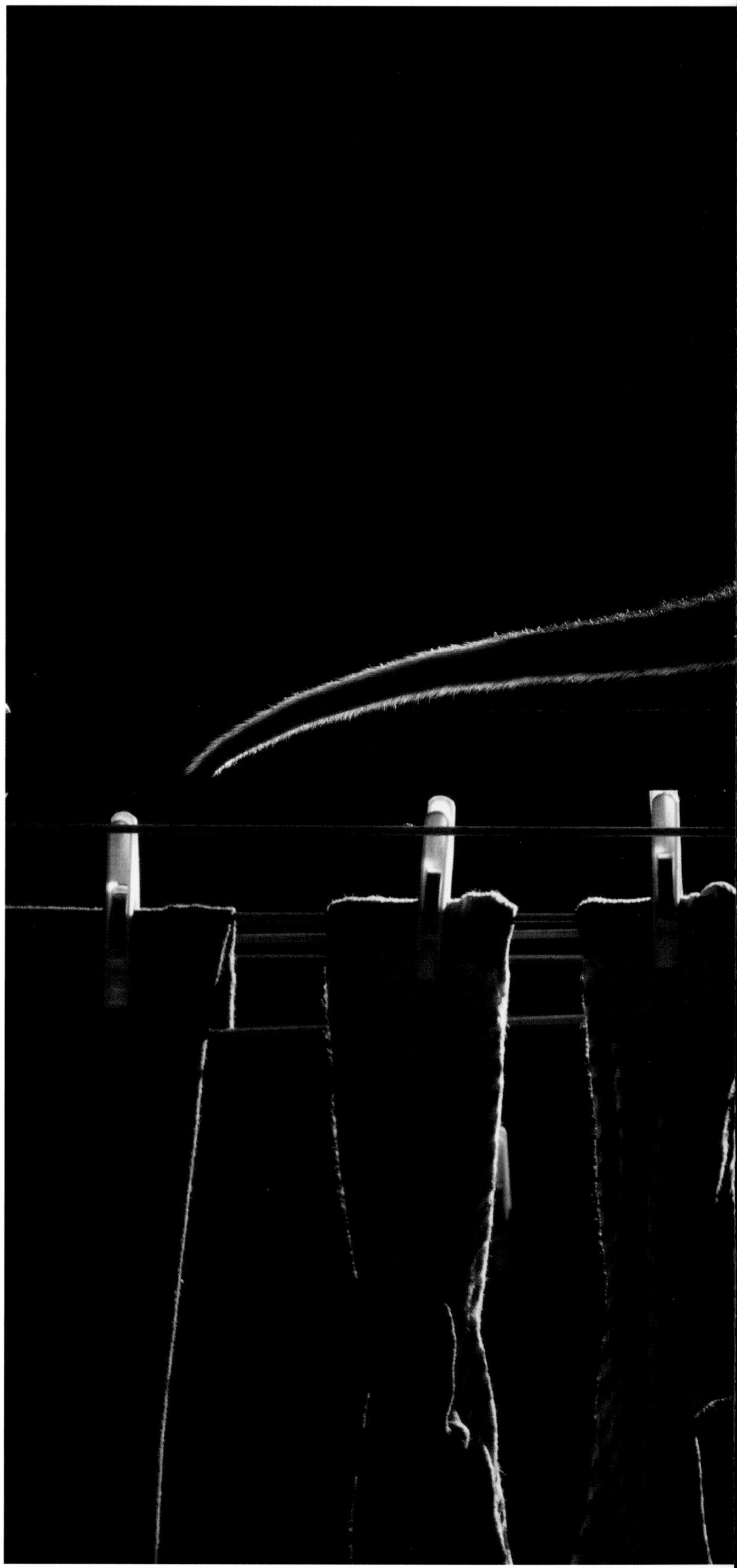

Laundry Night

Ringtail possum
(*Pseudocheirus peregrinus*)
Ethan Mann, Queensland

Ringtail possums frequent backyards and built up areas. I discovered that ringtails were using our clothesline as a walkway to scamper throughout the garden and trees – even our hanging clothes did not deter them. If only they would fold them for me.
Gubbi Gubbi Country, Sunshine Coast, Queensland

Canon 700D, Canon EF 40mm f2.8, 1/160, f/9.0, ISO 400, custom DSLR housing, Nikon SB-28 flash, Camtraptions PIR motion sensor v2, Camtraptions transmitter and receiver, Zomei M3 tripod

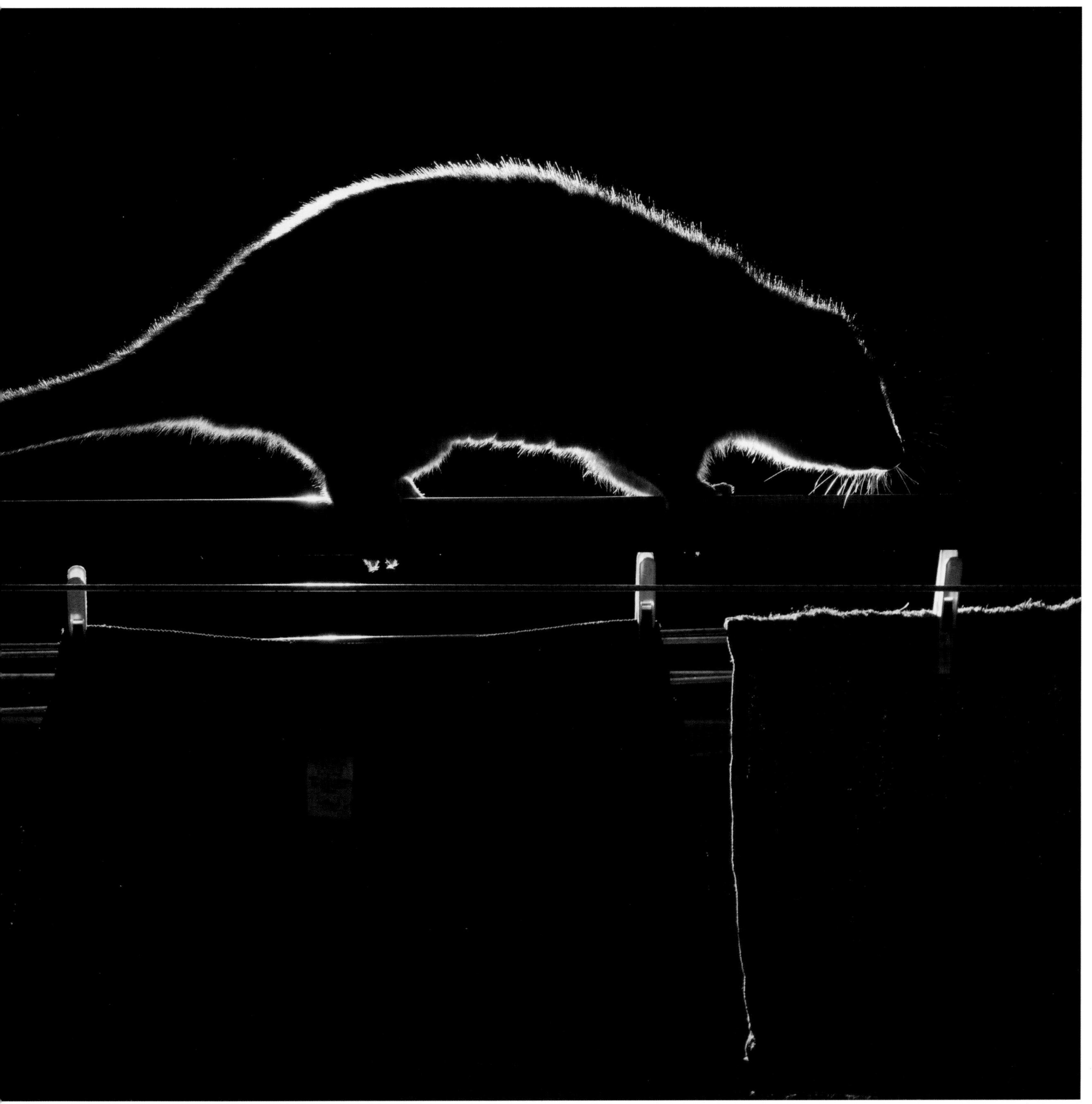

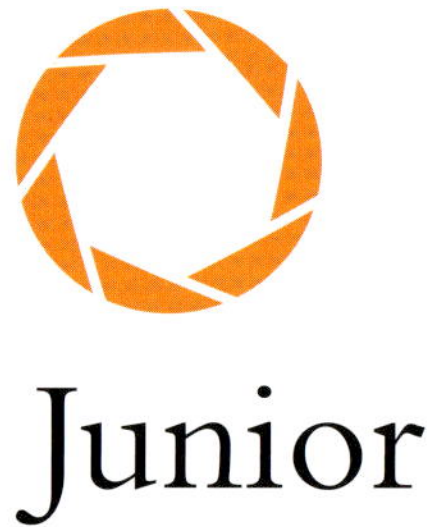

Junior

Junior Winner

You Can't See Me

Lichen huntsman (*Pandercetes gracilis*)
Georgia McGregor, Queensland
11 years old

I spotted this lichen huntsman waiting in ambush, perfectly camouflaged on a tree trunk near our campsite in the Daintree National Park. This spider, native to north Queensland, is one of the fastest moving of all known spiders, but harmless to humans.
Daintree National Park, Cape Tribulation, Queensland

Nikon D750, AF-S Nikkor 24–120mm, 1/60, f/4, ISO 900, handheld

Judges' comments:
A great reminder that interesting subjects can be found anywhere - close observation can reveal extraordinary things if we take the time to be still. Beautifully spotted with keen eyes, this spider reveals itself only after close study, hidden perfectly in the soft, mossy colour and texture of its environment.

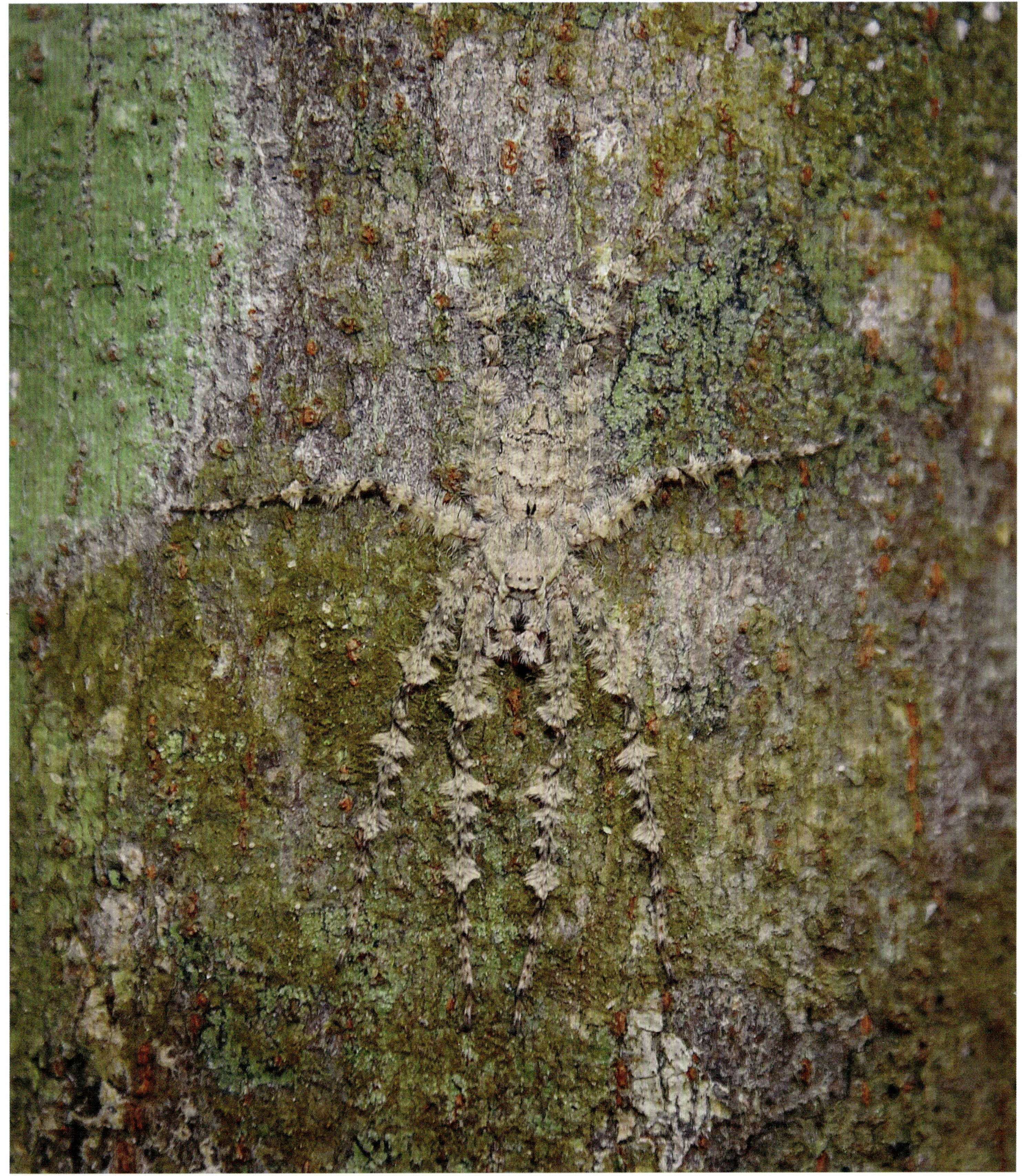

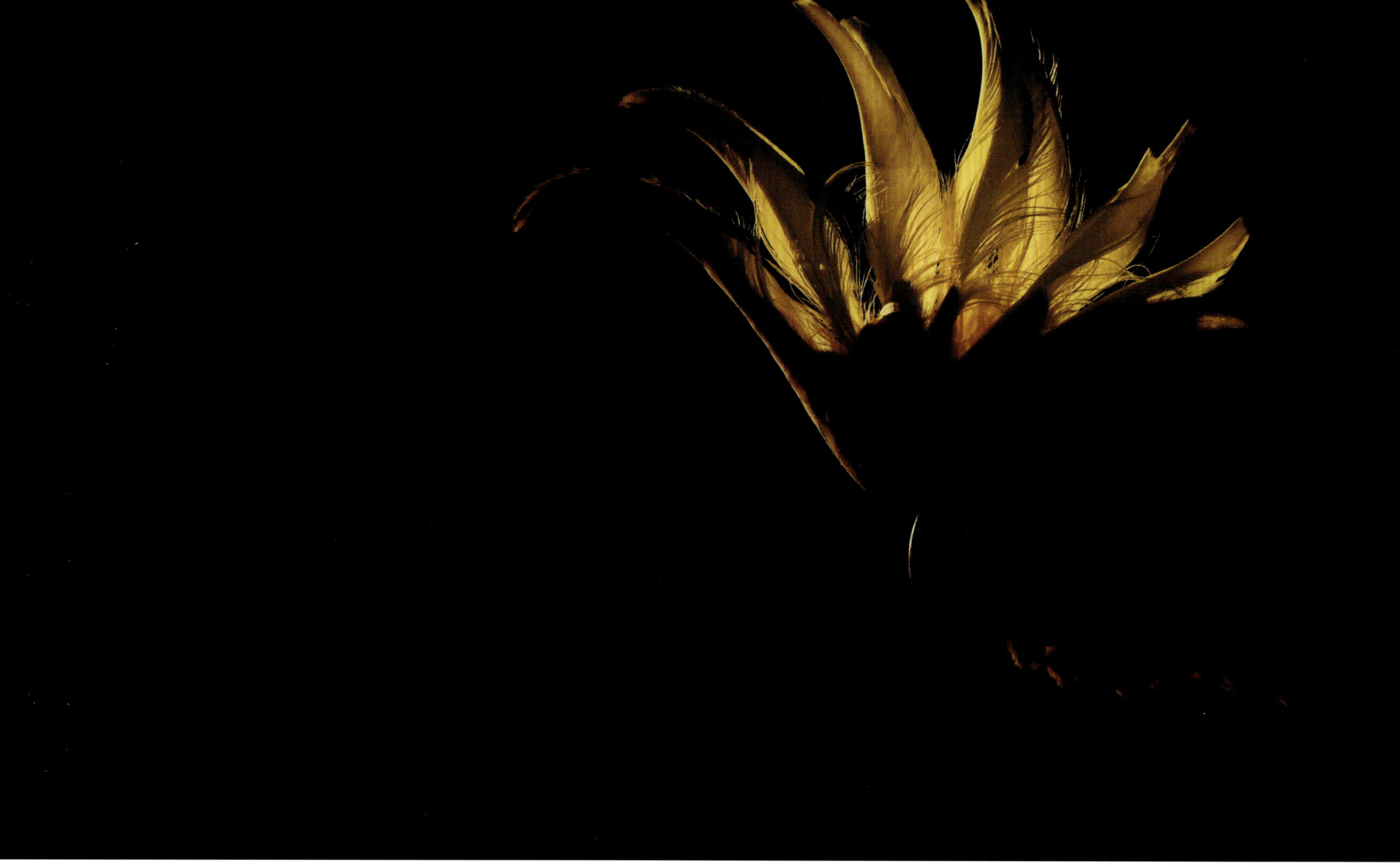

Junior Runner-Up

Cockatoo

Sulphur-crested cockatoo
(*Cacatua galerita*)
Aidan Cimarosti, New South Wales
16 years old

In my front yard on the Northern Beaches of Sydney, a group of cockatoos were gathering for some food. With the late afternoon sun on one particular cockatoo, I was able to photograph its crest in the golden light.
North Narrabeen, New South Wales

Nikon D7200, 18–300mm, 300mm, 1/3200, f/9, ISO 1250, handheld

Judges' comments:
An unusual composition and great light have been used to reveal a commonly photographed local. The yellow crest immediately identifies this familiar character, a perfect example of approaching photography from a different perspective. Good use of colour and light to turn something ordinary into the extraordinary.

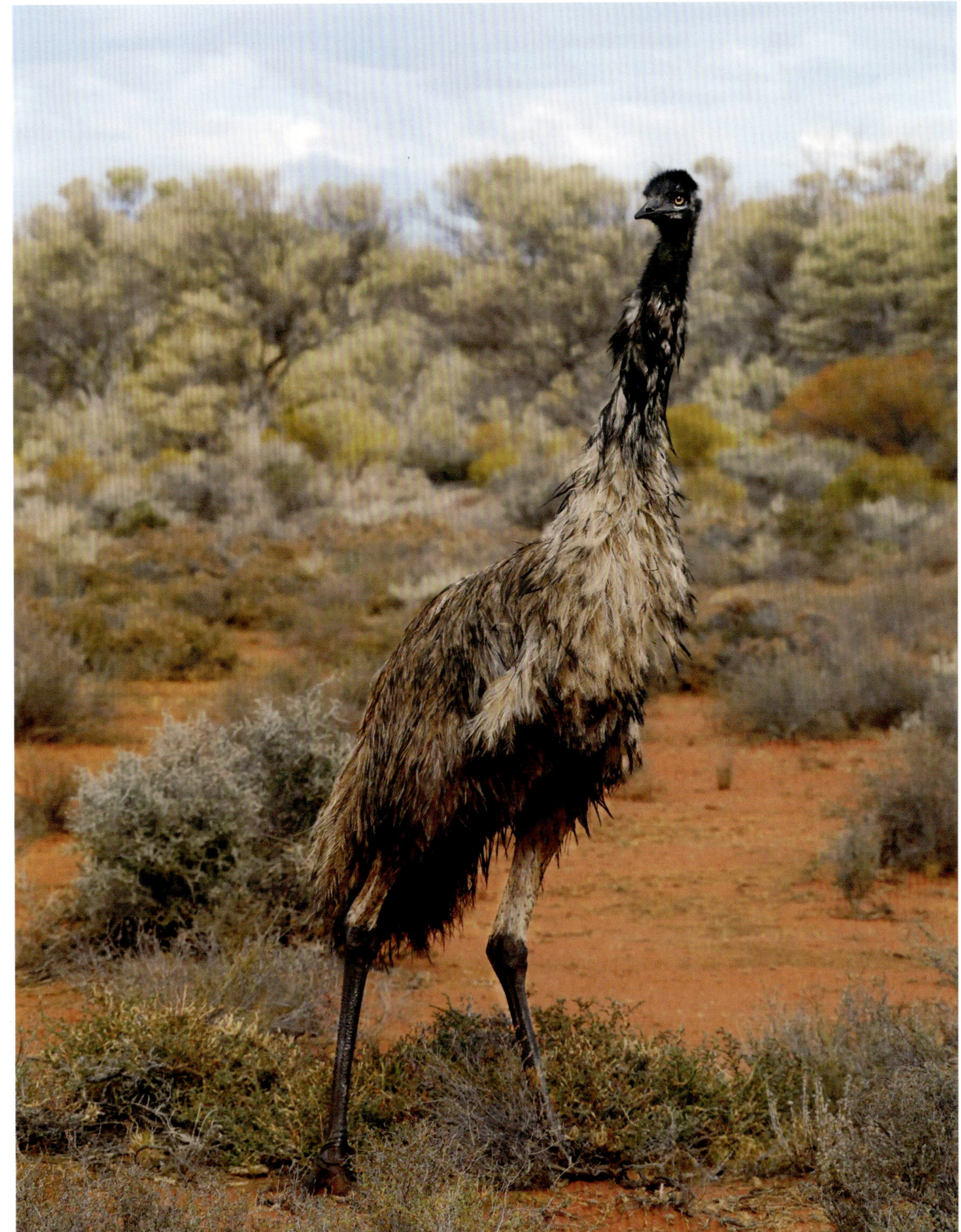

Standing Tall
Emu (*Dromaius novaehollandiae*)
Georgia Clifford, Western Australia
16 years old

On a drive through the Mount Elvire Station after a stormy night, we came across two emus. Despite the isolated location, these emus were extremely inquisitive and not bothered by the uncommon sight of a car. This allowed me to take this photograph of one of them checking us out.
Mount Elvire Station, Goldfields region, Western Australia

Panasonic Lumix G85, Panasonic G Vario 1:4.0–5.6/100–300mm, 1/2000, f/8, ISO 1600, digital, handheld

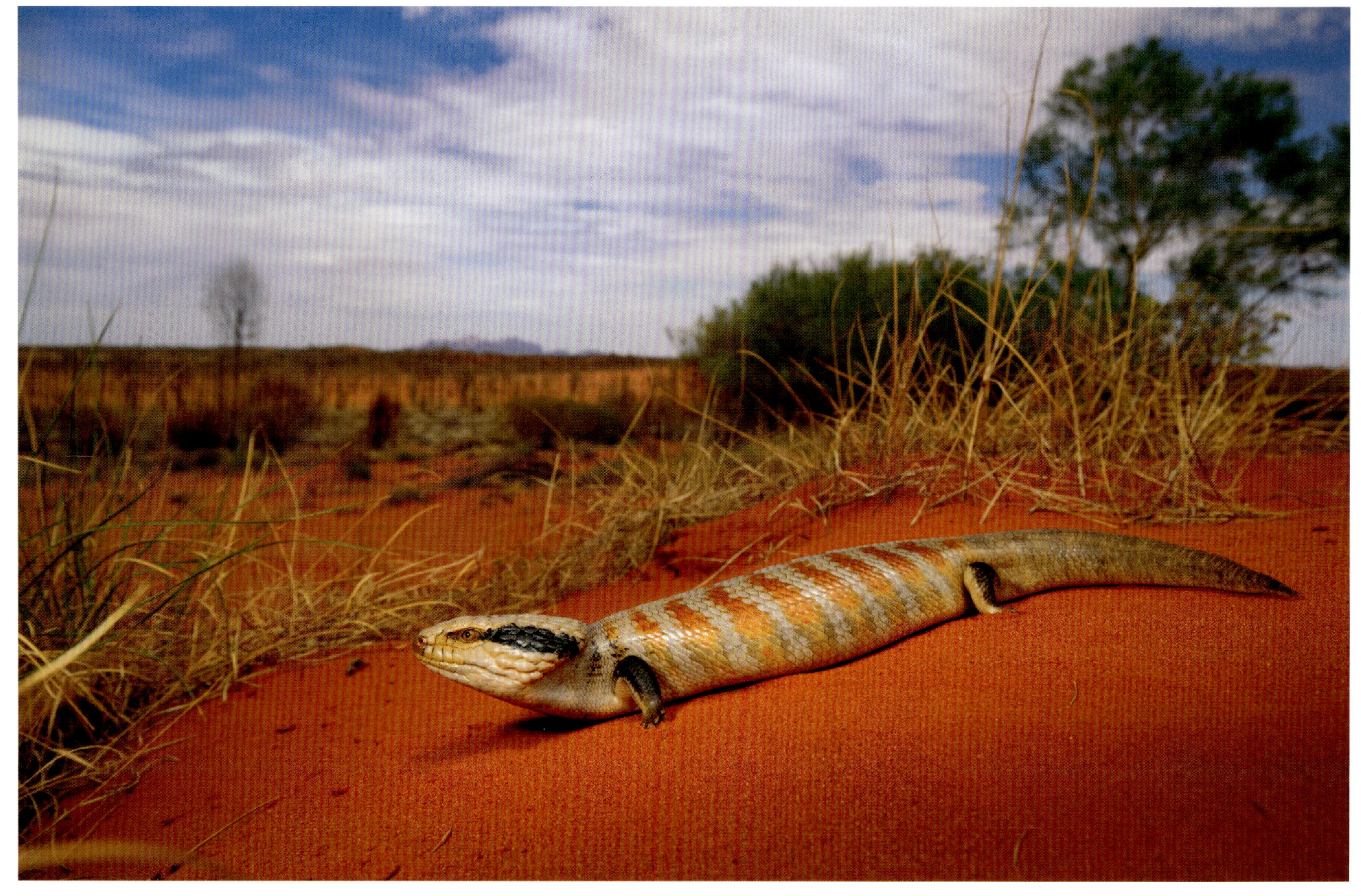

Centralian Blue-tongue Lizard
Centralian blue-tongue lizard
(*Tiliqua multifasciata*)
Robert Irwin, Queensland
17 years old

This species is an icon of inland Australia, exhibiting some of the most vibrant colourations of any reptile. On a trip to Uluṟu, I spotted it sunning on a dune. Using a flash and some careful framing I also managed to capture the outline of Kata Tjuṯa in the distance.
Uluṟu–Kata Tjuṯa National Park, Northern Territory

Canon EOS 1DX Mk II, Canon EF 16–35mm f/4L IS USM, 1/250, f/11, ISO 100, Canon Speedlight EX-600 RT II flash and transmitter

Eye to Eye
Leaf beetle (Chrysomelidae)
Isabella Balisky, Queensland
15 years old

This particular morning, the flowers had begun to bloom, the entire fence line sprinkled with flowers of all kinds. I spotted an unusual, reddish figure happily situated in the centre of one of these flowers – luckily I didn't walk straight past him!
Buderim, Queensland

Nikon D800, Nikkor Micro 105mm f/2.8G VR, 1/250, f/11, ISO 640, handheld

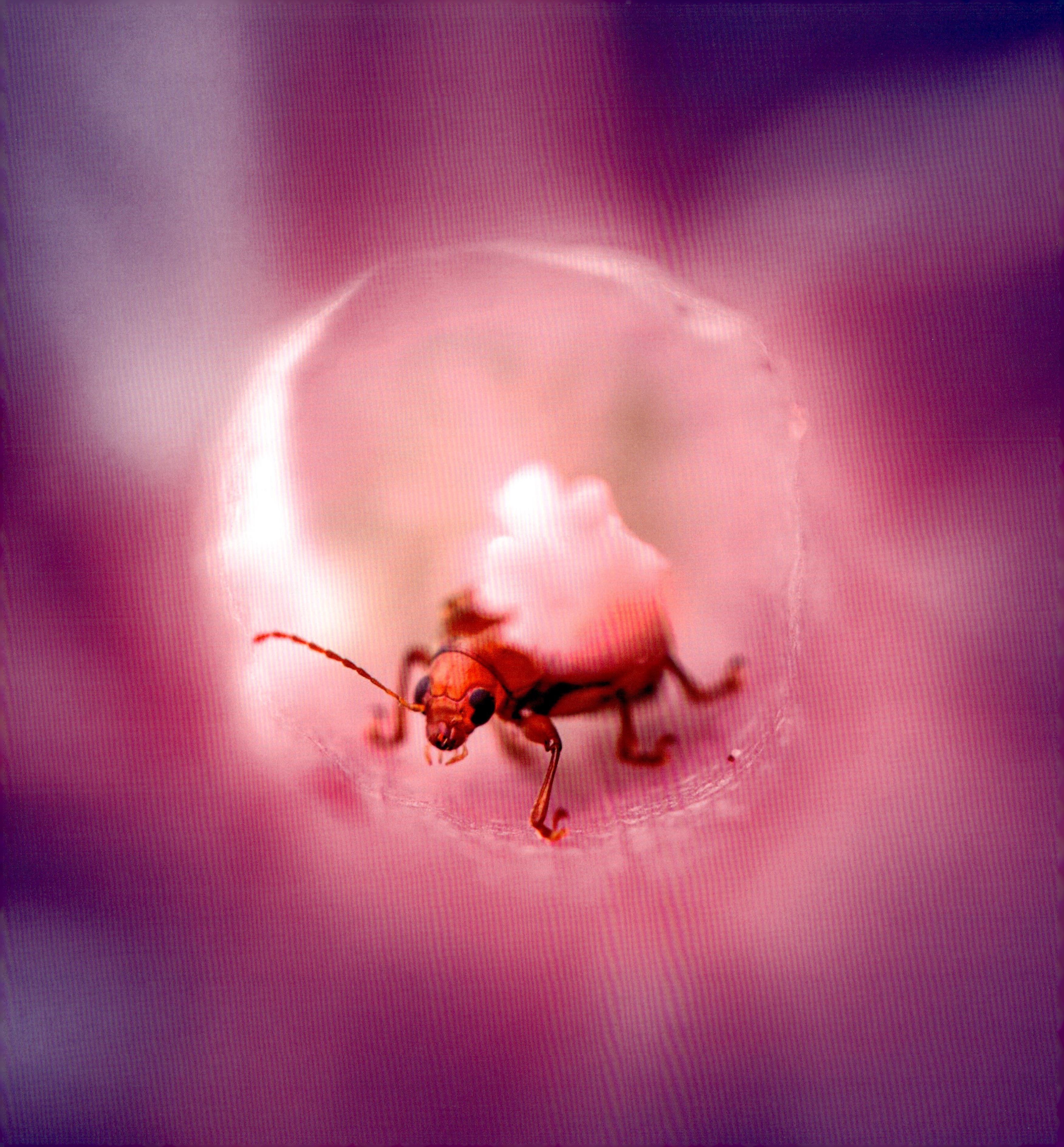

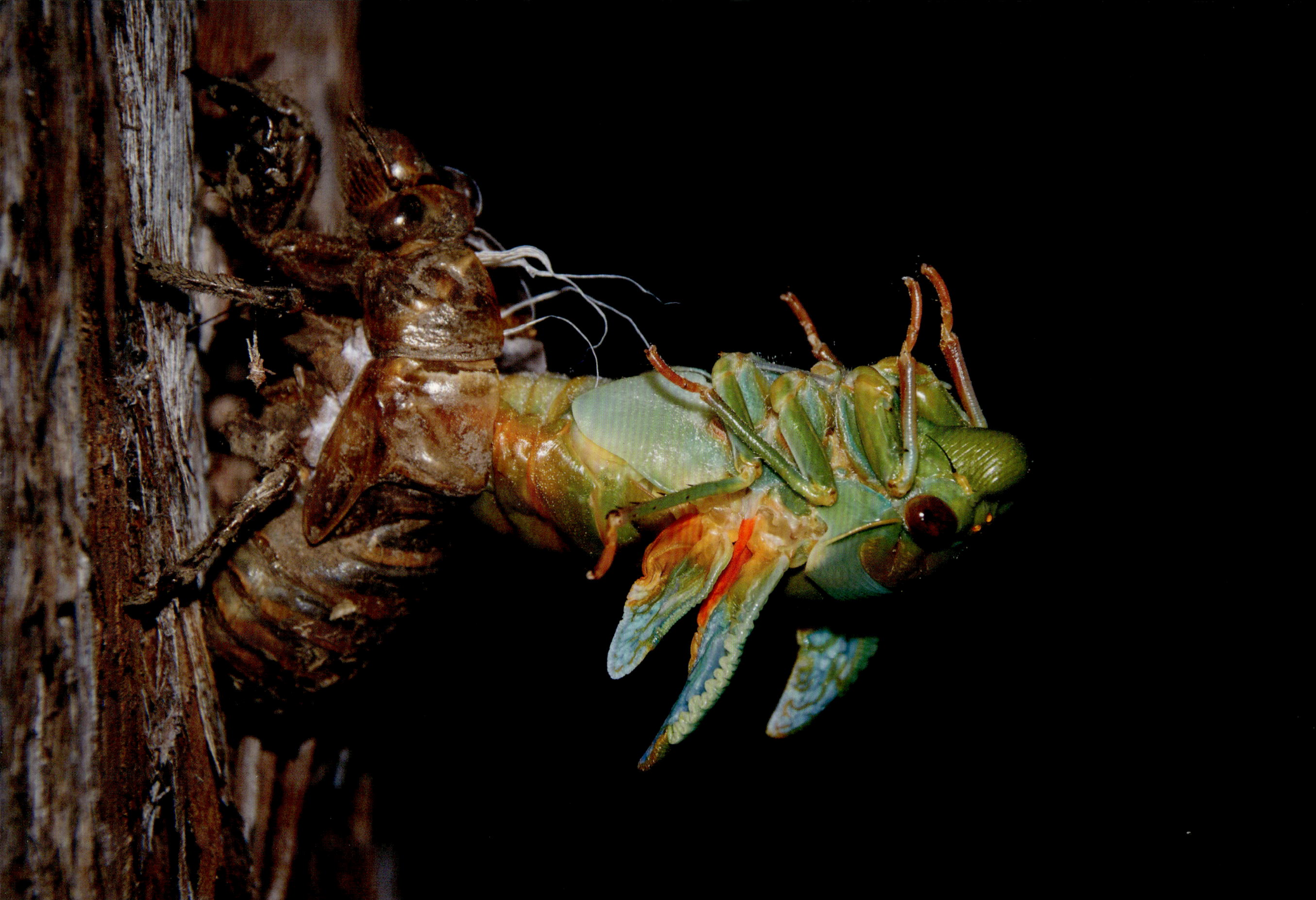

Emerging

Greengrocer *(Cyclochila australasiae)*
McKinley Moens, New South Wales
15 years old

It was a huge summer for cicadas this year, which meant that I enjoyed hour upon hour watching hundreds of them emerge each night. I was captivated by the intensely beautiful colouring of this greengrocer.
Blue Mountains, New South Wales

Sony A57, Sigma 18–250mm F3.5–6.3, 1/60, f/13, ISO ISO 100, flash and home-made diffuser, tripod

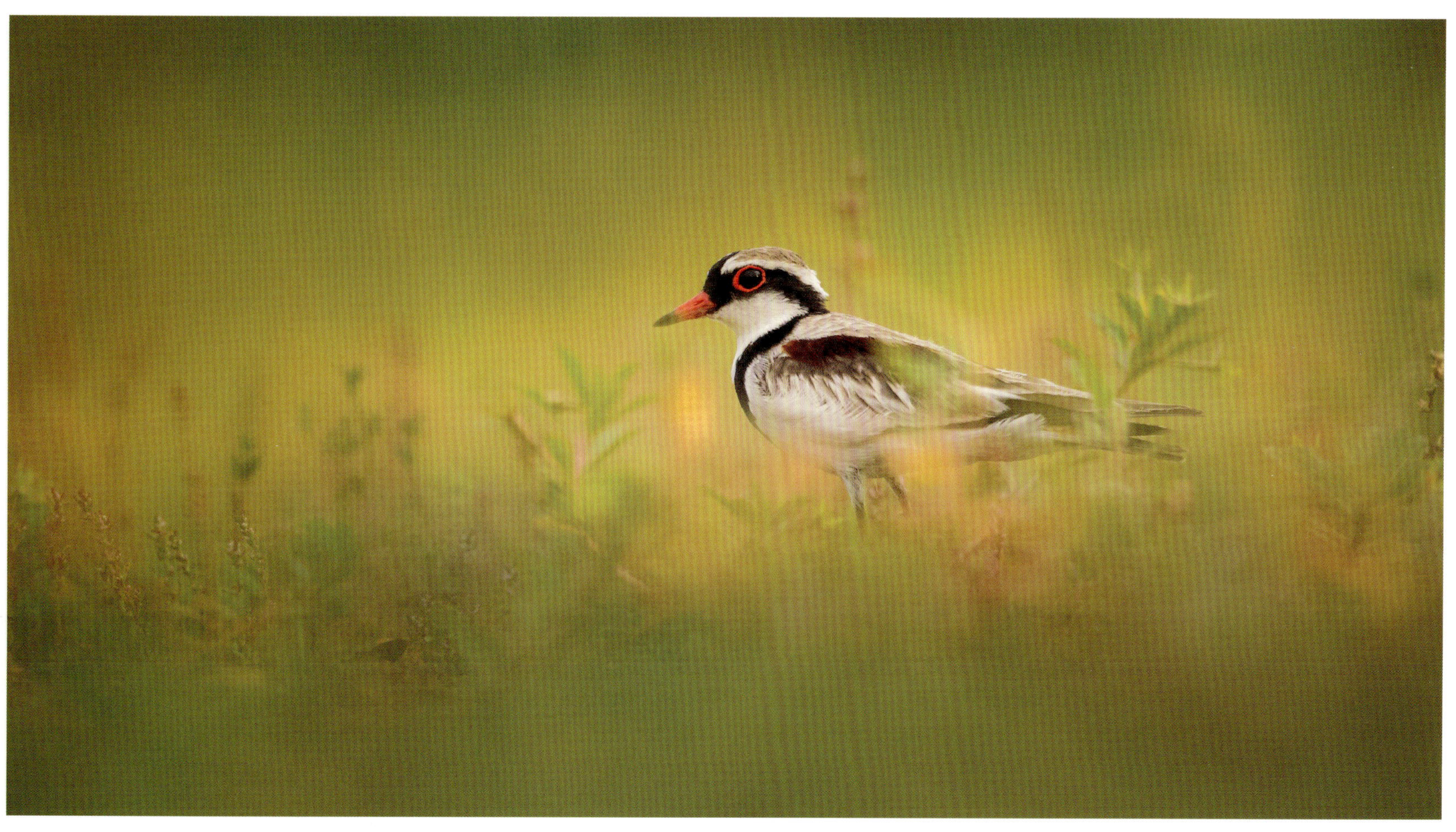

Hidden Dotterel
Black-fronted dotterel
(*Elseyornis melanops*)
Robert Irwin, Queensland
17 years old

A dotterel camouflages amongst a meadow of flowering plants around a waterhole in outback Queensland. I laid down in the mud to capture an eye-level angle. It took many attempts to photograph this speedy bird as he darted back and forth, feeding along the edge of the water.
Mourachan Conservation Reserve, St George area, Queensland

Canon EOS 1DX Mk II, Canon EF 500mm f/4L IS II USM, 1/1600, f/4, ISO 2000

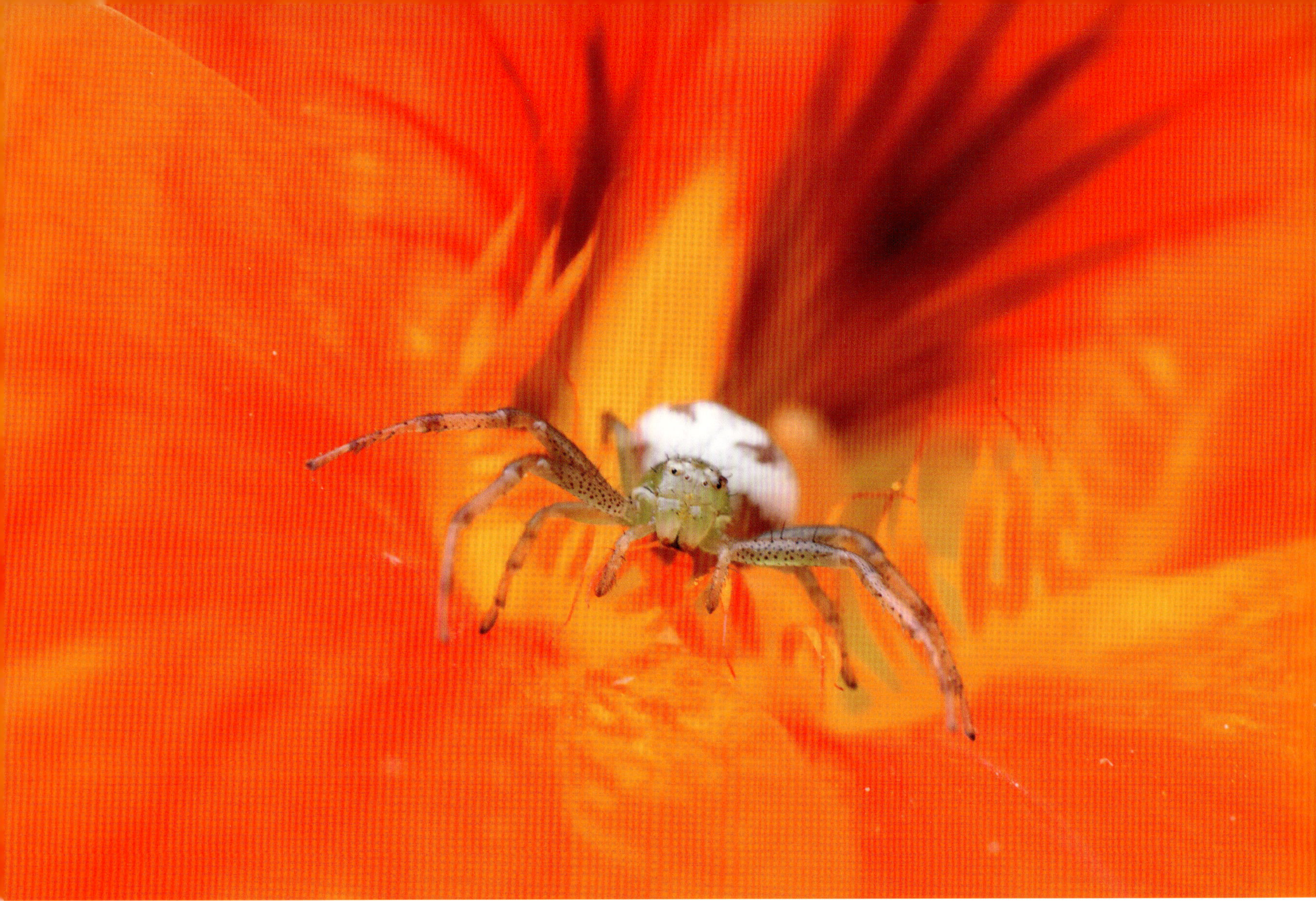

Hidden Hunter
Isaac Wilson, South Australia
12 years old

While photographing bees buzzing around my back garden, I noticed this tiny spider in a bright orange nasturtium. I think the spider was waiting for a pollinating insect to fly onto the flower. Unfortunately for the spider, the only insects coming to the flowers were bees, which were much bigger than it was. *Adelaide Hills, South Australia*

Nikon D7200, AF-S DX micro Nikkor 40mm f/2.8G, 1/250, f/14, ISO 4000, handheld

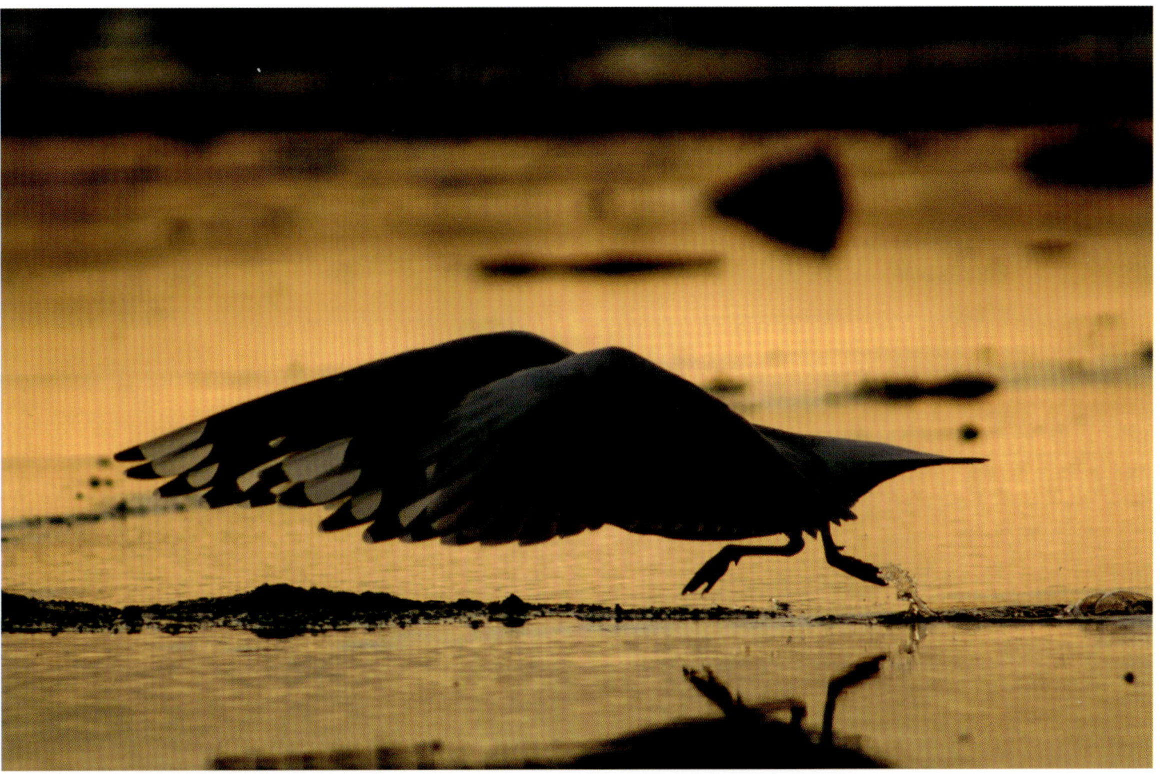

Long Reef Landing

Silver gull
(*Chroicocephalus novaehollandiae*)
Adie Connor, New South Wales
15 years old

I got up bright and early to go to photograph these birds at sunrise at Long Reef and was fascinated by the sheer number of birds coming in to land. I zeroed in on one gull in particular, taking the photo just as it skimmed the water's surface.
Long Reef, Sydney, New South Wales

Canon EOS 4000D, EF 75–300mm f/4–5.6, 1/2000, f/5.6, ISO 400, handheld

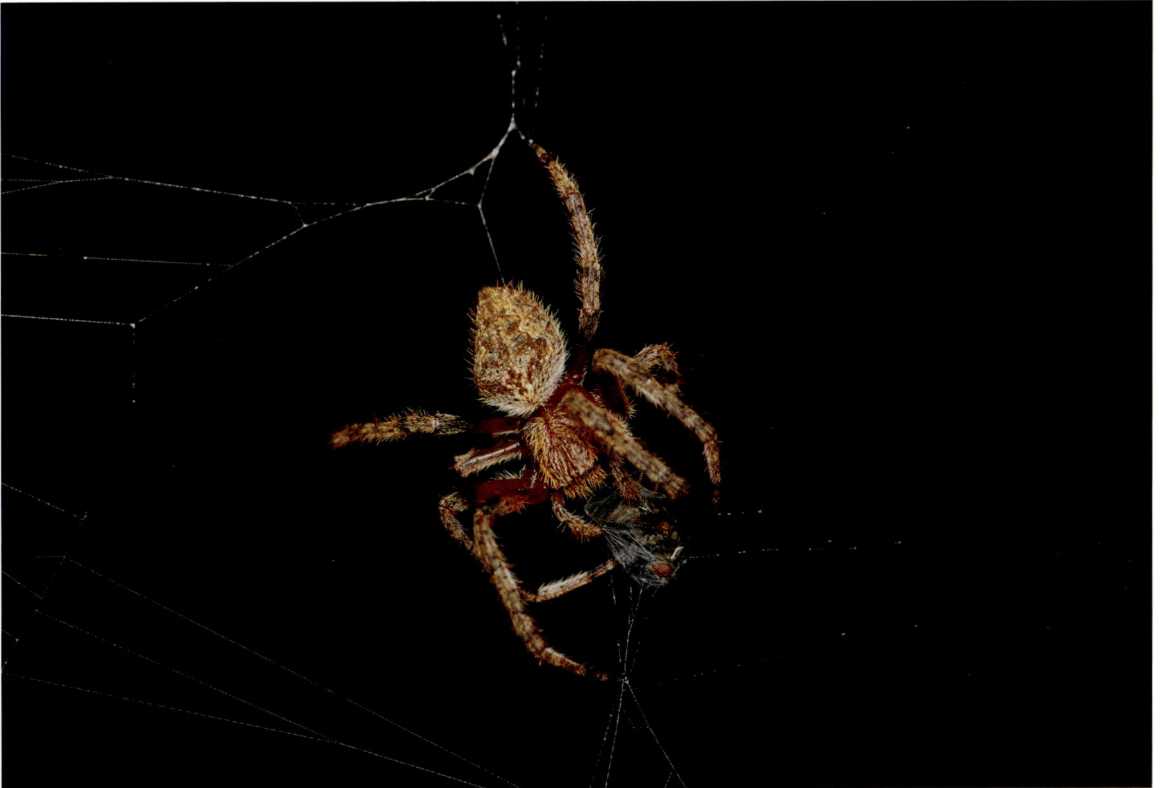

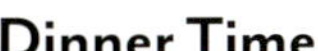

Dinner Time

Garden orb weaver (*Eriophora* sp.)
McKinley Moens, New South Wales
15 years old

The Australian bush really comes alive after dark! Where there is life, there is also death, as this garden orb weaver wrapping dinner for the evening shows.
Springwood, New South Wales

Sony A57, Tamron 90mm F2.8, 1/60, f/8, ISO 800, flash and home-made diffuser, handheld

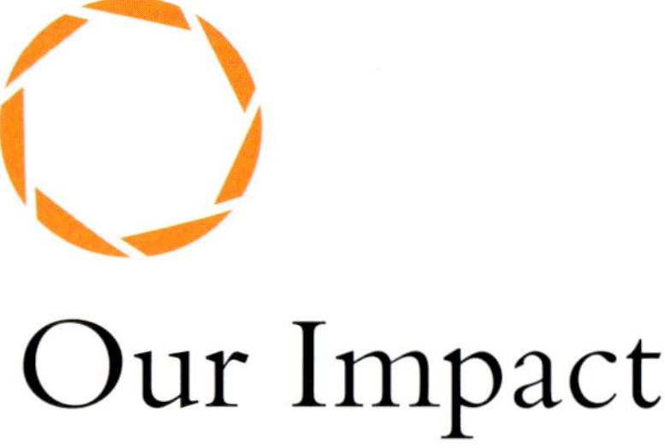

Our Impact

Our Impact Winner

Bound, jammed inside, and posted

Blue-tongued lizard (*Tiliqua nigrolutea*)
Doug Gimesy, Victoria

A wildlife officer measures one of two blue-tongued lizards found bound and stuffed inside a DVD player. Posted to Asia, it was detected at a Melbourne postage sorting facility. Luckily, both were still alive. Wildlife smuggling is so brutally cruel, with many not surviving their long trip.
Department of Environment, Land, Water and Planning (DELWP) facility, Victoria

Nikon D5, Sigma Art Series 35mm f/1.4, 1/250, f/8.0, ISO 1250, two soft boxes, handheld

Judges' comments:
Well executed composition with great contrast between the manufactured forms and the natural shape of the blue tongue lizard. This powerful image highlights the tragic plight of wildlife targeted by animal trafficking.

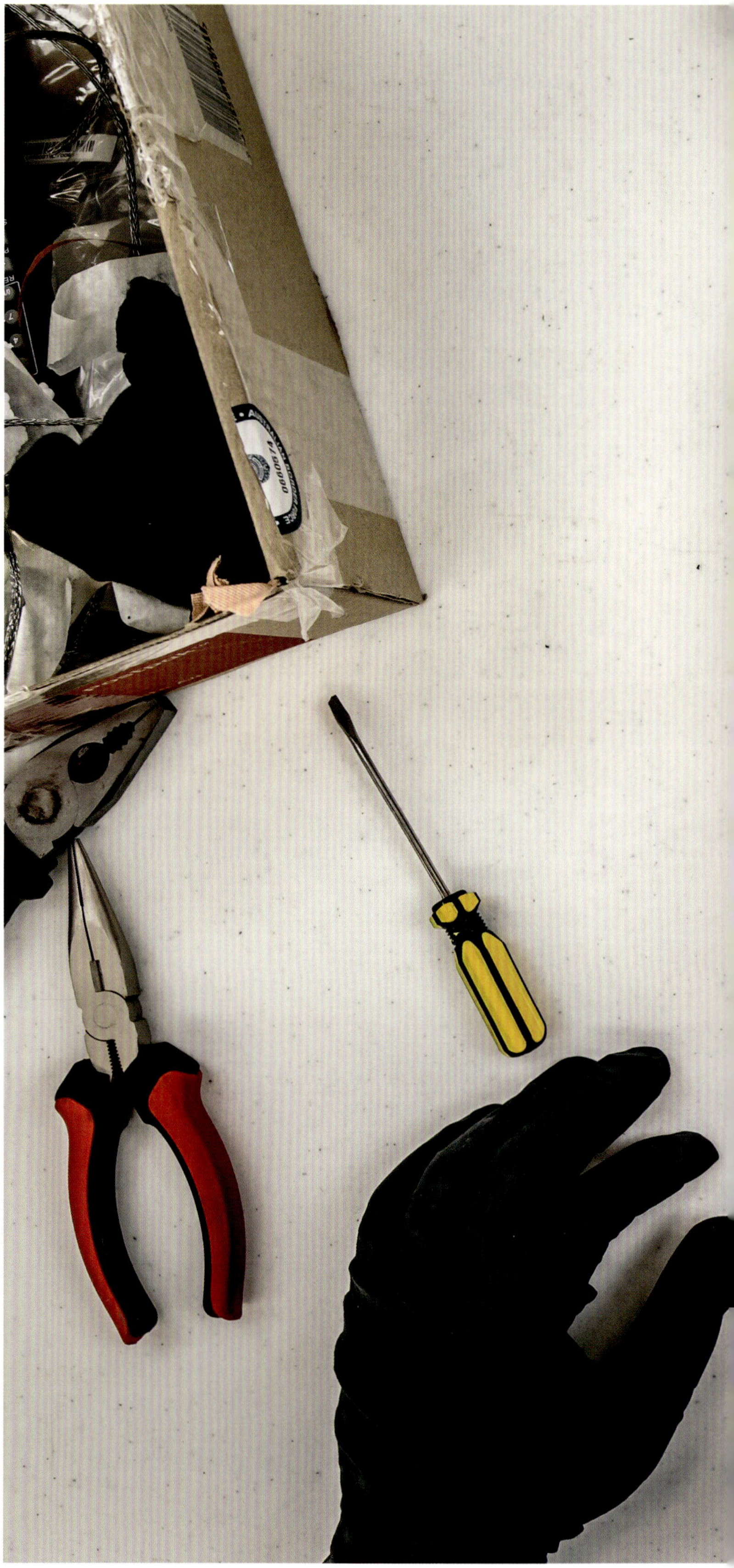

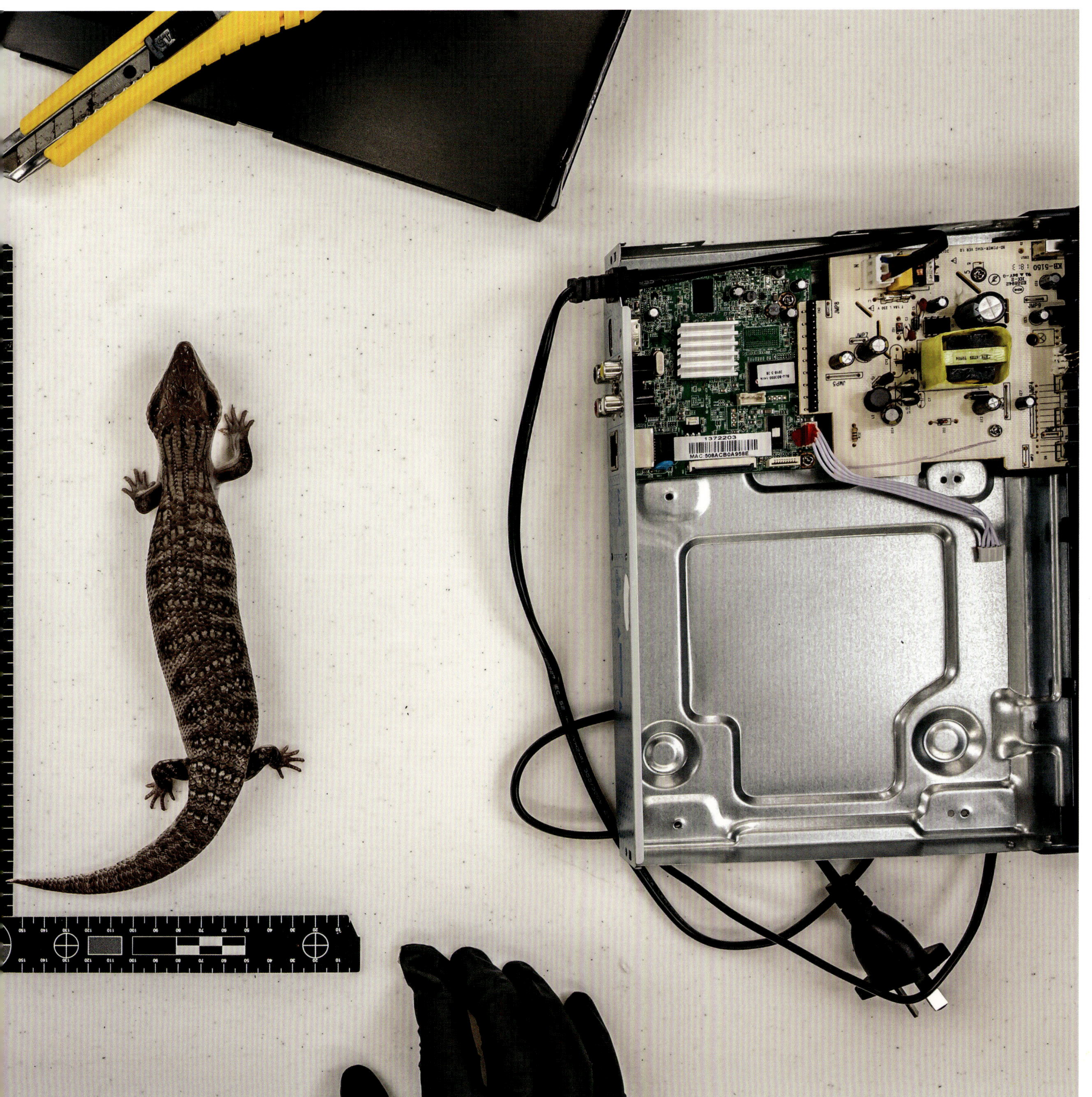

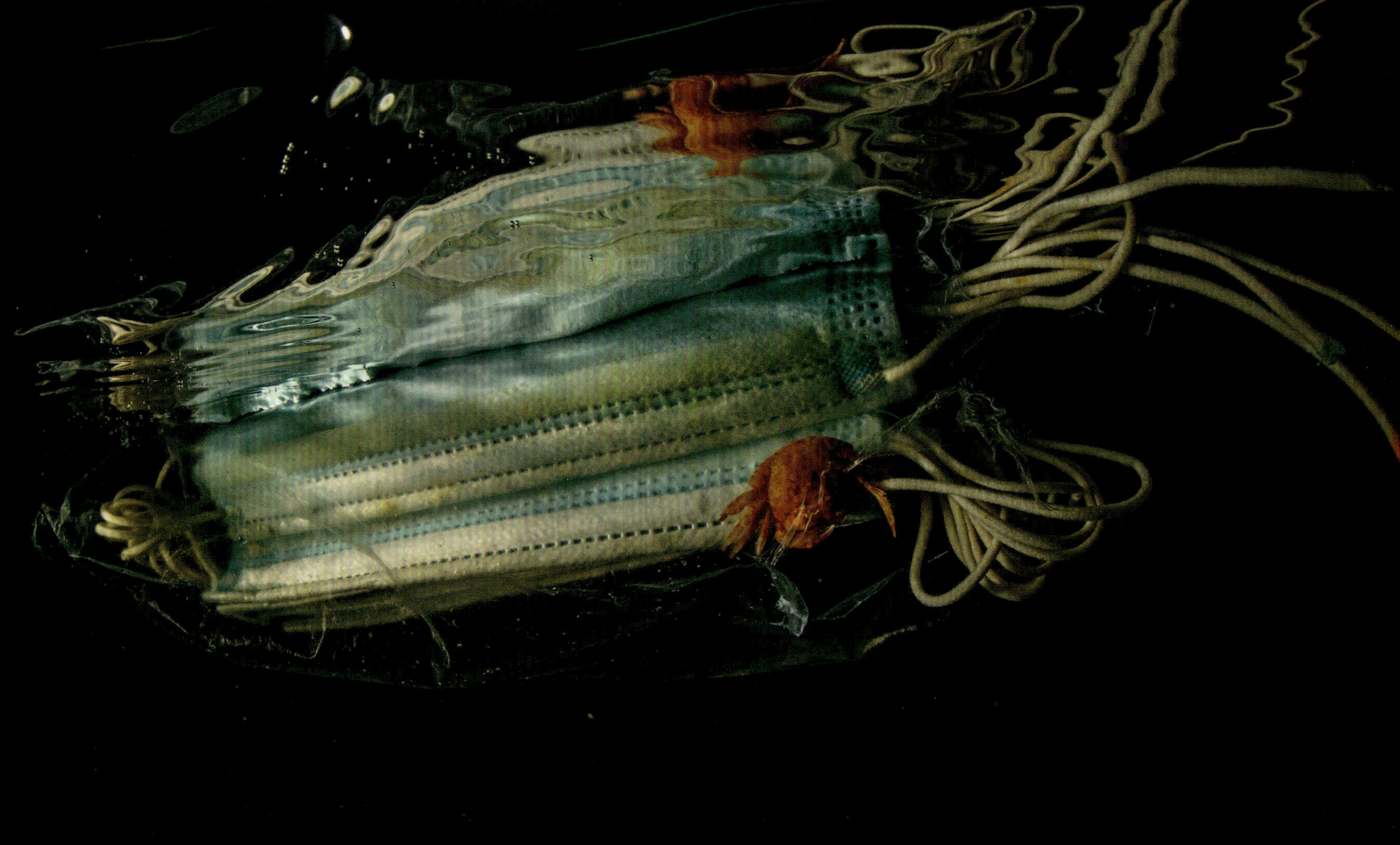

Our Impact Runner-Up

Single-use Drifter

Columbus crab (*Planes minutus*)
Justin Gilligan, Lord Howe Island

Face masks arrived at Lord Howe Island from a cargo ship that lost 50 containers in rough seas off Sydney. Over 1100 masks were collected during lockdown. In this image, a Columbus crab finds shelter in a plastic bag of face masks. The environmental impact will never be fully quantified.
Lord Howe Island

Nikon D850, Sigma 15mm +1.2TC, 1/15, f/22, ISO 400, Nauticam underwater housing, twin Ikelite strobes

Judges' comments:
At first glance this looks like a marine creature propelled by tentacles. On closer inspection, the reality is a stark reminder of the pandemic's impact, which has extended far beyond humans.

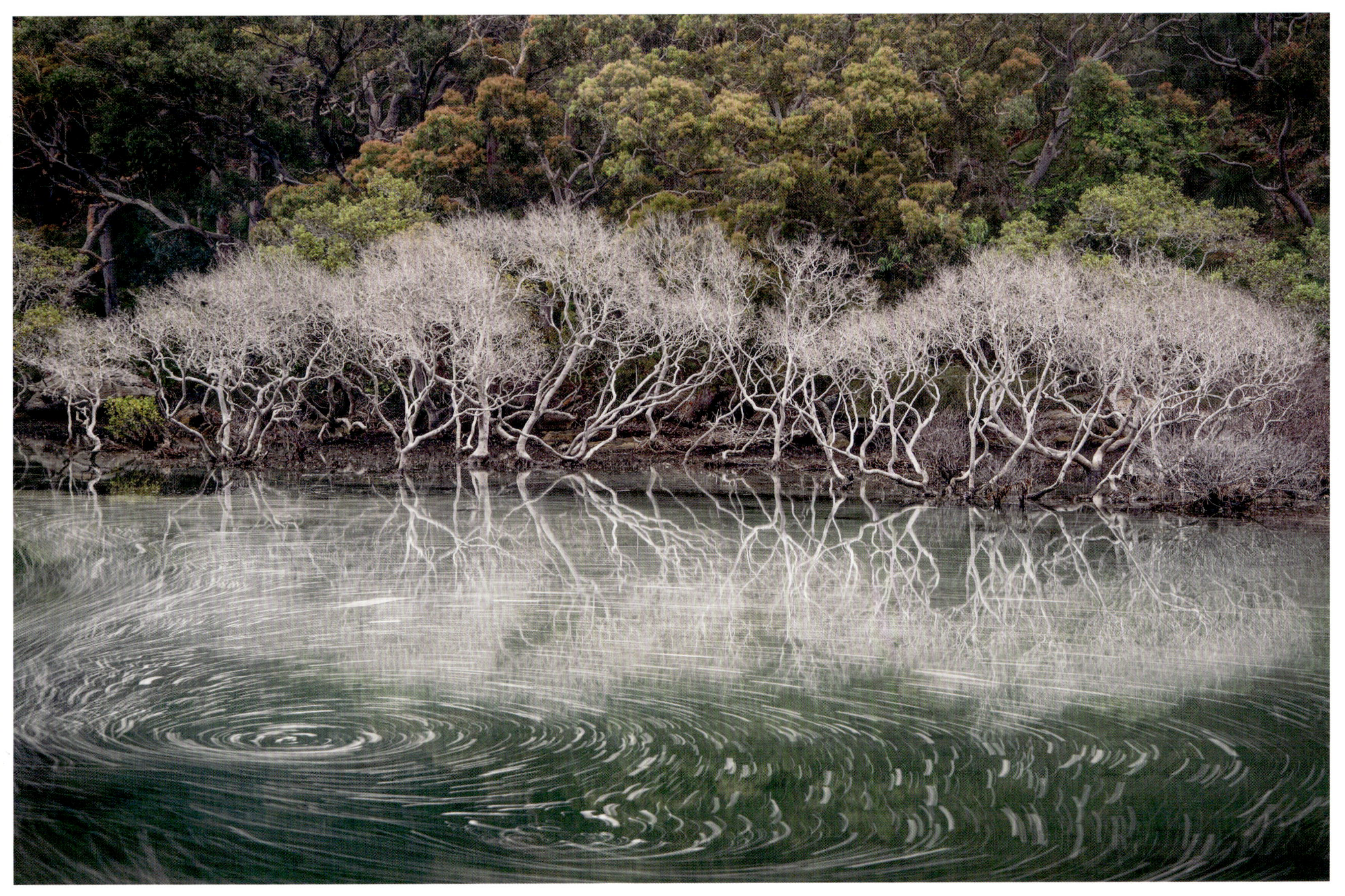

Spiralling away
Gary Dunnett, New South Wales

I watched with growing dismay as the mangroves around Cabbage Tree Basin began to die. Victims of storm and shifting sands, a foreboding of the changes to come with rising sea-levels. The slowly spiralling foam seemed to be draining away the vitality of the Royal, our first national park.
Cabbage Tree Basin, Royal National Park, New South Wales

Nikon D810, Nikkor 24–85mm AFS 3.5–4.5 G, 30 seconds, f/8, ISO 200, tripod, 66mm focal length cropped

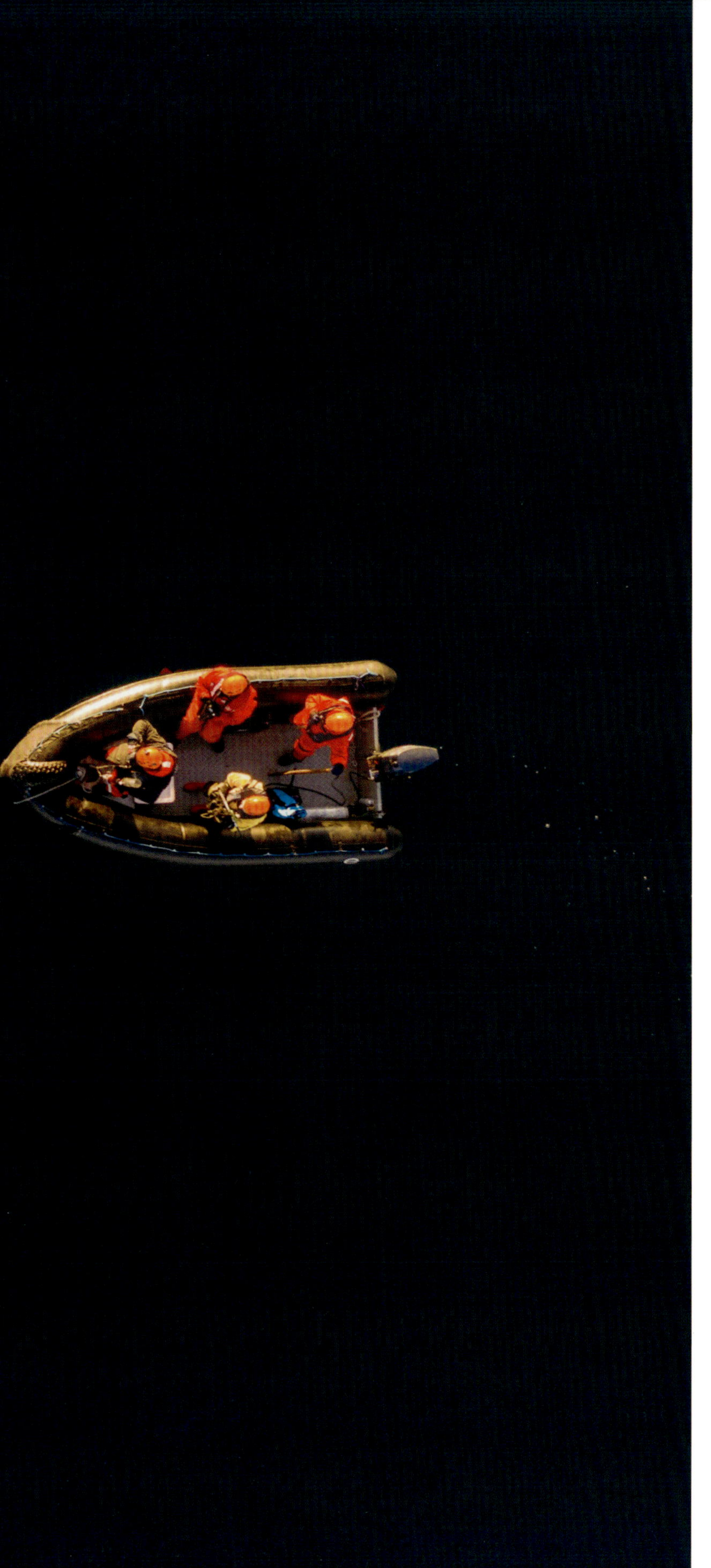

Tohorā
Southern right whale
(*Eubalaena australis*)
Richard Robinson, New Zealand

Two centuries after near extinction, southern right whales, also called Tohorā, thrive deep in the subantarctic. In 2020 a University of Auckland expedition, led by Dr Emma Carroll, visited to study the recovering population, using cutting-edge genomic techniques that will allow us to understand the complexities of these animals.
Port Ross, Auckland Islands, New Zealand

DJI Mavic 2 Pro, 28mm equivalent, 1/200, f/2.8, ISO 100

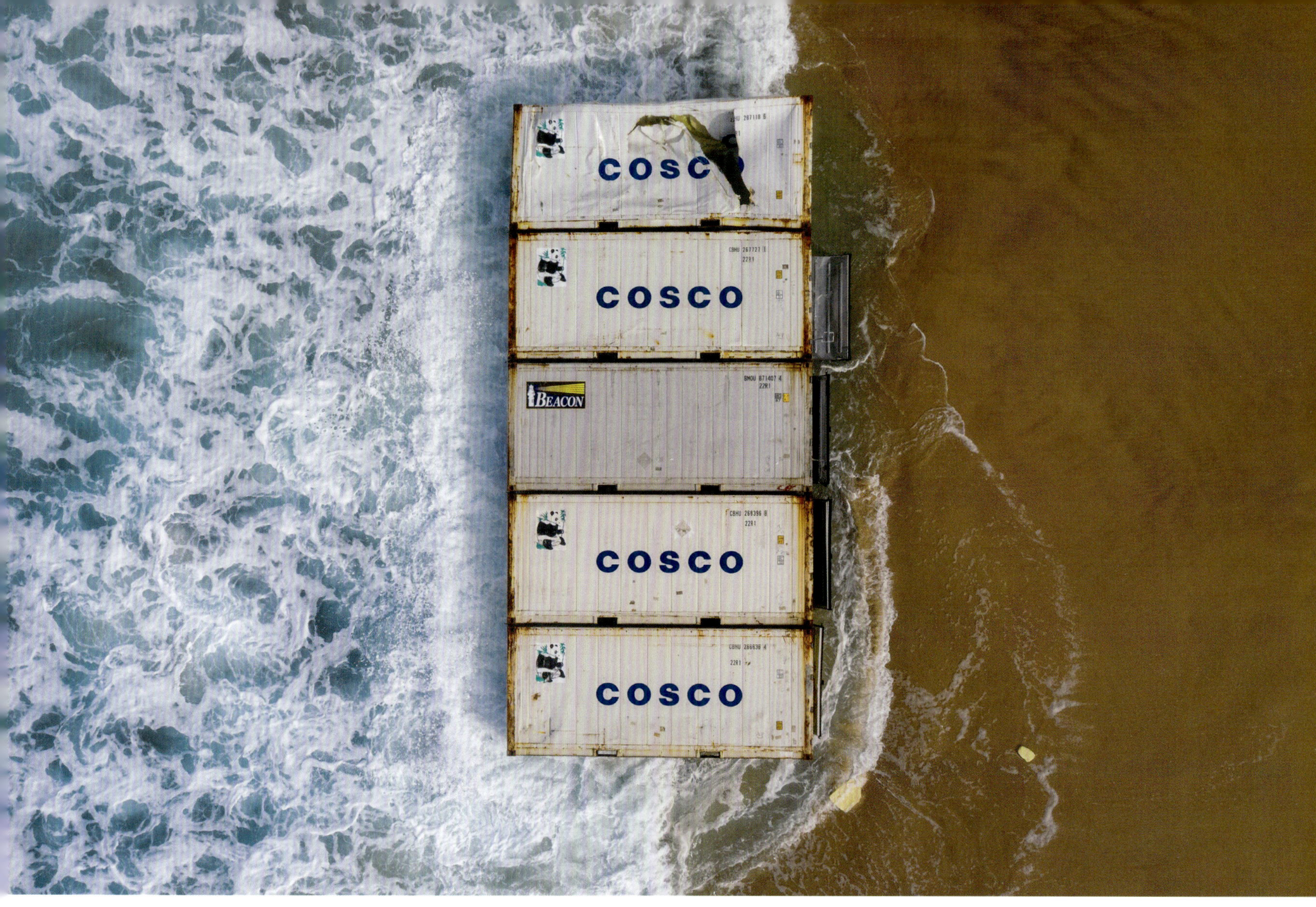

COSCO

Reed Plummer, New South Wales

Five shipping containers (of fifty in total) lost overboard the *APL England* wash up on Birdie Beach, New South Wales. Consequently, thousands of surgical face masks wash up along the east coast of Australia, at a time when this safety equipment is needed most.
Birdie Beach, New South Wales

DJI Mavic 2 Pro, about 77° 35mm, 1/400, f/11, ISO 100

Space invaders

Little penguin (*Eudyptula minor*)
Doug Gimesy, Victoria

In an attempt to capture a photo, tourists crowd a little penguin on the rocks of the St Kilda breakwater. Sadly, as happens too often with both amateur and professional wildlife photography, it seems little consideration was given to the potential stress this behaviour could cause.
St Kilda breakwater, Victoria

Nikon D750, Nikon 24–70mm f/2.8, 1/50, f/3.2, ISO 6400, handheld

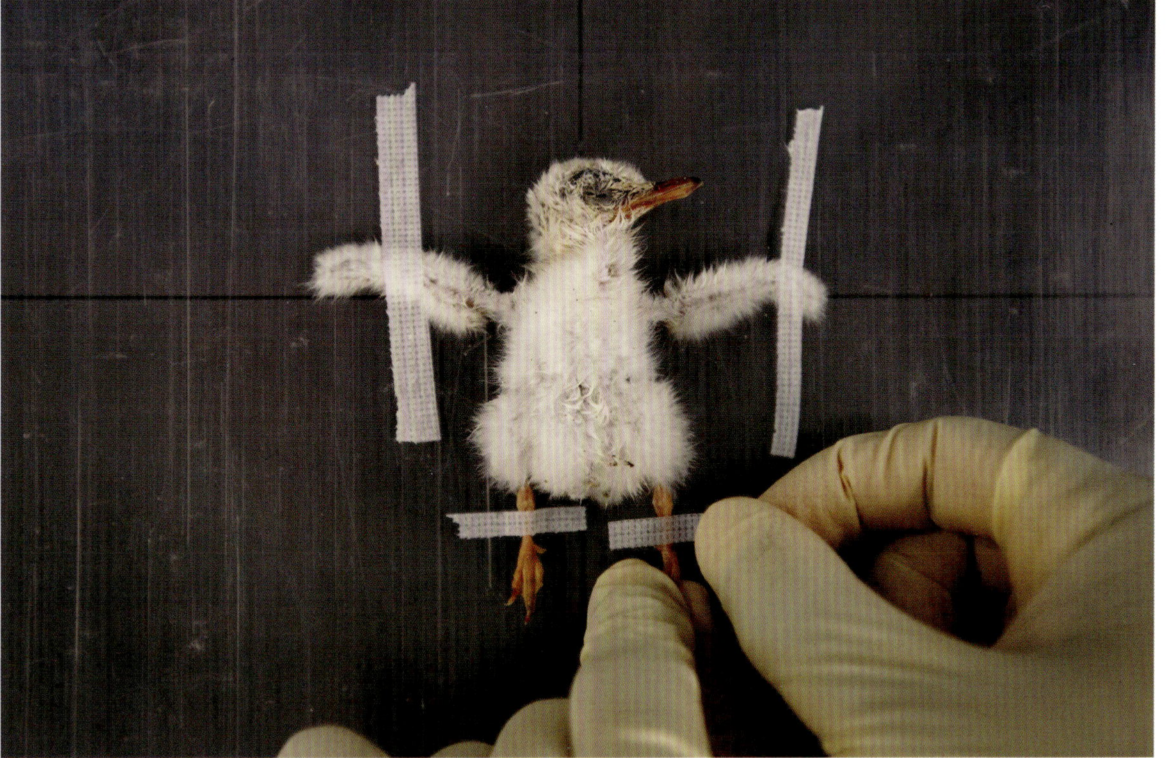

Fallen From Grace

New Zealand fairy tern (*Sternula nereis*)
Richard Robinson, New Zealand

A deceased New Zealand fairy tern chick is prepared for X-ray, looking for signs of trauma, before undergoing a necropsy. The fairy tern is the rarest bird in New Zealand, with perhaps 36 adults left in existence. It's got everything going against it: weather, cats, humans and its own DNA.
New Zealand Centre for Conservation Medicine, Auckland, New Zealand

Canon EOS-1DX Mk II, Canon EF 16–35mm f/2.8L II, 1/250, f/4, ISO 1600

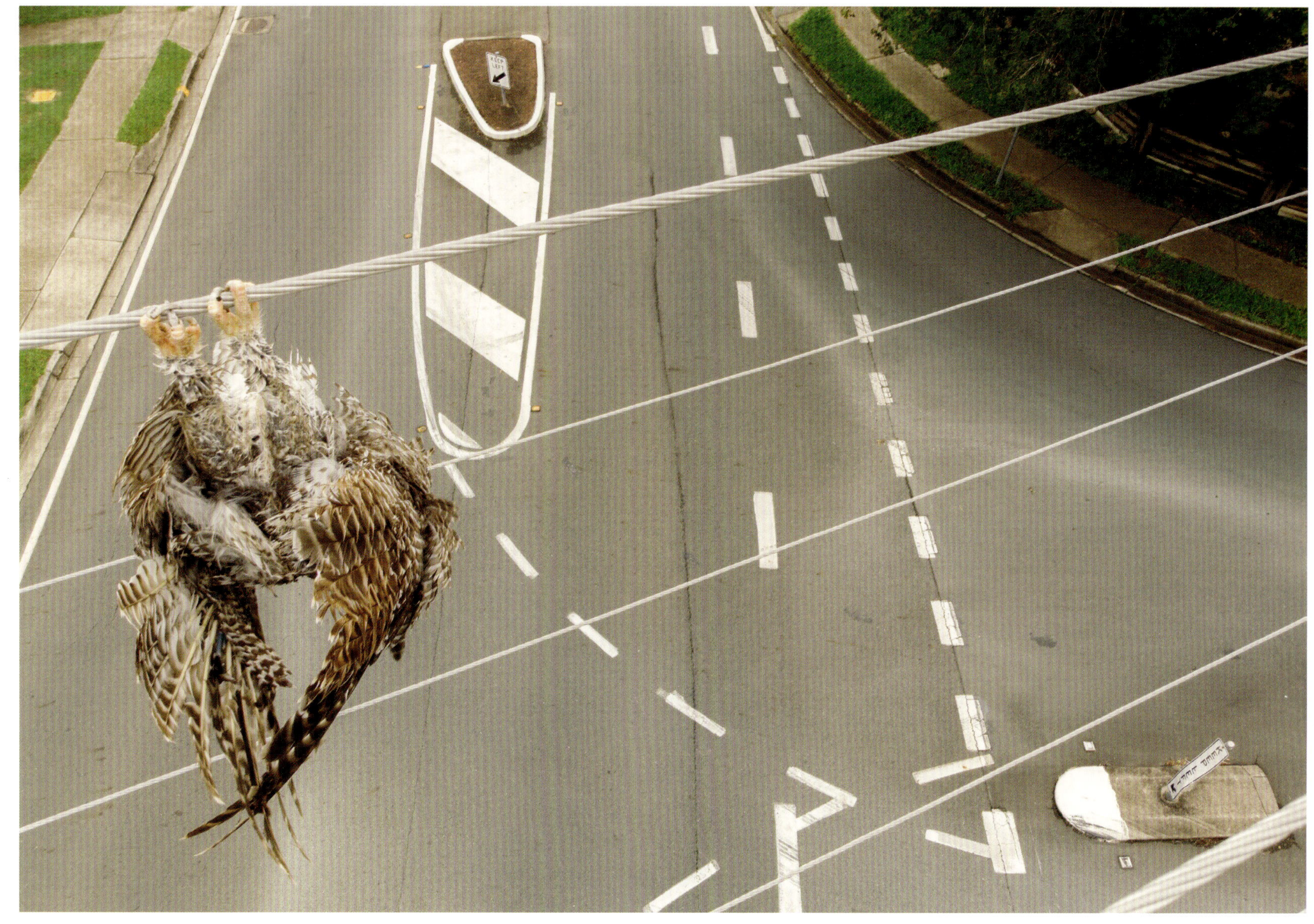

Power Outage
Powerful owl (*Ninox strenua*)
Matt Wright, Queensland

Mortality rates of powerful owls in urban areas are higher than that of their counterparts in natural areas. Electrocution is one of their biggest killers as they often target possums who use powerlines to navigate the concrete jungle. Urban powerful pay a hefty price for living in the big city.
Brisbane, Queensland

DJI Mavic air drone, 1/320, f/2.8, ISO 100

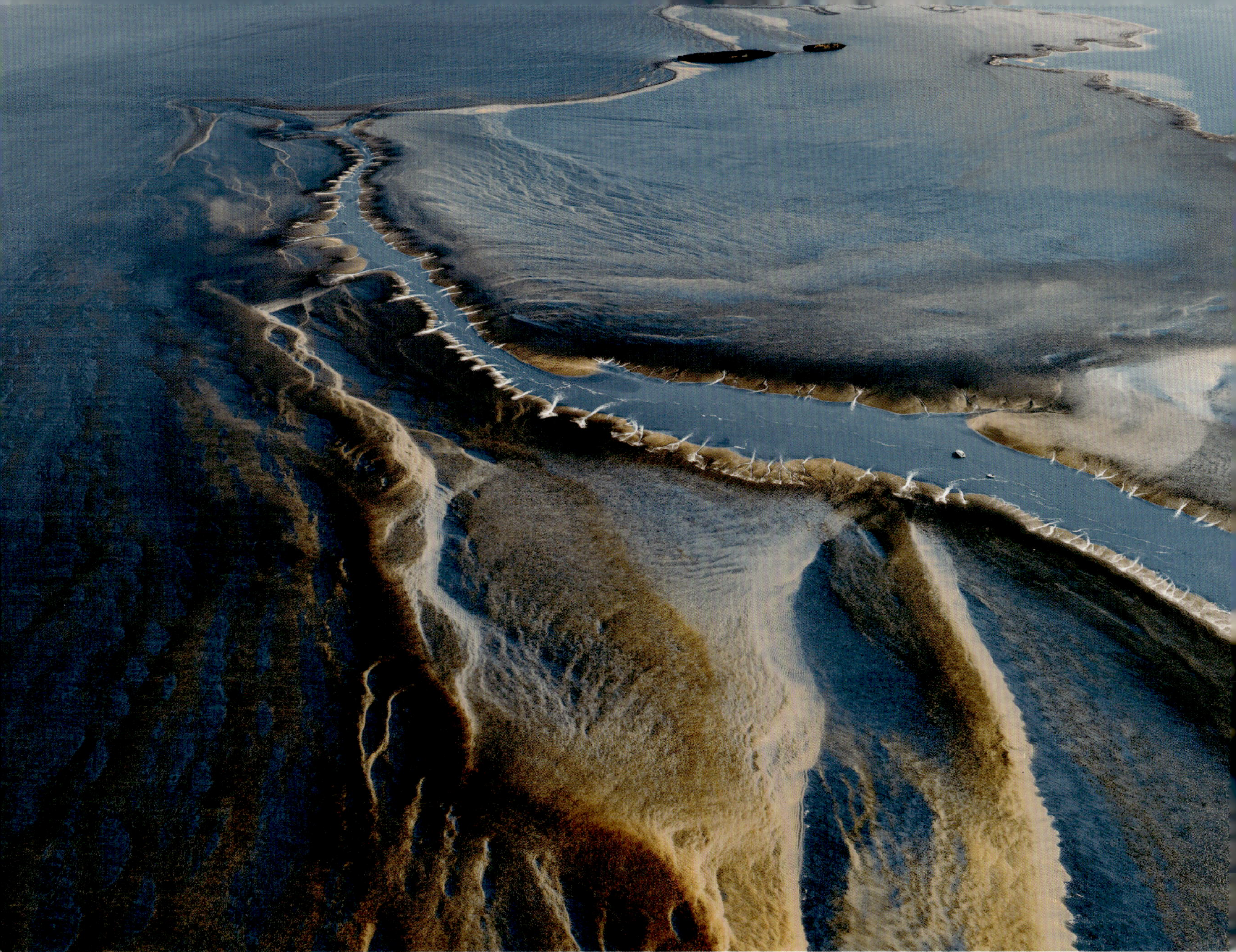

Fading Reef
Kevin Krautgartner, Germany

Today, coral reefs are dying at an alarming rate. Coral bleaching is caused by rising water temperatures which kills the coral. My image shows the beauty of these unique coral and algae systems and I hope it reminds us all that what we do on land impacts our oceans.
Kimberley Coast, Western Australia

Fujifilm GFX 50s, Fujifilm GF 32–64mm F4, 1/1000, f/7.1, ISO 400, handheld from a helicopter

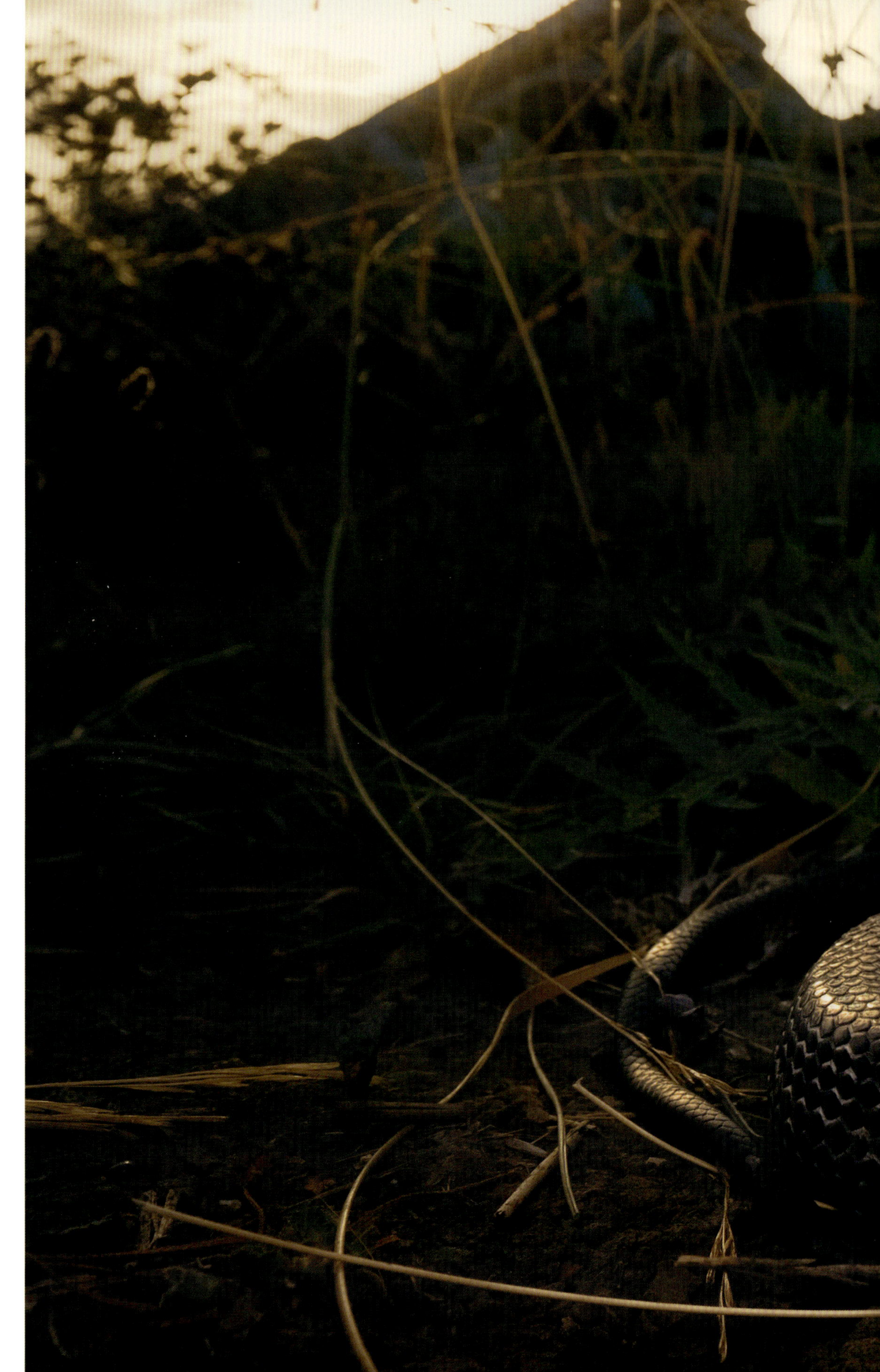

Mr Brown in the City
Brown snake (*Pseudonaja textilis*)
Kristian Bell, Victoria

A striking start to an intended walk around grasslands on Melbourne's urban fringe. This brown snake appeared to have recently had a meal and this may explain its reluctance to retreat, instead standing its ground in a defensive posture. The site where this photo was taken has since been developed.
Melbourne, Victoria

Canon EOS 5D Mk III, Canon EF16–35mm f/4L IS US, 1/60, f/11, ISO 100, single, diffused, on-camera flash, handheld

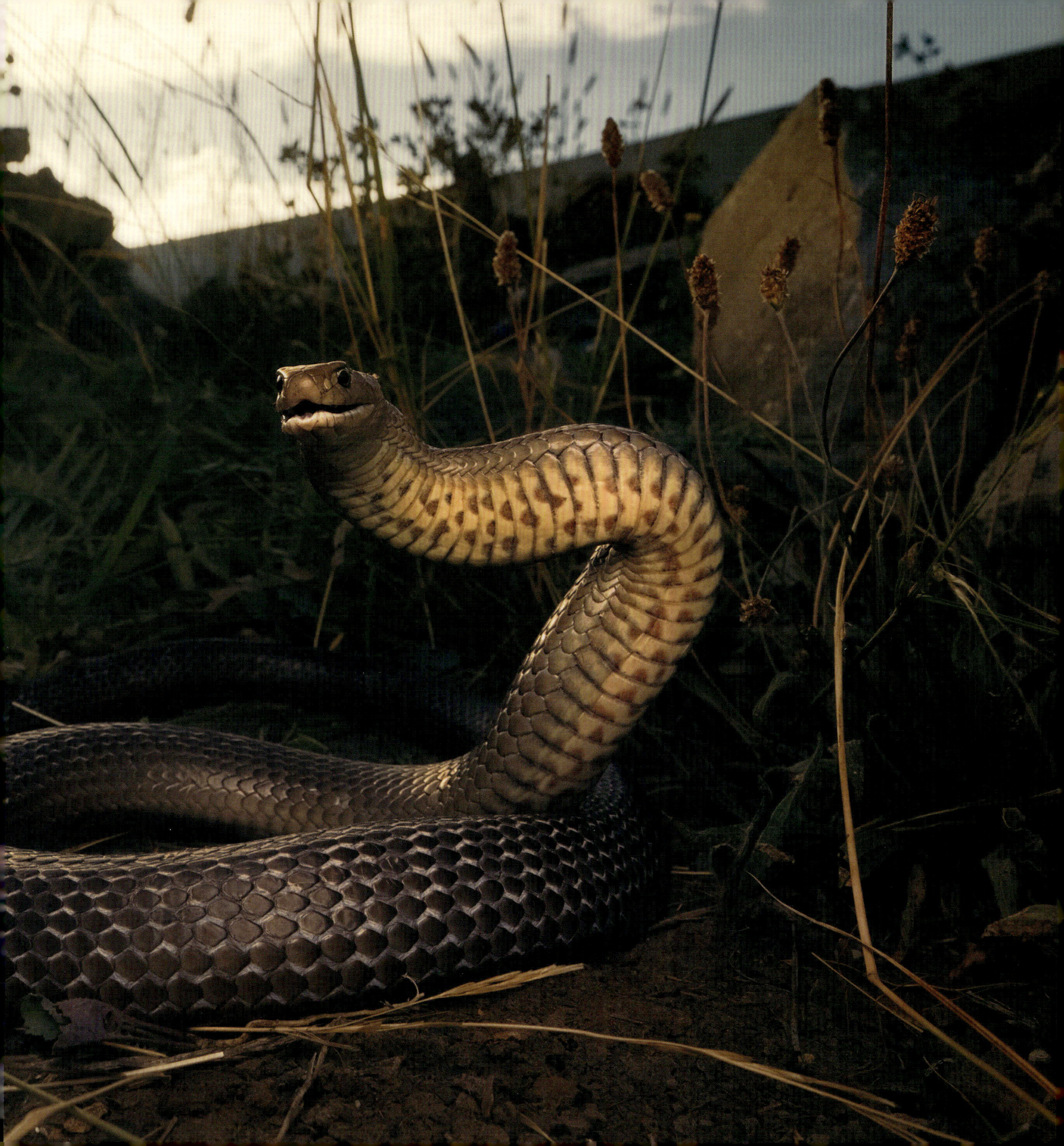

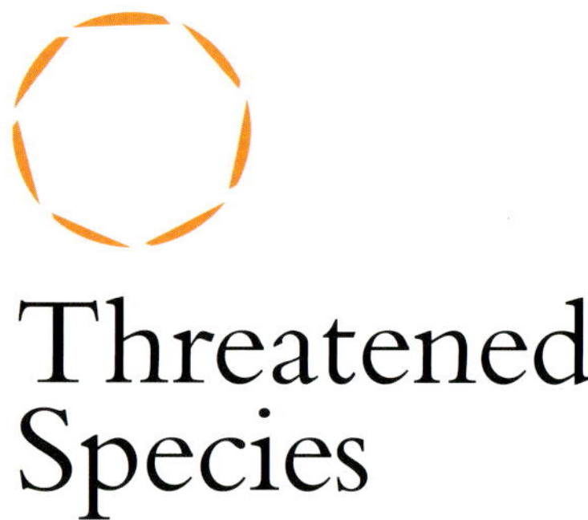

Threatened Species

Threatened Species Winner

Declining Species

Grey nurse shark (*Carcharias taurus*)
Status: Vulnerable
Scott Portelli, New South Wales

Populations of grey nurse sharks along the Australian coast are under threat and have suffered a decline over recent years. Current threats to the species are believed to be incidental catch from commercial fisheries, recreational fishing and, to a lesser extent, shark net programs run in New South Wales and Queensland.
Exmouth, Western Australia

Olympus EM1 Mk II, 8mm fisheye, 1/200, f/6.3, ISO 250, Olympus strobes

Judges' comments:
The shark is perfectly illuminated in its environment, captured in a beautifully balanced composition with great use of artificial and available light. The neighbouring schools of fish provide great texture and contrast.

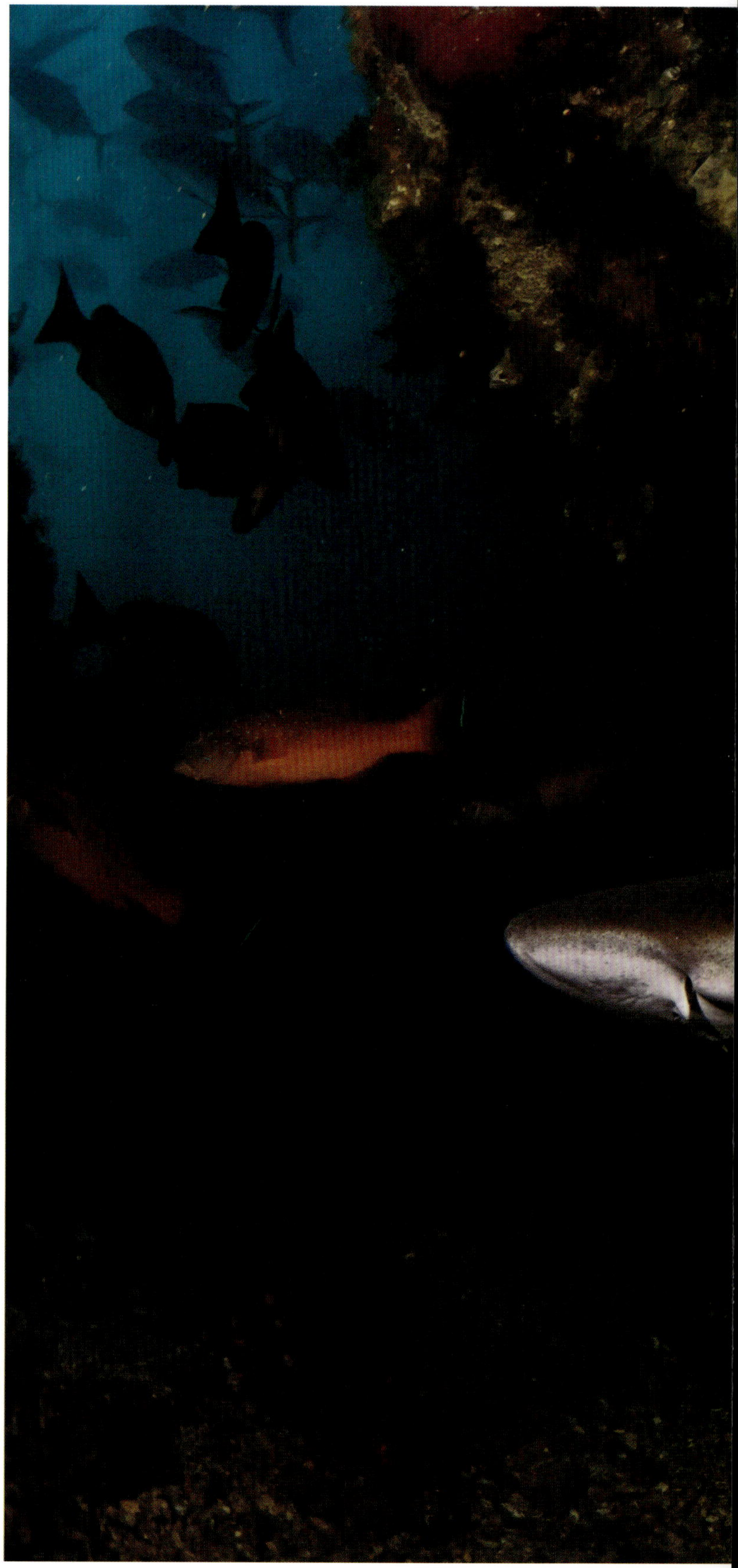

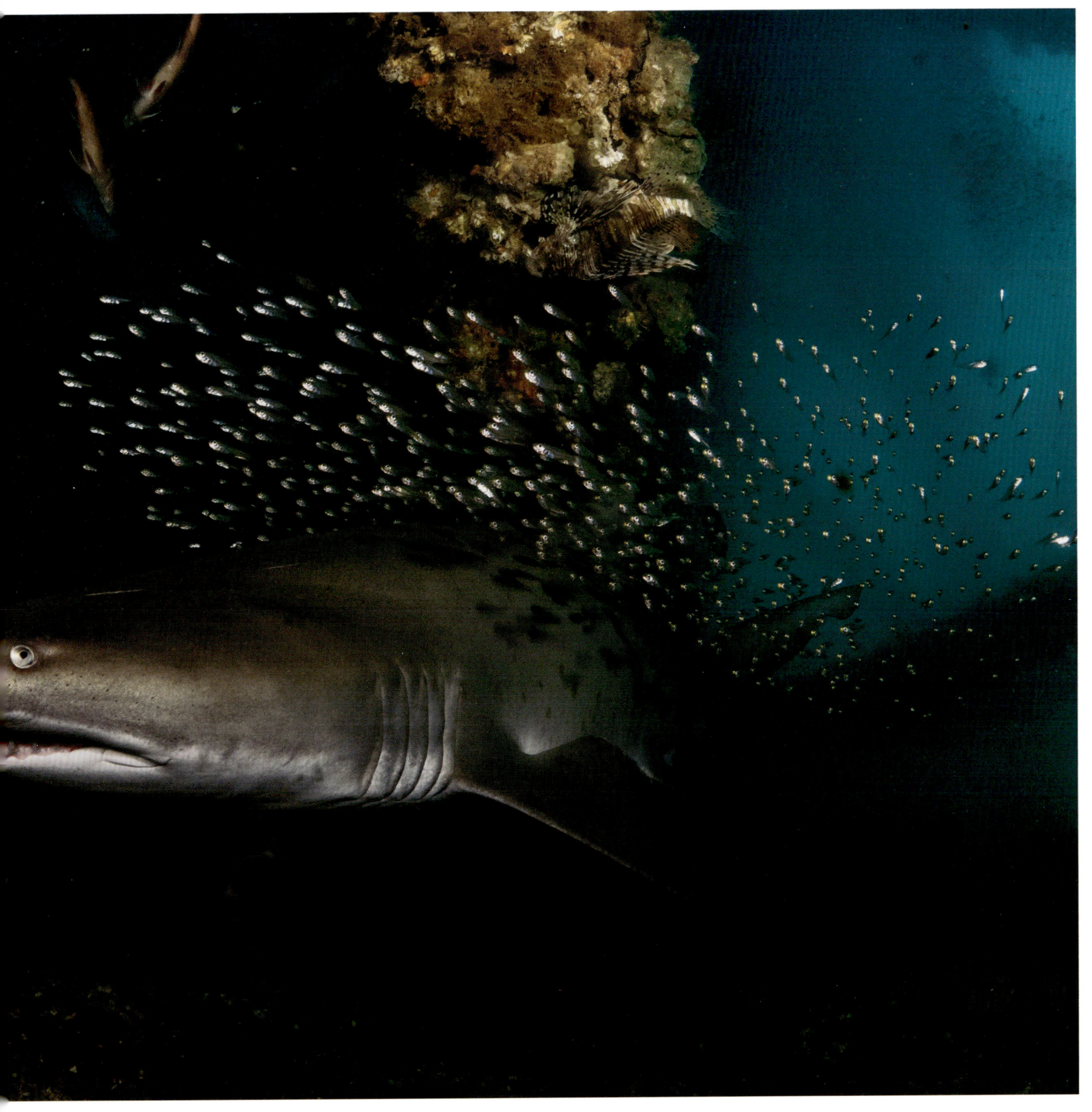

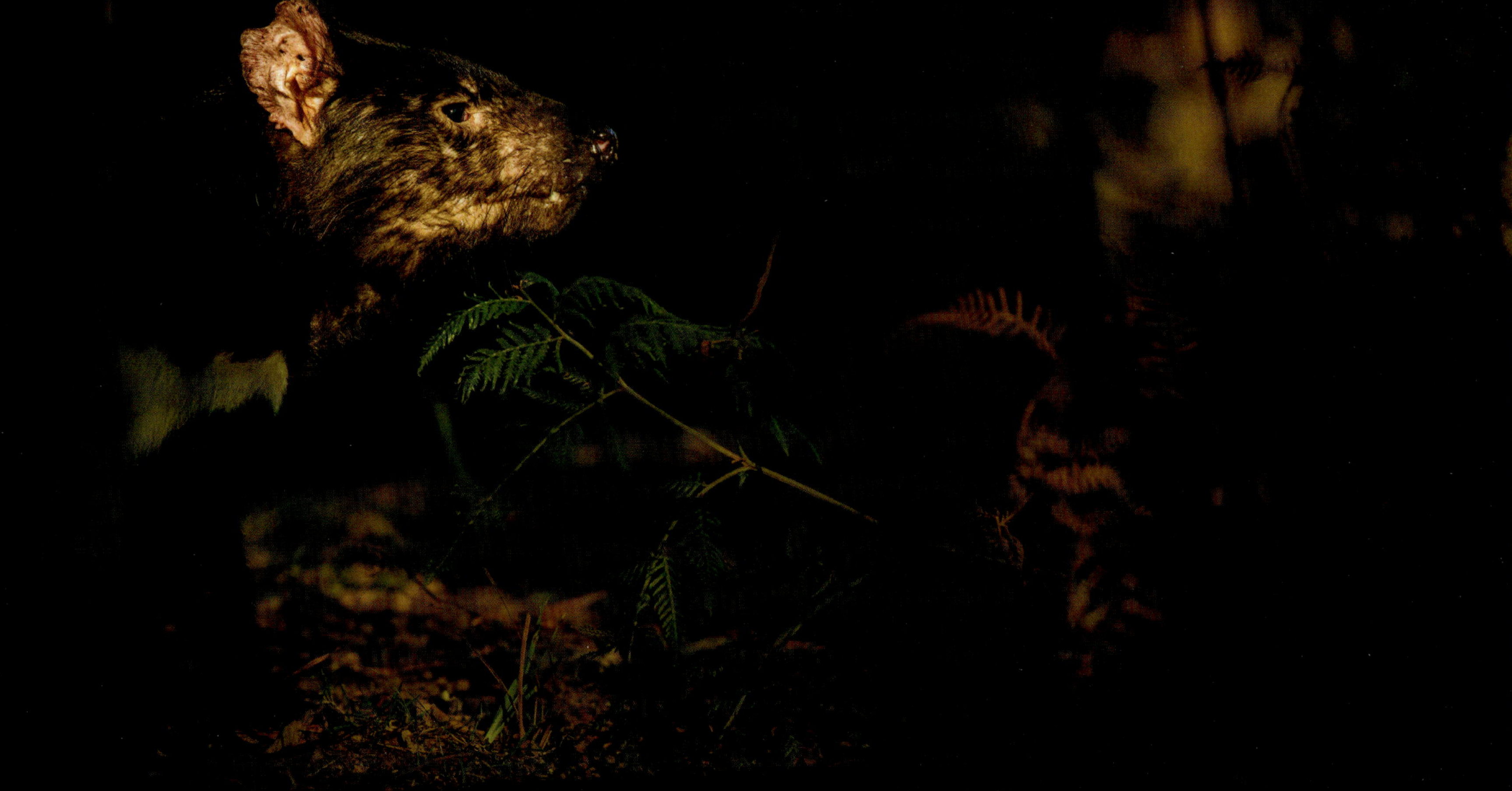

Threatened Species Runner-Up

In the shadows

Tasmanian devil (*Sarcophilus harrisii*)
Status: Endangered
Tom Svensson, Sweden

I spent 14 days on Maria Island and one day, I was lucky enough to see a devil running past. I could see him in the bushes and the sun shone directly on him. It was an amazing feeling to see one out during the day.
Maria Island, Tasmania

Canon 1DX Mk II, Canon 200–400mm f4L IS USM 362mm, 1/1000, f/5.6, ISO 3200, handheld

Judges' comments:
Caught in a shaft of light, this perfectly poised devil would otherwise disappear into the dark forest, blending in completely with the subtle muted colours of the background. A mysterious scene with a primitive ancient feel.

Cooling down

Grey-headed flying-fox (*Pteropus poliocephalus*)
Status: Vulnerable
Ofer Levy, New South Wales

I have been studying and photographing the grey-headed flying-foxes in the Sydney area for the last 15 years. These magnificent endemic Australian mammals suffer from persecution as well as the impact of global warming. Recent years' heat waves have killed a significant part of the wild population. They need our urgent help.
Parramatta River, New South Wales

Canon EOS 1DX, Canon 300mm f2.8 x 2 converter, 1/2500, f/7.1, ISO 3200, taken from a floating hide

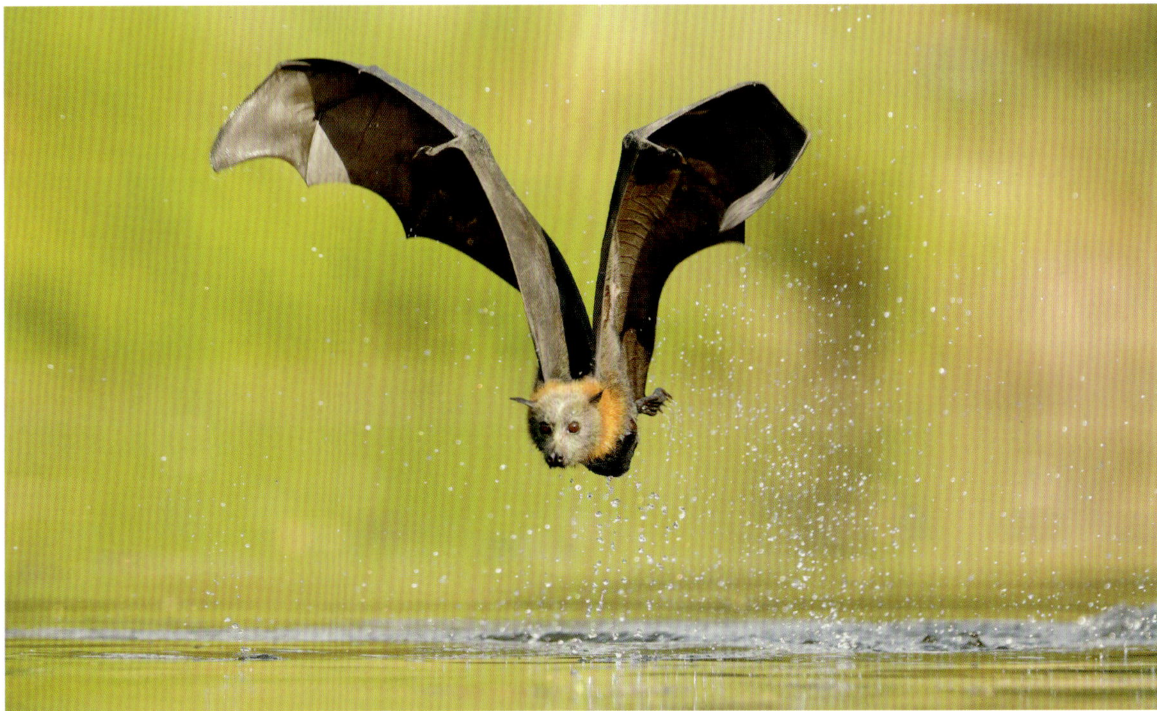

The Turtle Vortex

Green turtle (*Chelonia mydas*)
Status: Endangered
Jordan Robins, New South Wales

Using a slow shutter speed along with rotating my camera in a circular motion I aimed to create an abstract image of these two endangered green sea turtles to portray them as ghostly figures, emphasising that without proper protection they may one day actually become ghostly figures, facing extinction.
Lady Elliot Island, Queensland

Canon EOS 5D Mk IV, Canon EF 8–15mm f/4L fisheye USM lens, 1/4, f/18, ISO 100, 2 x Inon Z-330 strobes, AquaTech water housing

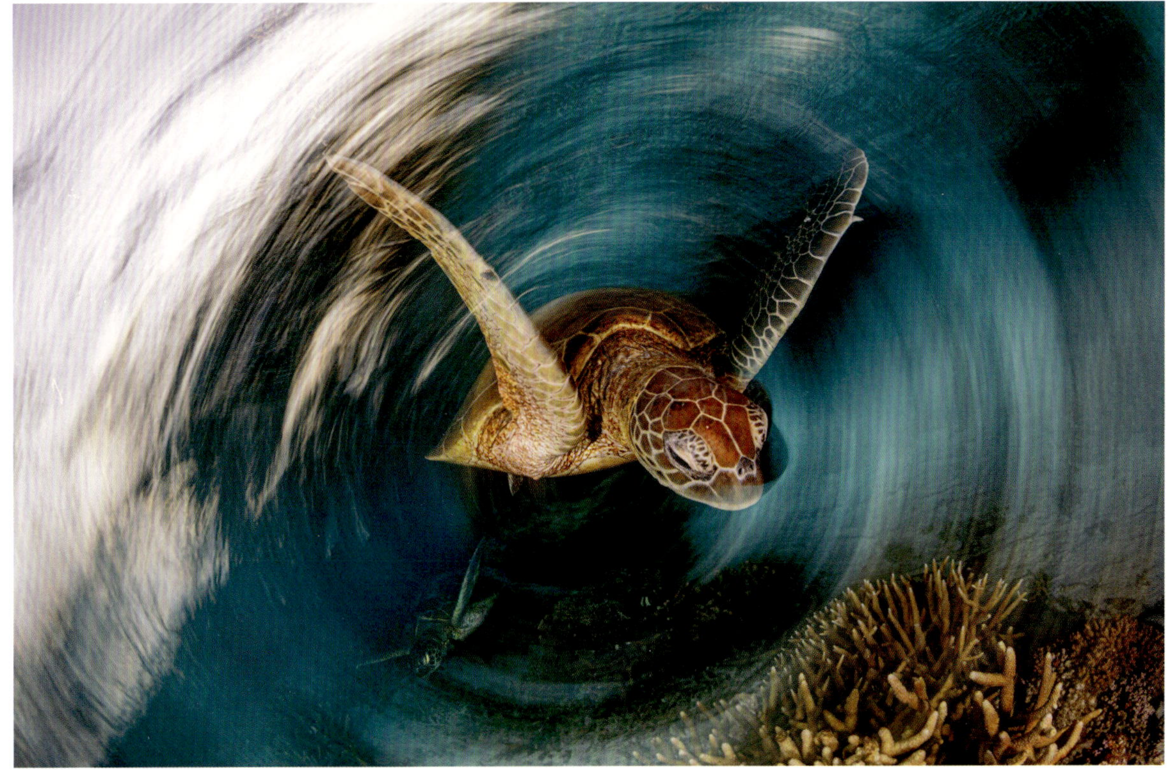

Burrow Maintenance

Greater bilby (*Macrotis lagotis*)
Status : Vulnerable
Brad Leue, South Australia

A bilby at the entrance to its burrow. Bilbies were reintroduced to Mallee Cliffs by Australian Wildlife Conservancy and NSW Government in 2019 to protect them from further decline due to feral predation. This is the first time bilbies have been present in the area in more than a century.
Mallee Cliffs National Park, New South Wales

Canon 5D Mk III, Canon EF 50mm f/1.4 USM, 1/200, f/9.0, ISO 320, 2 x Canon Speedlite 580EX, Camtraptions PIR motion sensor, tripod

Shy Quoll

Eastern quoll (*Dasyurus viverrinus*)
Status: Endangered
Matt Palmer, Victoria

This shy quoll is part of a breeding program managed by Bonorong Wildlife Sanctuary in Tasmania. I was quite lucky that there was a hole in the side of this log with which I could use some off-camera lighting to illuminate inside the hollow just enough to see the quoll's face.
Bonorong Wildlife Sanctuary, Tasmania

Sony A7RIII, Sony FE 100–400mm f4.5–5.6 GM OSS, 1/200, f/5.6, ISO 400, off-camera flash used from the right hand side, handheld

OVER PAGE

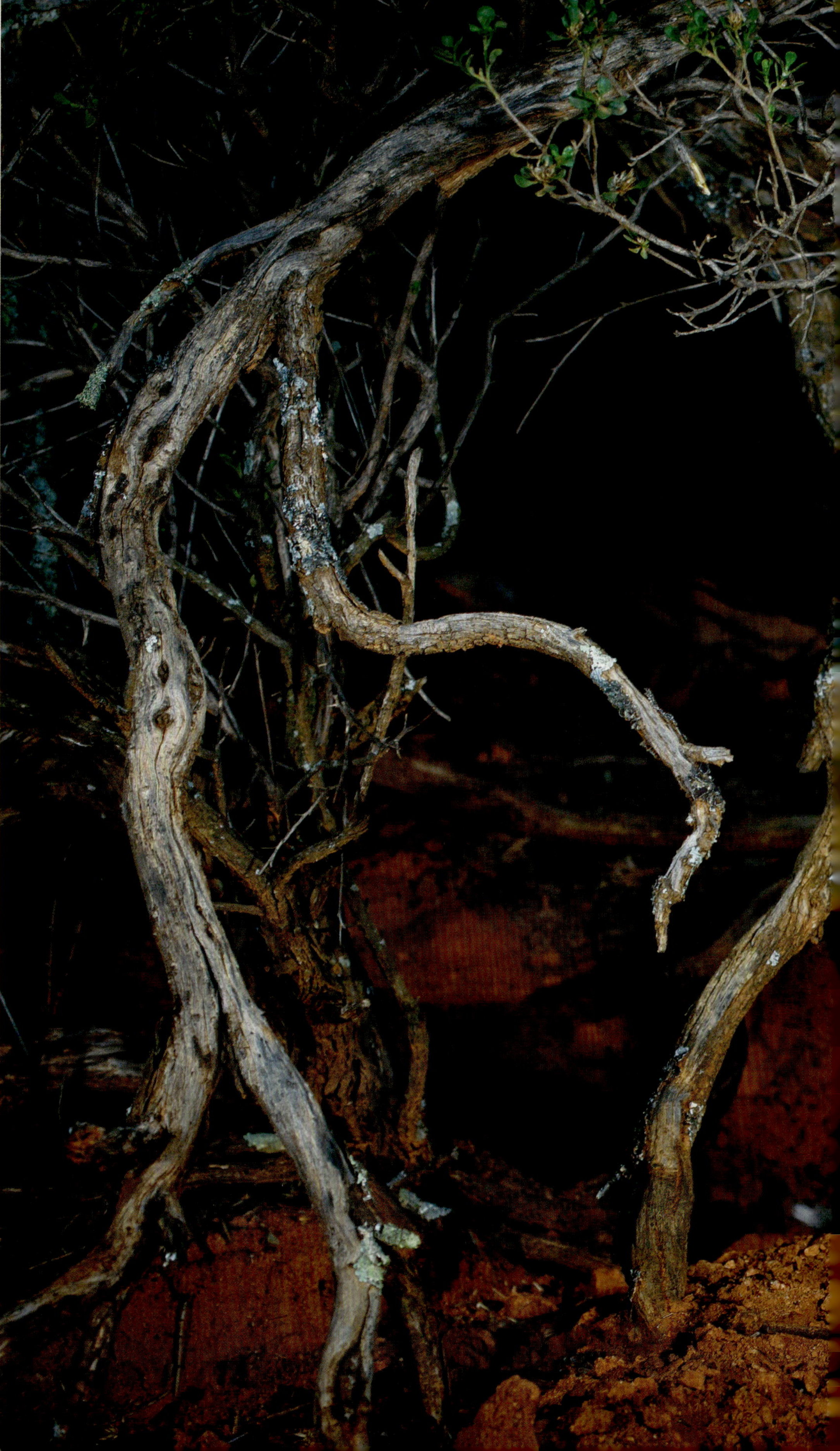

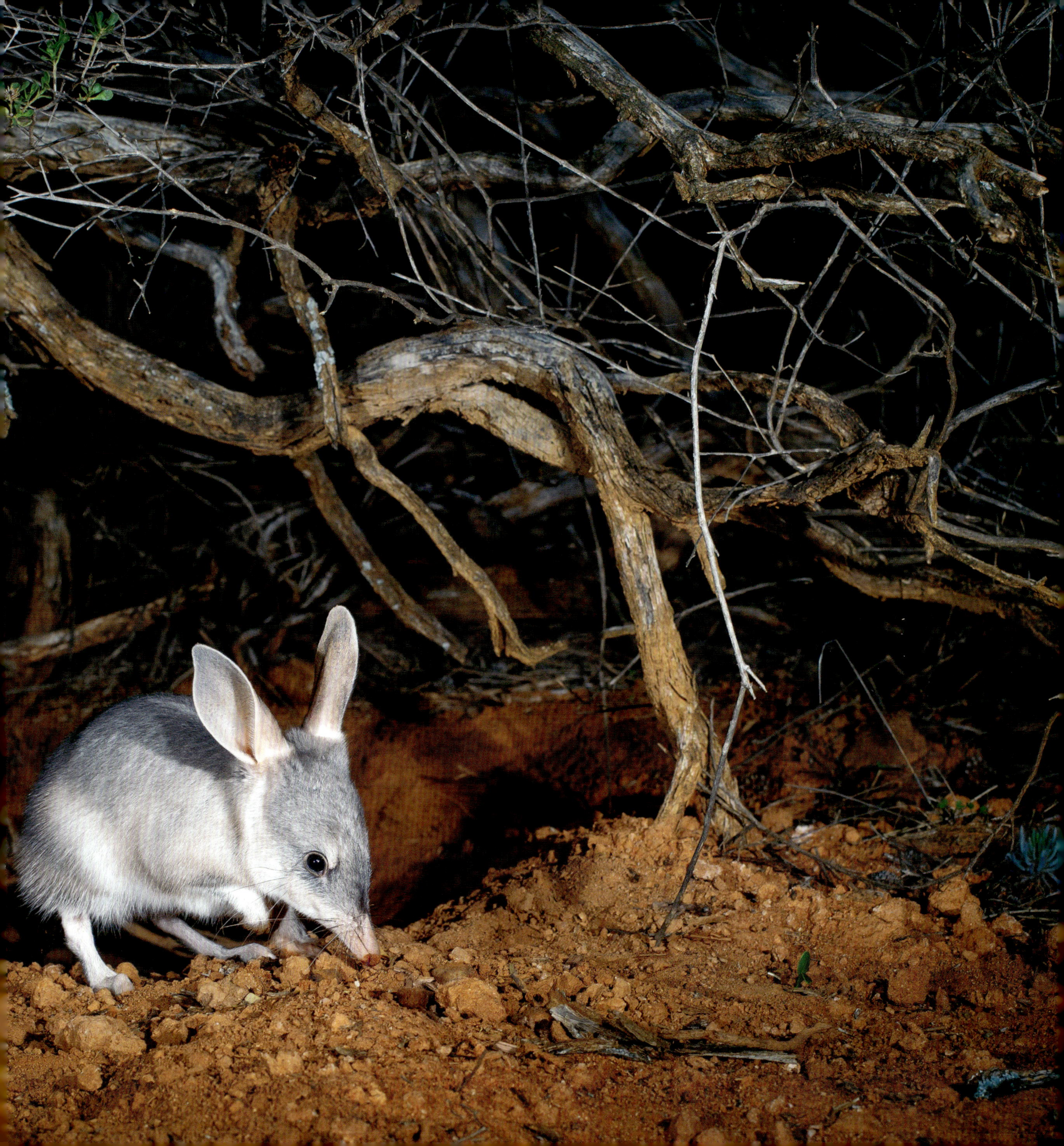

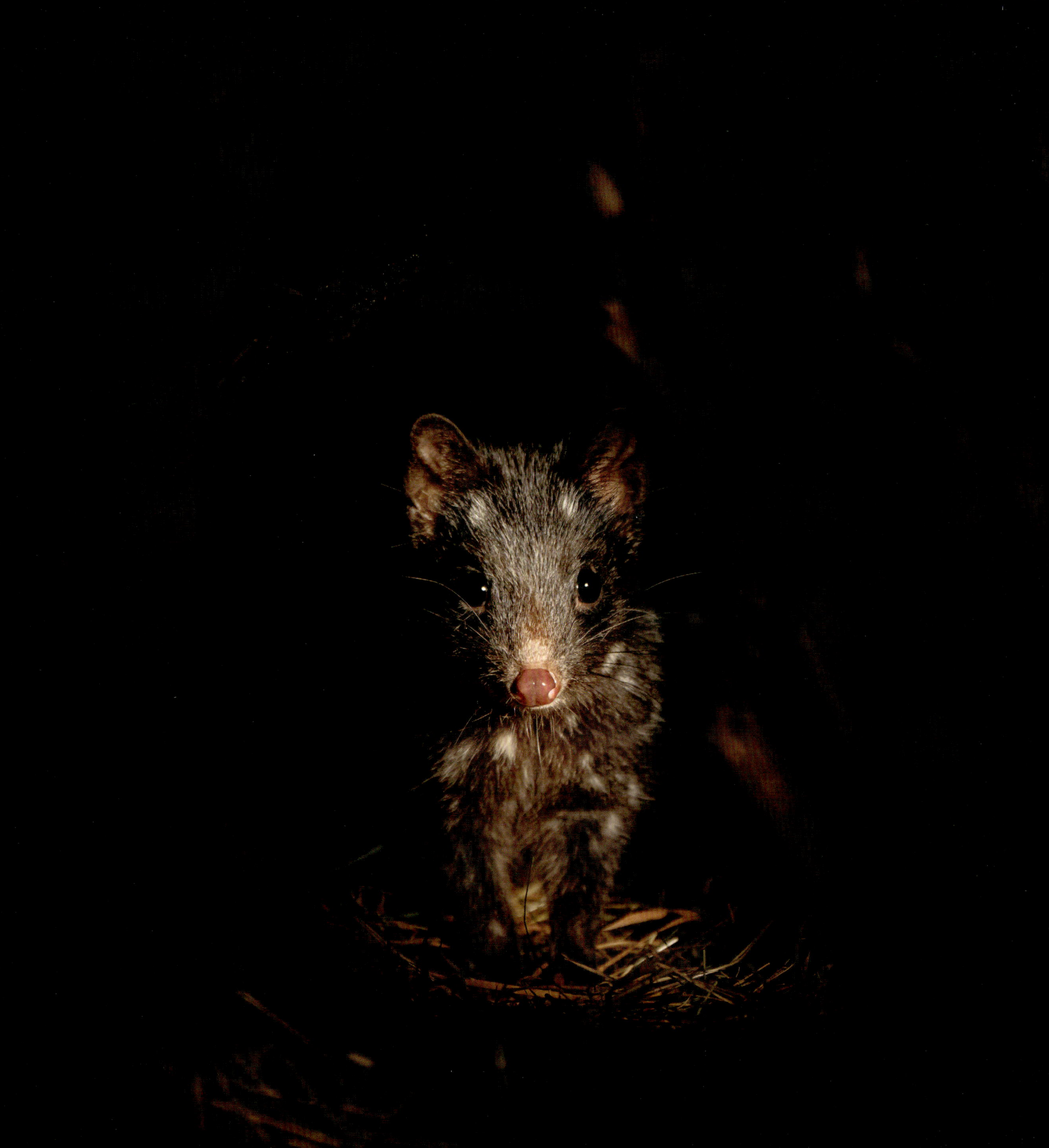

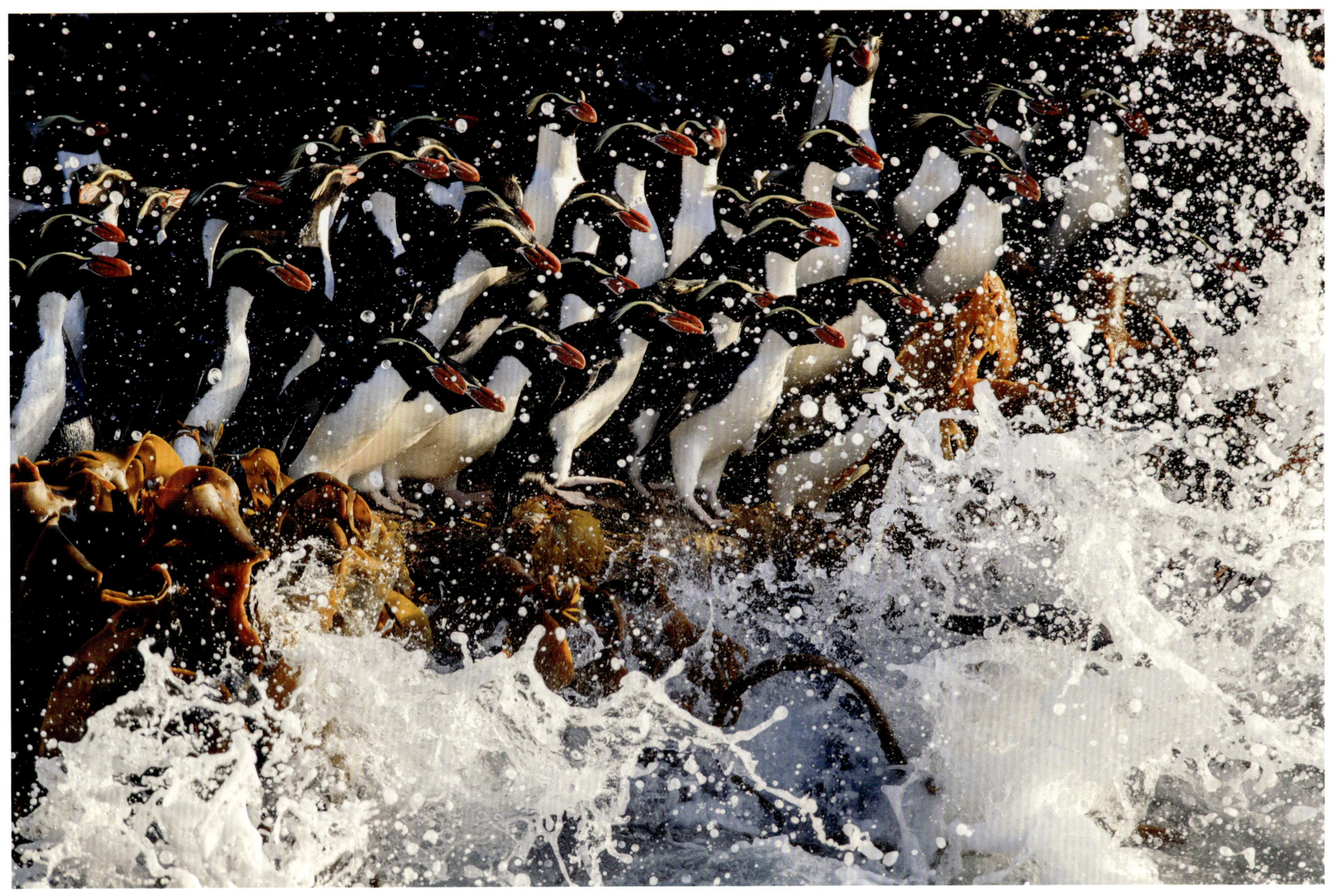

Life on the Edge
Snares crested penguin
(*Eudyptes robustus*)
Status: Vulnerable
Richard Robinson, New Zealand

Snares crested penguins are endemic to the tiny Snares island group, 200km south of mainland New Zealand. In search of food, they spend their winter migrating thousands of kilometres, clear across the Tasman Ocean foraging in Australian waters.
The Snares Subantarctic Island Group, New Zealand

Canon EOS-1DX Mk II, Canon EF 600mm f/4L, 1/1000, f/8, ISO 640

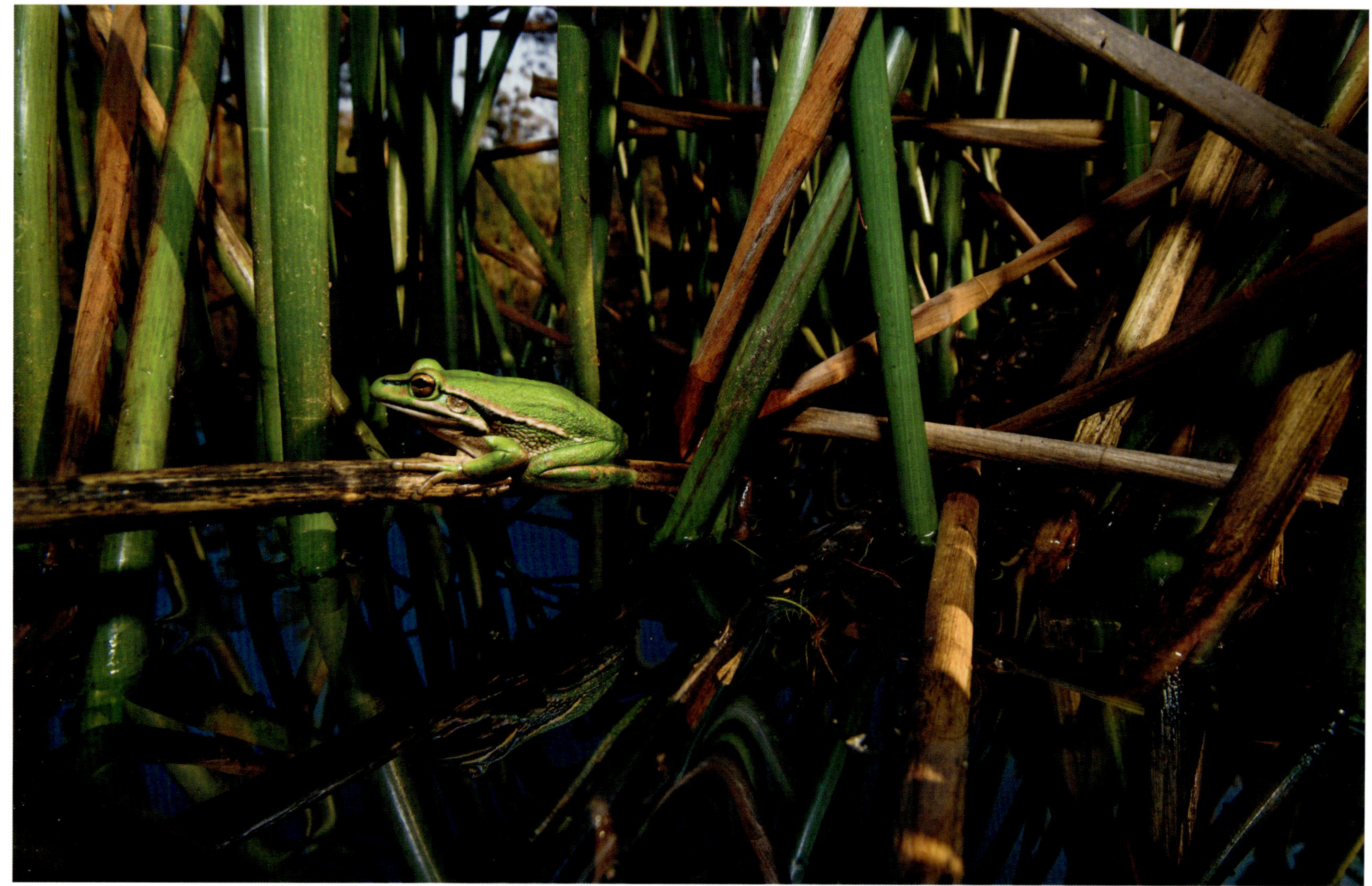

Hiding among the reeds
Green and golden bell frog
(*Litoria aurea*)
Status: Vulnerable
Chris Firth, New South Wales

The rapid decline of green and golden bell frog populations has been driven by habitat destruction, water contamination, introduction of predatory *Gambusia* fish and proliferation of chytrid fungus, which is impacting amphibians globally.
To photograph these frogs, I lay mostly submerged in a farm dam, which is a refuge from these threats.
Bendalong, New South Wales

Nikon D800e, Nikon 16–35mm, 1/200, f/13, ISO 160, Nikon SB-28, Camtraptions wireless trigger

Southern Royal Albatross

Southern royal albatross
(*Diomedea epomophora*)
Status: Vulnerable
Gillianne Tedder, New South Wales

A pair of majestic southern royal albatross on Campbell Island, New Zealand. Albatross are one of the most threatened birds in the world and we're the problem. Climate change, plastics in the ocean and entanglement in longline fishing poles are just some of the human activities pushing these birds to the edge.
Campbell Island, New Zealand

Nikon D750, 70–400mm, 135mm, 1250, f/9, ISO 400, handheld

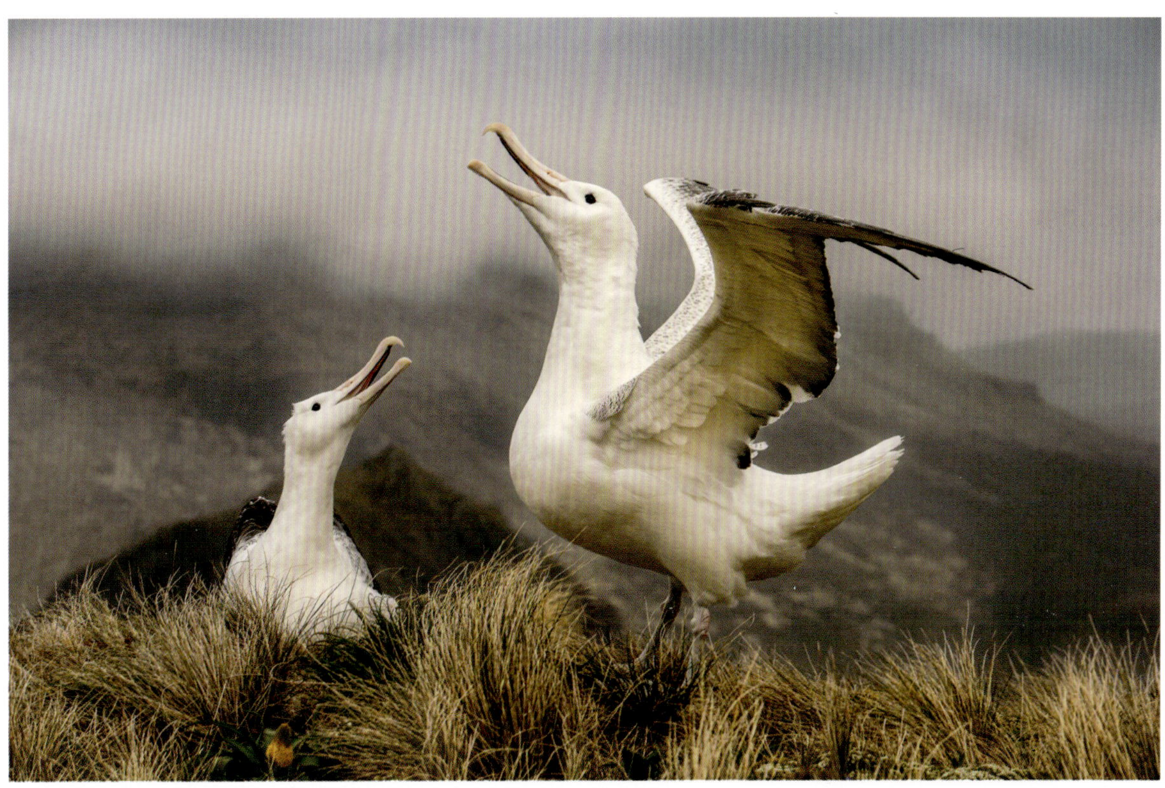

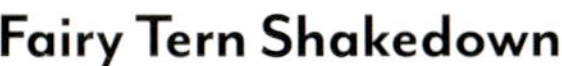

Fairy Tern Shakedown

Fairy tern (*Sternula nereis*)
Status: Vulnerable
Pam Osborn, Western Australia

With a spirited head flick, a fairy tern creates an arc of water droplets. Fairy terns are spring and summer breeding visitors and nest in shallow sand scrapes above the high-water mark on the island.
Rottnest Island, Western Australia

Canon EOS 1Dx Mk II, Canon EF 600mm f4L IS II USM lens, 1/2000, f/6.3, ISO 400, tripod

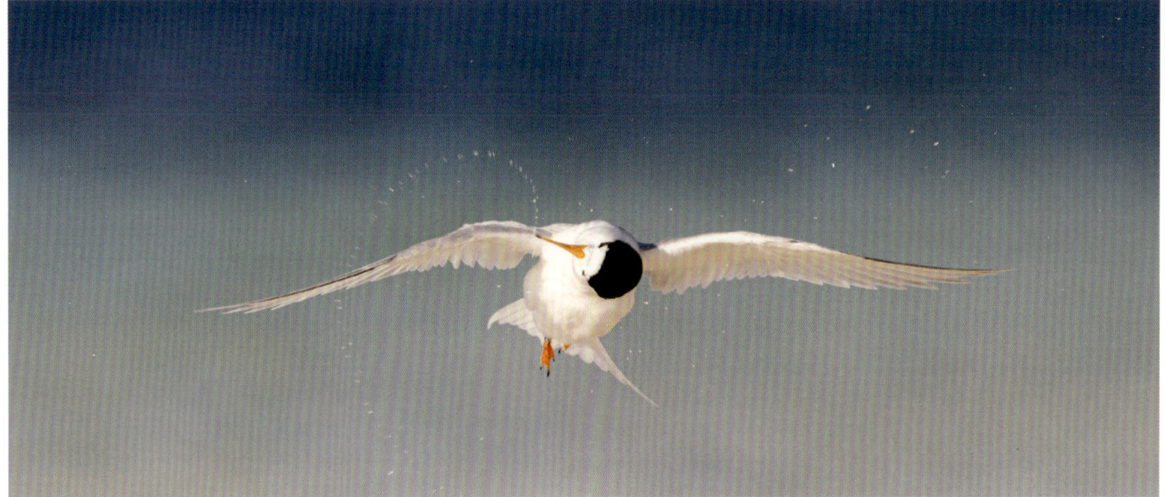